New Families, ND0175863

STUDIES IN DEMOGRAPHY

General Editors

Eugene A. Hammel
Ronald D. Lee
Kenneth W. Wachter

New Families, No Families?

**The Transformation
of the American Home**

Frances K. Goldscheider
and Linda J. Waite

A RAND Study

University of California Press
Berkeley / Los Angeles / Oxford

University of California Press
Berkeley and Los Angeles, California

University of California Press
Oxford, England

Copyright © 1991 by
The RAND Corporation

Library of Congress Cataloging-in-Publication Data

Goldscheider, Frances K.
  New families, no families?: the transformation of
the American home / Frances K. Goldscheider and
Llinda J. Waite.
      p. cm.—(A Rand Corporation research study)
  Includes bibliographical references and index.
  ISBN 0-520-07222-7 (alk. paper)
  ISBN 0-520-08305-9 (paperback)
    1. Family—United States   2. Marriage—
United States.   3. Home—United States.
I. Waite, Linda J.   II. Title.   III. Series.
HQ536.G65   1991
306.85'0973—dc20   91–15452
                                                 CIP

Printed in the United States of America

1   2   3   4   5   6   7   8   9

The paper used in this publication meets the minimum
requirements of American National Standard for Information Sciences—Permanence of Paper for Printed
Library Materials, ANSI Z39.48–1984 ∞

*We dedicate this book to our four daughters,
Sarah, Janet, Shana, and Nava, who also
contributed a great deal to this project, and
who face the challenge to establish, in their
own ways, "new families" of their own.*

Contents

Figures

Preface

This book is about two revolutions confronting the family. The first revolution is taking place inside the family, where changes in sex roles, which have increased women's participation in the paid labor force, are now challenging the rules underlying traditional marriage. As a result, many wives resent putting in a double day of employment and housework, while many husbands still resist their wives' urgings to share in family tasks. The second revolution is going on outside the family, where unmarried people are experiencing the privacy, dignity, and authority (and sometimes the loneliness) of living in their own home rather than living in a family as a child, relative, or lodger.

The first revolution is putting pressure on families to change by limiting the time and energy women have available for traditional family tasks. Slowly, "new families" are being formed, in which men and women share family economic responsibilities as well as the domestic tasks that ensure that family members go to work or school clean, clothed, fed, and rested, and come home to a place where they provide each other care and comfort. The second revolution, in which unmarried adults live independently, is providing an *alternative to change*, by giving men and women the opportunity to avoid marriage and parenthood or living in families at all. We call this option "no families."

Thus, American society confronts a profound choice: create "new families" or be left with "no families." The first choice requires changing our familiar family roles and experiencing the pain of innovation that will affect our most powerful and private relationships. The second option will come about, we argue, if we avoid change, leaving family roles much as they have been since the 1950s, with fewer and fewer adults who are willing and able to fill them.

Although the outcomes are very different, both revolutions are fueled by the same social priorities that value the workplace over the home. These priorities lead many women to want to escape from a life built exclusively on family relationships and the tasks of maintaining them, since they see them as burdens and barriers to their accomplishments in the workplace, where their work is valued and appreciated. These priorities also lead many men to stay away from the home, and to acknowledge the importance of family and family tasks only when they are urging them on women. And these priorities are now leading a new generation of children to learn little or nothing about the home and its tasks. School work, friends, and even their favorite TV programs seem to be taking precedence over sharing domestic responsibilities with their parents.

In this book, we use national data to document the historical roots of these options and to highlight the forces that are moving us and our sons and daughters—the young adults of the new generation—along one path or the other.

Some experiences are strengthening "new families" while others are leading to "no families." For example:

Children who grow up in a family disrupted by divorce delay their own entry into marriage and have few children; but boys with this experience tend to have more egalitarian marriages than boys who have not.

Leaving home before marriage to establish an independent residence results in a greater commitment among young women to have a career and reduces the number of children they expect to have; but this experience increases young men's likelihood of marriage.

Growing up in a female-headed household results in greater participation in household chores among children than growing up in an intact family, so much so that boys in mother-only families are more involved in household tasks than girls in two-parent families.

Our results indicate that it is by no means clear whether the outcome in the future will be "new families" or "no families."

We did not plan originally to write a book on such a broad theme. The project really began in bits and pieces, each published in professional journals, about the interrelationships among a few types of family changes. (The chapters that began life this way cite their origins and the professional journals that originally published them, and indicate as well how much our ideas have changed.) We are two demographers: one primarily interested in the changes in living arrangements that are leading unmarried Americans increasingly to live alone; and one whose research focused on the growth in women's roles outside the family and the decision to marry. We are also two friends, who found each other's work interesting and enjoyed working together. We wondered whether our research might not be connected—that young people who experienced nonfamily living in young adulthood might be less likely to marry as a result. We reasoned that those who might otherwise marry *in order to leave home* would be under less pressure to marry, and those who lived for a while away from their families, and had the chance to learn the survival skills of the opposite sex so that they could both maintain a car and cook a meal, would have less reason to marry. This line of reasoning led to a series of articles about the factors leading men and women to marry and the role of previous family-related experiences—both nonfamily living and parental divorce—in that process.

But in analyzing and thinking about these connections, we wondered whether these same experiences might also lead to more egalitarian families, and we explored this question in a paper on sex-role attitudes. In this as in all our other analyses, however, we shared a perception common among most family demographers: only women's lives were changing. Though these changes posed a threat to familism and family stability, men—like children— were passive bystanders. It was only when we immersed ourselves in the details of the division of labor in the home, tasks at which we ourselves are skilled, but which, as adolescents in the 1950s, we had learned to take for granted, that we saw very clearly what men and children could, with the encouragement of women, do to help. These analyses forced us to focus on the home and its social, human, and emotional tasks, as well as on the chores that still take many hours a week, and to see it as an undervalued treasure that is at risk. These analyses became the core of this book, and led to a nearly complete reinterpretation of the materials on marriage and sex-role attitudes that began our investigation.

Many have contributed to this book, although we realize that not all of them will agree with us, some because they think we have gone too far, and some because they think we should have gone further in clarifying our sense of the choices that lie ahead between "new families" and "no families." The research began when Goldscheider was at RAND, and all the analyses were carried out there, supported by contracts and grants from the Center for Population Research, National Institute of Child Health and Human Development (Grant No. P50 HD–12639 to the RAND Population Research Center and Contract No. NO1–HD–12814) and the National Science Foundation (Grant No. SES–8609092), as well as by RAND Sponsored Research from The RAND Corporation. It has been a long project, growing out of a collaboration that began a full decade ago, and was continued over thousands of miles, accelerated by intensive research stays at RAND, visits in Jerusalem and Providence, and more recently, by the power of electronic mail. We have been blessed throughout with a stalwart team of fellow researchers, each of whom contributed in his or her own way. We want to express our warm appreciation to our programmers, Pilar Rosenfeld, who helped us figure out how to get started; Christine Witsberger, who helped us out of tangles both in the data and of our own making; and David Rumpel, whose diligence and interest in our ideas contributed both to the quality of the analyses and to our feelings of accomplishment. We also greatly enjoyed the support of Eileen Miech at RAND, who read as she typed—and uploaded and downloaded—and always encouraged us in our efforts, as well as that of Sharon Norigian of Brown University, who also read and encouraged as she photocopied and express-mailed.

We are grateful to our colleagues, who have listened to and discussed our ideas with us at RAND, Brown, and the Hebrew University in Jerusalem, as well as at professional meetings. Jim Smith at RAND, and Arland Thornton at the University of Michigan, have been supportive throughout, though they might be the last to agree with our arguments. Others at RAND require special mention, including Peter Morrison, whose leadership first brought the pieces together and whose support remained constant; Julie DaVanzo, whose thoughtful challenges always helped us to improve our methods and our logic; and Arleen Leibowitz, who helped us fill the holes in our arguments. And Barbara Williams listened, shared our vision, and helped to provide us key support.

At Brown, both in the Department of Sociology and at the Population Studies and Training Center, we found colleagues who listened with patience and interest to reports of our results. And when research funds at RAND were nearly exhausted, the support of the Brown academic administration, via a faculty sabbatical, allowed the work to be carried through to completion.

We also want to express our appreciation to the Rockefeller Foundation, and the Rockefeller Study and Conference Center at the Villa Serbelloni, Bellagio (Como), Italy. As a retreat in time and space in the Italian alps, Bellagio provided the opportunity to draft a number of key chapters. The staff was marvelous, and should serve to remind all of us how much less scholarly work can get done when there are no others to help perform the daily tasks of cooking, shopping, and cleaning.

And finally, our love and thanks to Calvin and Rafe who, through their professional contributions to editing and presenting our work and their domestic contributions to our rich home and family lives, have shown us their love.

1

The New "Decline of the Family"

One well-known sociologist whispered to another sharing the podium at a session on family change, "I have to cook dinner every Thursday, and I hate it." A man in the audience complained during the discussion that followed that his wife "wouldn't let him" do the laundry, although he had volunteered. No doubt many men have wondered when, if ever, it is appropriate to hold the door open for a woman. Clearly men, including those who study the family, feel some anxiety about male and female relationships, particularly about a man's role in the home.

This anxiety may be the reason most male scholars ignore the changes that are underway in the home, even though they write extensively about the rapid changes that have occurred since the 1950s in almost every other dimension of family life. This writing is often pessimistic—greatly concerned about family instability and the risk of population decline—because of changes in marriage, fertility, and divorce that they link to the increase in cohabitation and childbearing outside of marriage and most dramatically and ubiquitously, to the growth in paid employment among women, particularly married mothers of very young children (Espenshade, 1985; Westoff, 1986; Bumpass, 1987).

But their explanations are incomplete, for what is at the heart of these changes is a restructuring of male-female relationships, both at work and at home, in which men are increasingly expecting their wives to share in economic responsibilities and women are increasingly expecting help with domestic tasks. They appear to believe instead that the only way to ensure that women stay married and raise two or more children is to turn the clock back to the time before this restructuring took hold; to go back to the 1950s by making women dependent once again on male incomes. They reason that

1

as women act increasingly like men by focusing on their careers, no one will be left to raise the children, maintain networks of family relationships, and manage the home, because most men today are uncomfortable doing these things. In studying the transformation of the workplace as women increasingly join men there, many social scientists assume the home will be abandoned.

Male scholars are not the only ones feeling anxiety about rapid change in family structure. New generations of children are growing up experiencing the pains of family revolution as their parents divorce and remarry or opt out of the fray to stand alone as single parents. The norms and expectations underlying married life in the 1950s—those "rules" that told couples what to expect—are no longer valid. Marriages formed under the old rules are being dissolved; new ones formed during the confusion of the present are not holding up very well, either. As a result, the children of divorce are increasingly choosing not to marry. They are cohabiting or living outside of familylike relationships altogether, afraid to risk such loss again, at least until it is clear what the new rules are (Thornton, 1990).

The option to remain unmarried has become increasingly attractive, and not simply because of the growing confusion about marriage. While female independence has been upsetting the rules of family life, a separate family revolution has also been in progress. A new alternative to family life—nonfamily living—has become available for the first time.

This revolution began in the 1940s with an increase in residential independence for the widowed elderly. With the advent and expansion of Social Security and the development of private pension plans, retired men and women—including women who had never worked outside the home—had enough income to maintain themselves independently, with no need to move in with their grown children. This "family change" has always been seen as benign, even welcome.

Then, beginning seriously in the 1960s, nonfamily living spread to young adults, who discovered that they now had the option of living independently before marriage. Only a generation ago, almost all unmarried people lived either with their parents, their married children (if they had them), or their married siblings. Most of those who did not have access to the homes of near kin boarded with other families rather than having their own home or apartment. They were either dependents or outsiders in someone else's home. The rise in nonfamily living has meant that for the first time the privacy, independence, and authority of having one's own place does not require marriage. The general scholarly view of this phenomenon (e.g., Michael et al., 1980) is that if all unmarried people had enough money, they would choose to be freed from the restrictions of dependency and live alone. Few consider that there might be some living arrangement *better* than living alone, that in an equal relationship—whether of roommates or of those with family ties—

people can find companionship while respecting one another's privacy and independence.

Thus, the family is undergoing two revolutions in the latter part of the twentieth century: one outside it, in the rise of nonfamily living; and the other inside it, as relationships between men and women change under pressure from the sex-role revolution. These are not by any means the first revolutions in family life. Another dramatic transformation of family life occurred in the nineteenth century when urbanization and industrialization took the production of many goods and services out of the home. As a result, men left the farm to earn money to buy these goods and services, leading to the physical separation of men's and women's productive work and to the notion of their lives as "separate spheres."

When central heating arrived, and families no longer needed to spend their leisure hours together in one room, like a long car ride, for all but the warmest months of the year, the transformation may have been even greater. And when the invention of the telephone meant that neighbors and family could be counted on not to drop in unexpectedly, the level of privacy and isolation of the American family increased to unprecedented levels.[1] Families no longer marry off their children by age order so that younger daughters need not wait for their older sisters to find a match; and fathers no longer can expect their sons to work alongside them and eventually take over their trades or their places on the family farm. Hence, "the family" has changed repeatedly. But family change has always led to "new families"—in some ways better and in some ways worse than those they succeeded. At least this was always the case for families in the past; the expectations—or *rules*—changed, and families changed with them. But what about changes in current rules? Will they also lead to "new families"? Or will the option of nonfamily living bring about "the end of the family"?

Hear again what family demographers, sociologists, and economists are saying. They define marriage as a relationship based on *trade*. "Marriage is an exchange of female services for male incomes" (Bumpass, 1987); ". . . [until now] when a man and woman married, the husband specialized in market work and the wife in home production, and then they traded" (Espenshade, 1985). Hence, "with men and women earning the same income . . . what then is the point of marriage?" (Westoff, 1986). Missing is any consideration of love as a basis for marriage, companionship as a basis for living together, or *shared* parenthood.

These scholars do not consider that a relationship can provide benefits, such as closeness and companionship, comfort in difficulty, and sharing of happy times, beyond the exchange of goods and services. They conclude that the economic basis of family relationships is crumbling, as women increasingly support themselves. By implication, they are arguing that if *women* have enough money, they will live alone. Their argument is the same as the one given for the rise of nonfamily living, in which living in families is seen as less desirable than living alone, not only for the unmarried, whose only other option is thought to be dependency on another's household, but *for all women.*

In many ways, this may not be an unfair description of many traditional marriages, in which the quality of the marital relationship is subordinate (for both partners) to their economic interdependence. Even at its height in the 1950s, romantic love as a basis for marriage, or "companionate marriage" as we will call it (Burgess and Locke, 1945), was little more than a myth, because such a marriage is founded not only on love but also on equality and mutual respect between partners. Women with no recent (or any) work experience or marketable skills have difficulty being equal partners in such a relationship unless they are extraordinarily desirable in the remarriage market.

Companionate marriage focuses on the quality of the relationship between the partners. It emphasizes interpersonal closeness, trust, communication, and mutuality as the foundation of a mature, romantic love. However, such a relationship is difficult to maintain when a wife and mother has few options for support except to find a "better" husband. Men can and do leave an alcoholic or abusive spouse (or even an unpleasant one) and can support themselves alone and expect to remarry. But women cannot leave their husbands as easily. Since many women cannot support themselves, all they can do is hope the alcoholism or abuse ends. Women have *needed* to please in a way men have not. Hence, women found they had to lie—about their grades, their tennis skills, their orgasms, and how they spent the housekeeping money— rather than communicate honestly, as required in a companionate marriage. So in many traditional marriages, women have in fact been dependents in their own homes, in many ways like unmarried children, parents, and siblings before they had the resources to live alone.

Married women have also had full responsibility for managing the home and doing many of the chores that, despite all the modern conveniences of washers and vacuums, take many hours a week. In many ways, women's domestic responsibilities have increased, since they have taken on the chores that men once performed, while their husbands work longer hours, commute more, and spend more leisure time away from home. They have taken on their children's chores with the expansion of education. The academic year is longer and the years of schooling necessary to function successfully as an adult have increased. Our conception of childhood has transformed the "useful child" into the "useless child" (Zelizer, 1985) and in the process, has created daughters who learn few household skills as children, and sons who learn fewer still.

Hence, living alone is not a great loss for many women, compared with a traditional marriage based on exchange (assuming they can maintain themselves financially); they have fewer rooms to clean and people to cook for, balanced against the loss of their partner's income. But what of young men? Does the same logic imply that if they all had enough money, and could purchase domestic services in the market, they, too, would live alone? Have they only married to get someone else to do the housekeeping? If so, the revolution that has created privacy and dignity for those living outside of families may well be the last family revolution, and the recent pessimistic scholarship about the family may turn out to be correct.

We do not think so. If the revolution in employment means that women no longer *have* to marry, it also means that the marriages they do contract are now voluntary in a way that was never before possible. Men and women have the opportunity to create "new families." They can do so by becoming partners again, sharing in home- and family-based tasks, as they did before men's work moved out of the home and they followed it into the factories and offices of the modern economy. The "no families" created by the rise in nonfamily living should not be as attractive as a companionate marriage. Most young adults can develop such a relationship if they work together not only to earn the resources to make a home but also to create family relationships and a physical environment that can provide them with satisfaction and beauty in their domestic lives.

"New families" are only possible, however, if men will share in family work more directly—including performing household tasks. A rewarding family environment rests on careful coordination and hard work, and women are beginning to resent having to take it all on, alone. If women are now refusing to marry, it may not be because they no longer "need" the earnings of men, as the family demographers think. It is true that their earnings can finally "buy" them out of bad marriages. However, there is no basis either in economic theory or in social psychology for expecting that women or men should use their earnings to forgo a good marriage with love, companionship, sharing, and the continuity of children and grandchildren. It is likely that women are, instead, *deferring* marriage, looking for an appropriate partner as most men and women always have, but are taking longer to do it. They are likely to have become much choosier because they fear the double burden of work and home—not just because they can now "afford" to be choosy. And they can wait in independence and privacy, living in their own place, rather than remaining daughters in their parents' homes.

To learn whether this is a realistic prospect—to find out whether "new families" or "no families" are more likely to result from the changes currently underway in family life—requires systematic study. We know much less about how things work in families than we do about physical and biological systems, political systems, or even economic systems. There is an enormous need for evidence about the way people function in families and outside them, and what factors affect our family lives. This book is meant to contribute to this task. Our results cannot be definitive. Predicting the future is always risky, whether for families or the weather. Most of our analyses do not even focus directly on *change*, as we discuss in more detail in chapter 3. What we try to do, in a scholarly and systematic way, is examine the family patterns that have emerged in the 1970s and 1980s and use these patterns to see what they portend for the future. The shattering of the family stability of the 1950s and early 1960s by the revolutions in divorce and in gender roles and the emergence of nonfamily living arrangements in early adulthood made the decades that followed critical for the future of the family. The young adults that we study are the first of whom a large proportion had childhoods disturbed by parental divorce and remarriage, and they are also the first to have started thinking about gender equality in childhood. The factors that influenced their attitudes about their future family lives, the process of marrying and having children, and the division of labor in their homes provide clues to assess the likely direction families will take.

Our view is that children's experiences in the home shape the families they later form. Factors that increase the involvement of children in household tasks should lead to men who are not tormented by sharing the responsibility with their wives for making dinner. The participation of fathers should make their daughters more optimistic that the "double burden" is not a necessary component of all marriages. Hence, in this study we look not only at the factors that affect the ways in which adults create and maintain families (or instead, lead them away from family living altogether) but also at the factors that might lead to "new families."

Specifically, this book is a study of the factors influencing the decisions of young women (and young men) to marry (chapter 5), have children, or divorce (chapter 6). As such, it is part of the tradition of studies that have led demographers recently to write pessimistically about the "decline of the family." But it differs from them, in that it is also a study of the development of egalitarian gender roles (chapter 4), particularly in *the home*, and the factors influencing the extent to which men and women—and boys and girls—share in its care (chapters 7–10). The critical question is whether these trends in nonmarriage, nonparenthood, and divorce are leading to a future of "no families," or whether the family can become again a sharing partnership between men, women, and children, and thus ensure its future.

2

Family Trends Since the Baby Boom: Decline or Restructuring?

Many of the trends currently affecting family relationships and family living are familiar. Most people know that there has been an increase in divorce and in women's employment and that young people are not getting married as young as they "used to" and are not having as many children.[1] However, other changes, particularly the increase in nonfamily living (in which unmarried people live alone or with nonrelatives), are much less familiar. To understand how families have changed, we must begin with the way they *were*. What were the families of the past? How long had they been that way? And how should we interpret current trends?

In this chapter, we review the central changes that have occurred since the 1950s in family life and in the relationships between the sexes. These changes have created the two options that now confront the family: "new families," in which men and women increasingly share not only the economic but also the domestic responsibilities of the household, teaching their children to do so, as well; and "no families," in which men and women forgo marriage and children and support themselves (and only themselves), living apart from each other and often from any family setting.

We will also look back into earlier periods whenever possible, because beginning with the 1950s creates its own distortions. That was the middle of the baby boom, a period in which more people got married and married younger than in the past, and when more people were having children, and having them younger, as well.[2] It was also a time in which the public and private spheres of men's and women's work were most separated as a result of the dramatic growth of the suburbs. Freudian psychology and a host of other ideas reinforced and glorified the differences between men and women, and overlooked or even denied their similarities.

Yet even during this high-water mark of marriage and family, strong forces were developing that contributed both to a fundamental restructuring of male and female roles outside the home (making them more similar) and to a long-term decline in the family-centeredness of adult lives. These forces also contained the seeds of a rejection of the home and a devaluing and trivializing of housework and child care, a rejection that came to color the views of traditionalists and radicals alike. What was happening, and how have the 1950s left us a legacy that can lead, at the extreme, to "no families" or to "new families"?

New Families: The Revolution in Male and Female Roles

The changes having the most powerful impact on restructuring the family are those that are breaking down the separation between male and female adult roles, although thus far, this revolution has taken place almost exclusively in the work force. As we will discuss in more detail in chapter 7, men only left the home as the base for their productive activities during the nineteenth century—relatively recently, in terms of change in traditional family relationships. And it is even more recently (and hence, more briefly) that most men expected to be able to earn a "family wage" that would allow their wives to stop taking in washing or boarders and to devote themselves full time to the domestic arts being developed by the emerging middle class (Matthews, 1987). It is also only in this century that men's incomes were sufficient enough to allow their children to attend school throughout childhood rather than to work in the field or factory (Zelizer, 1985).

By the 1950s this increase in the specialization of men's and women's "spheres" had taken place, reaching almost complete segregation at home and at work. Many of our current trends are reactions against that specialization, but other trends now in progress break new ground in defining adult roles for men and women, impelled by women's rapid increase in paid employment outside the home.

Work Outside the Home by Wives and Mothers

Work outside the home has always been a necessity for the poor—including men and women—since for them "the home" did not include a farm, family business, or the resources that would allow them to confine their activities there. Poor people have always left their homes to sell their labor to others.

For them, being able to work at home—either by producing goods or services or tending to the family—may have been a goal, but was almost never a reality.[3]

Families in more comfortable circumstances, however, confined the productive activities of women exclusively to the home. In the Victorian era, unmarried daughters in such families often spent their young adult years in relative inactivity, and married women worked outside the home only if starvation loomed (Huber and Spitze, 1983). At the beginning of the twentieth century, fewer than 1 woman in 5 was working or looking for work outside the home. Among white married women, fewer than 2 percent were in the labor force.

Since the turn of the century, we have seen a remarkable transformation of women's lives, from exclusive focus on the home and family to what is often called "the double burden," or more recently, "the second shift" (Hochschild, 1989). Employment is now normative among women in the prime working ages of 24–54, with over two-thirds in the labor market. Even among mothers of children under 1—the group historically least likely to work—over half are in the labor force (Bureau of Labor Statistics, 1988).

This growth in female employment in paid jobs has been fueled by generations of increases in women's education and work experience. And the changing structure of the economy has greatly increased employment opportunities for women in positions as clerical workers, teachers, nurses, and other service and production workers (Smith and Ward, 1984).

The entry of women into the paid labor force represented a major shift from earlier periods, since for most of the nineteenth century and early twentieth century, it was *men* who were moving into the paid labor force from joint production with their wives and from continuous involvement in the lives of their families. During the same period, as men specialized in paid work, women increasingly specialized in family tasks, so that by the 1950s, they were responsible for a very broad realm of activities connected with it. In addition to continuing to care for infants (and stay home from work when their school-age children are ill), women keep social calendars for their children and spouses, plan the graduations and weddings of their children and the anniversary parties of their parents, and generally do the social, emotional, and physical work associated with maintaining the family. What have been the consequences for women as a result of the increase in their paid employment?

To a large extent, working mothers still manage all these family-related responsibilities. All they have relinquished is part of the daily supervision of their children. Although there have been a few studies of how women have managed to do all this (Berk, 1985; Pleck, 1985), an entire industry of studies on the fate of children of working mothers has emerged. As recently as the early 1960s, college students in child development courses learned that children of working mothers became psychological misfits or even sometimes died. Only later did research reveal that early twentieth century theories of "maternal deprivation" were not useful guides. Such theories were based on studies of English children of the blitz, sent abruptly away from home to the countryside while their parents fought the war, and on infants in foundling homes left almost totally alone except for bathing and feedings (Bowlby, 1956; Spitz, 1956). They bore no real relationship to what could be expected to result if infants grew up in homes in which their mothers left and returned home on a regular schedule, and the child spent the intervening hours being cared for by someone else either in the caretaker's home or in some other familylike setting.

Since the 1950s, attitudes about whether working women can be successful parents have continuously become more favorable. Studies of the effects of working mothers on their children have found few, if any, adverse effects (National Research Council, 1990). Nearly everyone has had some relatively direct experience with this phenomenon, as children have grown up with working mothers, as parents have scrutinized the effects of their daughters' (and their daughters'-in-law) employment on their grandchildren, and as men have learned to live with and appreciate earning wives. The trend toward more egalitarian sex-role attitudes is apparent within each younger generation reaching adulthood, as well as within the generations whose members have grown older (Miller and Garrison, 1982).

Husbands' Help Around the House

The growth in female labor force participation sharply unbalanced the traditional family. When only men worked outside the home, the total amount of work effort of married men and women was approximately equal. However, this was clearly not the case among two-earner families. Beginning in the 1960s, studies were undertaken that asked people to keep diaries of the amount of time they spent in various activities over the course of a day (Walker and Woods, 1976). Although *children* of working mothers might not suffer ill effects, this was not the case for working wives themselves, particularly compared to their husbands. The "second shift" means that employed women work many more hours—at their jobs and at home—than either men or women who are not employed outside the home. This inequality is exacerbated by the presence of young children; employed mothers of young children appear to meet their responsibilities to job and children chiefly by taking time out from their own leisure, such as reading or watching TV, and from sleep (Stafford, 1980).

The substantial disparities between the sexes in time spent on household tasks extends also to the kinds of tasks men and women perform. Men specialize in yard and home maintenance both as sons and after marriage. As they often discover when leaving home before marriage or after divorce, experience with such chores is not as critical as knowing about cooking, shopping, and cleaning. The successful performance of these daily tasks is fundamental to the quality of life when one is living alone, and it is just these tasks, such studies showed, with which men had no experience.

Until recently, no study of time use in married-couple families was able to document much difference in housework hours between husbands with employed wives and those whose wives worked only in the home, or any increase in husbands' housework time as greater numbers of their wives began working. Until the late 1970s or early 1980s, employed wives simply added the demands of a job to their traditional responsibilities of running a household. Husbands' *share* of housework increased when wives worked, but almost entirely because women cut down the number of hours they spent on housework when they took a job outside the home (Spitze, 1986).

However, there is now some evidence that by the mid-1980s, after a generation of employed women worked a second shift in the home, men are actually *increasing* the number of hours they spend on household work. Married men are spending more time on routine domestic tasks, shopping, and child care not only in the United States but also in Canada, the United Kingdom, and Norway (Gershuny and Robinson, 1988). Women still put in far more hours at these tasks than their husbands, but gender differences at home are apparently beginning to erode, with some hope that this change may eventually rival those in the workplace.

That there has been much less change in gender roles in the home than in the workplace is reflected in people's attitudes, as well. More people approve of women working in the labor force under almost all circumstances[4] than they do of men sharing in the responsibilities of the home. In 1985, 83 percent of men over 30 said they "approved of a married woman earning money even if she has a husband capable of supporting her," but only 42 percent disagreed with the statement that "it is much better for everyone involved if the man is the achiever outside the home and the woman takes care of the home and family."[5] Though most respondents approve of women's working outside the home, a majority are still concerned about the man's role in caring for the home and family.

The gap, however, between these two versions of gender role equality— work and home—has been closing, particularly among younger people and women. The proportion of men under 30 approving of married women working increased from 81 to 90 percent between 1977 and 1985, and those disagreeing with the view that it is "much better" for a woman to take care of the home and family increased from 50 to 64 percent. Comparable percentages for women under 30 in 1985 were 88 percent approving of married women working and 72 percent disagreeing that it is "much better" for a woman to take care of the home.

Similarly, a substantial change in attitudes has taken place toward husbands' helping with housework. In 1962, a majority of a sample of married mothers thought it unreasonable to expect their husbands to help in any way with housework. However, by 1985 fewer than a quarter of those women, still married to the same husband, felt that way. And there is at least some evidence that parents are beginning to prepare their children for more egalitarian roles in the home. Mothers in 1971 were less likely to endorse sex-role differentiation in children's chores than mothers in 1955, even after controlling for differences in education, labor force status, and race over the 18-year period (Duncan and Duncan, 1978).

The trend toward "new families" has proceeded extremely unevenly. More than a generation of women carried the double responsibility of working at home and in the workplace. They also worried about their children's well-being while they were at work and felt a profound unwillingness to be "unwomanly" by asking their husbands to do "female" tasks in the home. Only very recently have men begun to relieve women by taking on more domestic responsibilities.

We believe that this is a profoundly "profamily" trend. The traditional male sex role is essentially *antifamily*. It encourages men to put career success ahead of everything else and reinforces the idea that tasks relating to family matters are women's work and are thus inappropriate and even demeaning for men.

But this profamily trend has been a long time in coming, and may be too little or too late. During the long period in which men's and women's family burdens remained unbalanced, there was a major shift to "no families." Attractive and remunerative employment outside the home became increasingly available to women, making it less necessary for them to specialize in family roles, and the rise in divorce made such a strategy too risky even for women who preferred traditional family roles. Ultimately, many women did not marry and refused to assume the major responsibility for small children by not bearing them. What was happening?

"No Families": Trends in Childbearing, Marriage, and Divorce

Several trends seem to signal an absolute decline in the centrality of the family, with perhaps a weakening so great that the necessary tasks it once performed—such as providing warm and supportive relationships for adults while at the same time supplying society with a new generation—will not be performed in the future. Trends in the demographic phenomena of childbearing and marriage are of critical importance to the increasing move toward "no families."

Childbearing

The primary concern with fertility is that it has fallen to levels that will lead to a natural decrease in population, since births will not replace deaths. The baby boom that lasted from the late 1940s to the early 1960s ended fairly abruptly, after a decade in which American women were bearing on average about 2.8 children. Since then there have been major declines in fertility, particularly in the late 1960s and early 1970s, with no real sign of any increase (ignoring the ripples created by baby boomers passing through their own childbearing years). The current generation of women is likely to bear about 1.8 children (taking into account those who never have children); they need to average 2.1 children to offset mortality and guarantee the replacement of the adult generation of men and women.[6]

Part of the decline in fertility is likely to benefit everyone. It should increase the well-being of children, since later-born children and those closely spaced between older and younger siblings achieve less on a variety of education-related measures, controlling for the level of family economic resources (Blake, 1989). If families put a fixed amount of resources into children, those with fewer children can invest more time, energy, supervision, and enrichment into each child.

Nevertheless, young people in the United States are currently not bearing enough children to reproduce themselves, and in Scandinavia and parts of Western Europe, which have experienced many changes in the family earlier than the United States, the deficit is even greater. This, despite the fact that young American men and women still *expect* to become parents. Among seniors in high school in 1986, few thought it "fairly unlikely" or "very unlikely" that they would want to have children eventually (fewer than 7 percent of young women and fewer than 5 percent of young men).[7] This suggests that the decline in childbearing results not from the desire to avoid parenthood but from the costs and difficulties along the way. Chief among these difficulties, we suggest, is the problem of finding and keeping a suitable spouse with whom to raise children.

Marriage and Divorce

Since the 1950s, the American family has retreated from a pattern of early and stable marriages, with extremely high proportions marrying. Not only are young people marrying later but more appear not to be marrying at all. And those who do marry are increasingly likely to end their marriages by separation or divorce. Between 1960 and 1985, the proportion of women in their early twenties who were single doubled from 28 to 58 percent. Among those in their mid- to-late-twenties, the proportion never married rose from 10 to 26 percent (Westoff, 1986). And although virtually all—90 percent or more—will marry eventually (Schoen et al., 1985), these marriages are much less stable than they were in the past. Recent studies estimate that about 2 out of 3 first marriages will end in divorce or separation (Martin and Bumpass, 1989), a rate much higher than a generation or two ago.

Again, although these trends represent a retreat from the centrality of family roles in adult lives, they also provide many benefits. Delaying marriage and parenthood allows more time for increased education and work experience for both men and women, so the families they later form should be more secure, both financially and emotionally. Women who are older when they first marry are much less likely to divorce (Moore and Waite, 1981). The current average marital age and projected proportions marrying are not at all exceptional in contrast to the more distant past; it is the baby boom period that was unusual.

However, the vast majority of young men and women still expect and prefer to marry and remain married. Among high school seniors in 1986, almost none said they "definitely" or "probably" preferred not "having a mate for most of [their] life" (fewer than 3 percent of young women and only 5 percent of young men) (Thornton, 1989). This represented essentially no change from the answers high school seniors gave 10 years earlier (an increase of one-half of 1 percent for women, and seven-tenths of 1 percent for men).

The rise in divorce has often been interpreted positively as evidence of the growth in importance of the ideal of romantic love and companionate marriage. Married men and women have reported greater satisfaction with their marriages over time, presumably because unhappy marriages are now more likely to break up (Thornton and Freedman, 1979). This argument once was persuasive, because, until recently, divorce was followed by rapid remarriage for both men and women (Davis, 1972). Couples who had made a mistake in choosing a mate were able to recover from their error and try again. Furthermore, many scholars expected the divorce rate to decline quickly, as well, since the very high divorce rates that first appeared in the 1960s and 1970s were due at least in part to the widespread liberalization of state divorce laws. Those laws allowed separated or unhappy couples (many of whom had been separated or very unhappy for many years) to divorce, resulting in a piling-up effect.

Thus far, however, no evidence exists for any substantial decline in the divorce rate. It is likely that some part of the high divorce rate reflects the working out of the sex-role revolution, in which couples have become increasingly dissatisfied with their original bargain, but cannot find a way to change the terms without dissolving their marriage. Women still expect their husbands to share responsibility for household chores more than men do (Thornton, 1989). Both men and women can still draw comfort and support from their friends for their differing positions. Evidence that part of the problem with marriages lies in its traditional definitions can also be found in the rise in nonmarital cohabitation. Increasingly, divorced persons are not remarrying, choosing instead to cohabit (Bumpass, Sweet, and Cherlin, 1989).

New trends in marriage and divorce may be having a greater effect on family roles than on the decline in fertility within marriage. Part of that decline has been offset by increasing fertility outside of marriage, keeping women in parental roles to a greater extent than men. Women are evidently still willing to bear children despite the risk of divorce and to raise them as single parents. To the extent that declines in fertility and marriage represent a rejection by employed women of the double burden of family responsibilities, being married seems as problematic to them as being a parent.[8]

The Role of Children in Families

For many children, however, the decline in marriage and the increase in divorce have led to a childhood in one-parent and stepfamilies. Many bad marriages result in poor parenting, so that divorce benefits many children, as well as their parents. But many with marital problems nevertheless are able to parent quite effectively. Divorce and remarriage upset both parents and children, but children are less likely to benefit from them (Wallerstein and Blakeslee, 1989).

Children's experience of divorce and remarriage has grown rapidly since the 1950s. Although 84 percent of children born during the first half of the 1950s were living with both natural parents at age 14, one estimate is that only one-third of the children born in the early 1980s will still be living with both natural parents by that age (Hofferth, 1985). That same study shows that another quarter of these children will be living with a stepparent. Therefore, in nearly half the families with two parents, one parent will be a later arrival. And with the decline in remarriage and the rise in out-of-wedlock parenthood, the largest percentage of children (greater than 40 percent) will be living in one-parent families (Hofferth, 1985).

These trends in divorce and out-of-wedlock parenthood indicate that the axis of the family may be shifting away from men, both as spouses and as parents, and more toward women and children. This raises an important question: what part do children play in families, and how do these changes affect them? Interestingly, this is an area in which we have almost no information.

Our *theories* about fertility decline imply that whereas children once provided economic benefits of considerable value to parents, making it prudent to have many, their *economic* value to the family has become almost entirely negative. Families now resist having more children than they can "afford"—which might be very few (Caldwell, 1982). These theories argue that in the past, children helped their mothers and fathers with the many tasks centering on the household. But as these tasks have left the household, the economic value of children decreased (Zelizer, 1985). But in fact there is little evidence on children's contribution to household labor in traditional societies, and almost none for industrialized countries. A recent study shows that American children in the mid 1970s spent nearly as many hours as their fathers on household tasks—1.2 versus 1.7 hours per day (Sanik, 1981)—but we do not know whether this represents a decrease or an increase over the 1950s.

Some evidence suggests that in traditional families, parent-child relationships focus on obedience; children expect to obey parents and parents expect to be obeyed. But in more modern families, parents report that in teaching their children, independence is a much higher priority than obedience (Alwin, 1988).

It is unclear how this works in practice for children's involvement in household tasks. We will explore this issue in considerably more detail in chapter 9 and argue that the child's role in household tasks is likely to have decreased significantly in the recent past. Younger parents and those with more education seem to involve their children much less in dishwashing, laundry, shopping, and cleaning up, reducing the participation of their teenage daughters in these chores to little more than the extremely low level that characterizes the involvement of almost all teenage sons.

It may be that parents need to exercise a substantial amount of authority in order to involve children in housework and to establish patterns of interaction and *interdependence*. Many parents trying to raise independent children may actually be facilitating their children's noninvolvement in the life of the family, producing children who are not competent to help around the house. If so, one result of this new form of parenting may be that children are learning less and less about the tasks associated with maintaining a pleasant and smoothly running home.

Family Decline Via Nonfamily Living

The rise in living alone (or with nonrelatives) among unmarried adults is rarely considered in discussions about "the decline of the family."[9] Yet this has been one of the biggest changes in family life since the baby boom. More and more unmarried adults are living apart from their immediate families, forming nonfamily households at a rate far exceeding the growth of the adult population. During the 1970s, nonfamily households increased 73 percent while family households increased by only 13 percent (U.S. Bureau of the Census, 1980).

For the unmarried, *family living* means family extension. Until very recently, those who did not have families, or whose families could not provide them living quarters, lived in boarding houses or as lodgers and servants in someone else's home. The rise in residential independence for the unmarried, then, has been viewed as a family change entirely for the good (when it has been considered at all). This is because family extension has been equated with a loss of privacy for the immediate family as well as with a feeling of dependency for the unmarried relative. Any benefits of sharing—whether of expenses, tasks, or companionship—are considered to come at a high price. Before 1950, the majority of widows over 65 lived with their married children; by 1980, barely one-quarter did so (Kobrin, 1976; U.S. Bureau of the Census, 1983). Older unmarried persons report they are afraid to be "in the way" when asked about the possibility of living with their children (Lopata, 1973).

The rise in nonfamily living among younger adults has also been rapid since the 1950s. While nonfamily households increased their share of U.S. households from 15 to 22 percent between 1960 and 1975 for all ages, those with heads under 25 increased from 13 to 30 percent (Frey and Kobrin, 1982). Since World War II, the age at which young adults have left home has fallen both in the United States and in other developed countries (Young, 1987).

Until the mid-twentieth century, most young people lived in their parents' home until marriage. Since people married later before the baby boom, they remained at home for a decade or more after completing schooling to contribute to the family economy (Kett, 1977). Those leaving home before marriage rarely formed an independent household, going instead either to institutional housing, such as dormitories or barracks, or to lodge in another family's home (Katz, 1975). In Rhode Island, the percentage of sons still at home at age 26 dropped from 50 percent for those reaching that age between 1930 and 1950 to 20 percent for those reaching that same age between 1976 and 1979. The comparable decline for daughters was from 37 to 13 percent (Goldscheider and LeBourdais, 1986).

Although part of the decline in age at leaving home during the early years of the baby boom was being driven by the falling ages at marriage, premarital household headship was also increasing, incorporating young people into the broader phenomenon separating residential independence from marriage (Kuznets, 1978). Among *unmarried* males 18–24 in the United States, for example, the percentage of primary individuals (household heads living alone or with nonrelatives) was 1 percent in 1940 and 1950, 3.3 percent in 1960, and 13.3 percent in 1980 (Goldscheider and LeBourdais, 1986). By 1950, relatively few young adults were living as boarders and lodgers (Ruggles, 1987), which means that full residential independence before marriage was increasingly becoming the new route out of the home for young adults. And by 1980, only 30 percent of high school seniors expected to wait until marriage for an independent residence (Goldscheider and Goldscheider, 1987). Evidently, young people feel that continuing to live in a family setting reflects unfavorably on their maturity.

The rise in nonfamily living for the unmarried is not a particularly significant event for society at large so long as most adults are married. When most people marry young and stay married, and the elderly are a small fraction of the population, those living alone are not very *visible*. Most adults are living in families.

But the American population has changed since the 1950s in ways that make the nonfamily option more common. The increase in marriage age and the rise in divorce, as well as the aging of the population, have combined to dramatically increase the proportion of the population that is unmarried. As a result, nearly 1 in 4 American households does not contain any kind of family. These are homes for unmarried people, in which most (90 percent) are living alone. Are these phenomena linked? Does the option of living independently lead young people to forgo marriage—or to end one—more easily than when their likeliest choice was to move back in with their parents or live with a married sibling? Have our family and marital relationships become so difficult that if we all had enough money, we would each live alone?

A recent argument pulls together all of these trends—nonfamily living, declining marriage and increasing divorce, and even the fertility decline (Burch and Mathews, 1987). That discussion explores the problems of living together with *anyone* except a spouse, and then probes the difficulties of modern marriage in the midst of the sex-role revolution. The authors assume that the relationships of people living together in households are normally hierarchical, all descending from the household head. Living together is only feasible in traditional, hierarchical (sometimes called patriarchal) families, in which everyone knows his or her place: adult male relatives do not challenge the head's decisions, adult female relatives do not criticize (publicly) how the kitchen is run, children do not talk back, and wives defer to their husbands whenever there is a difference between them.[10] The household head controls the financial resources, and all are bound to the (usually male) head through economic need.

In this view of the household, it is not surprising that someone lower in the hierarchy would be happy to escape such dependency when resources become available. Grandparents, adult offspring, and wives flee if they can, according to this view, by moving out to live alone, leaving the former *pater familias* to live by himself. Only minor children would never have this freedom, since although their resistance to obedience has grown, they cannot exercise their independence. However, adults have learned a new method for protecting themselves against the friction of living with the children they are now expected to raise to be independent rather than obedient. They do not have them. In this view, the rise of nonfamily living is but one indication of the declining importance of the family, a consequence of changes leading modern societies not to "new families" but to "no families."

The Changing View of the Home and Family

The view of human and family relationships as having an economic component, which creates hierarchies based on inequalities of resources and power, is undoubtedly true. But there is much more to these relationships than economics. People are inherently social creatures, their sense of self-worth and their very identities molded and maintained in interaction (Mead, 1934). Sharing an idea, an experience, or a memory, even without domination or competition, can be rewarding in itself. The overlap between family and economy that characterized human societies until the industrial revolution meant that economic exchange was tied to social and family relationships, but these relationships are not less important now that the economic threads no longer run through them so tightly. People still need warm and supportive relationships.

In relationships that are not characterized by dominance and control, separate residence is not necessary for privacy and independence. In close relationships, respect and consideration can be reciprocal, not simply hierarchical. In this context, one of the most powerful threats to families and relationships is that by the 1950s, the task of maintaining them had been assigned to women both inside and outside the home.

As we are increasingly learning, building and maintaining relationships, just as organizing and caring for a home, takes work, time, and energy. One of the most interesting results of recent research on kin contact and friendship patterns is that the modern separation of male and female "spheres," in which men earn and women manage families, has resulted in women becoming increasingly specialized in human relationships (Di Leonardo, 1987). They have been characterized as "kin keepers."

One of the consequences of this development is that people are normally closer to their *mother's* relatives than to their father's, since these ties are more actively maintained (Rossi, 1989). Another consequence of this "division of labor" between men and women is that information—both scholarly and practical—on how to strengthen and support relationships, increase communication, and develop mutuality is targeted at women. It appears almost entirely in women's magazines rather than in general mass-market or male-oriented outlets.[11] And of course, the key consequence is that men have become relatively less competent in the social skills needed to nourish and maintain relationships.

The assignment of home- and relationship-maintenance to women has also had another unfortunate consequence. It means not only that women become less willing to take on these responsibilities while they attempt to achieve parity with men in the world of paid work but that these tasks lose status as unpaid and unimportant "women's work." Since the 1950s, men and women have increasingly disparaged family roles, with men denying their advantages and women sharing in the view that they are low status or dirty work.

There is some evidence that the denigration of homemaking skills is very much a twentieth century urban phenomenon. A generation of women lost touch with the skills of their older kin because industrial development and mass production made the "old ways" of doing things "unscientific." Science was used to justify marketing new food processing and preparation techniques—canning, freezing, and prepackaging (such as mixes)—to overcome the inertia of long-established patterns (Matthews, 1987). It was not enough that commercially baked bread was a time- and labor-saving product; it was also sold as nutritionally more complete, "building strong bodies 8 (or 12) ways." As a result, the younger generation did not learn that homemaking is a sophisticated skill, as necessary in "new families" as in "old families."

Homemaking can also be an act of love. Everything people do to help, cheer, or please one another shows their love and care. Working overtime to earn a little more to buy a spouse a present, making something at school for a parent, or preparing a favorite dish for a grandchild are all ways people can express their love to warm and strengthen each other's lives. The home touches people's lives at rest, at meals, at play. As such, it is perhaps the richest environment of all for this kind of interaction. The ability to function there successfully may be the most important skill families can teach both men and women.

Experiences in the Home

It is our view that what is happening in the home today will be the key to how family changes of the last generation will affect American lives as we enter the twenty-first century. The revolution in the world of work has been extremely important, and will continue to be so, as young men and women increasingly prepare themselves in school and through their early work experiences for economic independence. But for this revolution to lead to "new families" rather than to "no families" will require recognizing the importance of the tasks and skills necessary to carry them out that are associated with making a home and developing personal relationships. This will need to happen *in the home*.

Children learn best from what they learn at home. The effects of these experiences can be seen in a wide variety of adult outcomes. Other things being equal, the number of siblings positively affects actual and expected family size; teenage parenthood is more common among daughters of teenage mothers; and divorce increases the likelihood of divorce for children (Terhune, 1974; Waite and Stolzenberg, 1976; Pope and Mueller, 1979; Baldwin and Cain, 1980).

We are particularly concerned about the effects of parental divorce on the families children later form, because in many ways divorce is a very painful experience for them, one more likely to teach young people lessons that will lead them to "no families" because they too divorce or avoid marriage altogether rather than take a risk on the even more unknown family form we call "new families." There is, however, one potentially positive effect of living in a nontraditional family during childhood. Several studies have shown that children in such families often become much more involved in household tasks, with effects that appear to be far greater than simply having a working mother in an intact family (Peters and Haldeman, 1987). If this greater involvement extends to boys as well as girls, and particularly to "female" tasks for boys and "male" tasks for girls, it could lead young people to more satisfying and less stressful marriages in later life.

Even in families in which parents remained married, children in American homes are having a variety of experiences. Children are exposed to egalitarian practices and ideas about men's and women's roles more in some families than in others. More commonly, they are seeing new roles for mothers in the workplace, as more are working, but in some cases, children are seeing new roles for men and women in the home. This should also affect the families they later form.

But increasingly, young people's experiences are taking place outside the home altogether. Nonfamily living in early adulthood may have critical effects on whether the future holds "new families" or "no families." One of the most dramatic aspects of the rapid increase in nonfamily households is its concentration among very young adults. Together with delays in marriage, nonfamily living means that more young people are spending an important part of early adulthood with no family roles.

This is likely to be particularly important for women, since nonfamily living provides a "role hiatus." For those who experienced the traditional role of daughter, nonfamily living can give them alternatives to the traditional roles of wife and mother (Presser, 1971). And for young men, nonfamily living can help them appreciate the complexity of homemaking tasks. Thus, this new living arrangement may help young adults develop skills that will lead to more egalitarian "new families." But it may also atrophy other skills that are developed by living together, such as negotiation, communication, and compromise, that allow people to realize the benefits of sharing their lives with others, which may lead as a result to "no families."

Our Study and Its Goals

The choice of "new families" or "no families" is a critical one that needs to be examined systematically using a rich body of data on young adults and their families. In our study, after introducing our data sources in the next chapter and our approach in using them, we then examine in the remaining chapters *which* families are likely to be changing, and ask how these changes within and outside families are affecting young people.

We will look at the effects of parental divorce and remarriage in childhood as well as the effects of nonfamily living in young adulthood on "no families" and "new families." We will also examine if it matters whether mothers work, how many hours they are away, or how much they earn. We will compare these effects with those resulting from growing up in homes with more egalitarian sex-role attitudes, having more educated parents, and living in less traditional regions of the country or in larger or smaller communities.

We will first consider the effects of these experiences on young people's plans and attitudes to see whether they are likely to form more egalitarian families—or any families at all. How do childhood family experiences influence a young woman's plans to work, have children, or do both? Do they influence whether young men and women approve of mothers' working, or whether young women take a more egalitarian stance on women's roles in the workplace and in the home? In chapter 4 we will examine in detail how experiences while growing up and in early adulthood affect a young person's plans and preferences for their later family lives.

But since there is often a gap between what people *want* and what they do, we then follow these young people further into adulthood and examine the choices they actually make to marry and become parents. In chapter 5, we examine the factors affecting marriage for both men and women, looking at parental family structure, nonfamily living, and at other experiences that affect the *value* of traditional marriage to young men and women. In chapter 6 we see whether the same factors that lead to marriage also affect parenthood and divorce.

Though we care about what affects family formation and stability, we are more concerned about *the kinds* of families that young people are forming. Are they egalitarian families, in which husbands and wives share in the process of raising children and making a home? Are children participating in household tasks, as well? How are experiences in and outside the family influencing the way men share in household labor (chapters 7 and 8), the share of household work contributed by children (chapter 9), and the whole family economy (chapter 10)? And most important, we ask what our analyses suggest about whether these families will provide the next generation of children with experiences and skills that will help *them* to achieve "new families."

3

Studying Family Change

In the last several decades, the American family has been challenged internally by the sex-role revolution and from the outside by the rise of nonfamily living. Associated with these challenges are the increase in divorce, the consequent increase in children's experience of family breakup and living in a mother-only or "blended" family, and marriage delay and fertility decline (chapter 2). Our task in this volume is to evaluate these two challenges. Are "new families" likely to increase, thus completing the sex-role revolution, whereby men participate in the household and help perform its tasks and their sons and daughters are trained in its maintenance? Or will there be more "no families," with low levels of marriage and childbearing, as people increasingly avoid the problems posed by family change by choosing to live unmarried or alone?

To understand this larger picture, we pose a series of questions: How are young people's work and family-related plans and attitudes influenced by their family background and personal characteristics? How do these characteristics influence whether they marry, have children, or divorce? And do they also influence the *kinds* of families young people create, involving husbands and children in household tasks? We focus particularly on how growing up in a mother-only or stepparent family or living alone in early adulthood are echoed in young people's new family experiences. But we are also interested in how other factors affect young people and their family lives, including such childhood influences as growing up in a relatively educated family or in a large community, as well as such adult experiences as marriage and parenthood.

23

Data for Studying Families

Our work rests on the results of a number of ways of studying families. Repeated surveys on sex-role attitudes have been taken, which have shown a strong increase in egalitarianism in the latter part of the twentieth century (Thornton, 1989). Wallerstein and Blakeslee (1989) studied the consequences of parental divorce on children by following patients at a counseling center in Marin County near San Francisco over a 20-year period after divorce. And several studies of the household division of labor contain intensive interviews of a small group of families. These studies have focused primarily on husbands and wives, although some have examined children's roles. Each of these studies has contributed hypotheses for us to test. We have also drawn from the work of historians who have studied the family, looking at the changing roles of children, husbands, and wives.[1]

These in-depth studies provide a wealth of detail, offering insights into the processes underlying behavior. But they usually include such a small number of individuals, often from one particular environment, that we cannot be certain about the extent to which these studies are revealing general trends or just the influence of unusual individuals or situations. Researchers are reluctant to generalize to the nation as a whole from these small, local samples. And often factors that might be making a difference do not appear to do so at all, since it takes many cases to see small differences. A few flips of a coin will not show whether it is a "true" one. But a coin loaded to flip heads 52 percent of the time will make a lot of money for its owner over the long run. Since the questions we ask focus on social change—often changes that are just appearing or may have consequences only for some groups of people—it is often necessary to study large numbers of individuals to see these trends emerging.

By being so specialized, these detailed studies also make it difficult to make clear comparisons. Many studies do not include those who did not have the experience under analysis. Wallerstein and Blakeslee's divorce study includes no children from nondisrupted marriages, whether happy or unhappy, so it may be that the traumas the authors ascribe to divorce are simply due to growing up in Marin County. Such studies are rich in insights, but they do not allow for *the systematic testing* of them. And cross-sectional studies, such as those of sex-role attitudes, preclude seeing whether those attitudes affect people's lives differently.

Our approach allows us to consider and test the insights drawn from other studies. We use a related series of surveys—the National Longitudinal Surveys of Labor Market Experience (NLS)—that includes large numbers of individuals who were selected to represent the entire population of the United States in particular age ranges. These surveys each started with about 5,000 individuals and followed their respondents over more than 15 years, allowing us to look longitudinally at early events and their later consequences. Two of the surveys focus on the transition to adulthood, taking young men and women aged 14–24 and following them as they make decisions about family and work. Another targets mature women (age 30–44) and asks detailed questions about their family and work patterns. (See Appendix A for more detail on these surveys.)

Thus we study a large and representative group of Americans, interviewed across the country, asked comparable questions, and followed over time. These data sets lack the detail that researchers achieve with small samples, especially those in which researchers themselves talk to each respondent and probe for the thoughts or events behind a particular choice or attitude. But by and large, these surveys contain the information that small studies have shown to be important, allowing us *to test* their tentative conclusions. We can turn to these in-depth studies as well to speculate about the processes underlying our results. These data give us the ability to speak about the social processes underway in the entire United States. By working within the constraints of a structured survey questionnaire, these data give us consistency across individuals in the information they provide and assurances about its quality. And most importantly, the surveys follow people over time, which is critical for a study of how young people's families evolve, and how experiences at one point in their lives affect them at later periods.

Studying Change Over the Life Course

Retrospective Longitudinal Data: Childhood Family Structure

The young adults in our study were at least 14 years old when they were first interviewed, but they were asked questions that tell us quite a lot about the structure of their childhood family. In some cases, the questions were specifically about the past; in other cases, the information was current, but is unlikely to have been different at earlier ages. Few parents increase their education during their children's teenage years or change their region of the country.

A key example of a specific question respondents were asked about the past was whom they lived with at age 14. Most reported living with both biological parents but others only lived with one (usually the mother) or lived with a parent and a stepparent. These were by far the most important groups, although a few lived in various other kinds of households.

Of course, these groups probably differ in many ways. For example, mother-only households are often poor. But by having large samples with many cases, some of which are more and some less affluent, we can take these differences into account statistically. This allows us to compare people who were raised by two natural parents with those raised in stepfamilies or by a single mother, but who were otherwise similar. Then if these groups differ in either their willingness to marry or in the age at which they do so, we can conclude that the experiences during childhood somehow "caused" the differences in marriage later.[2]

Our results will be limited, since the NLS does not tell us how long children spent in these different types of families nor how they got there. Therefore, some children raised in stepfamilies would also have experienced their parents' divorce, others a parent's death, while others would have been born out of wedlock. For those living with their mother only, some will have spent only a short period in this situation, while others will have spent their entire childhood. Lumping together different experiences within a category such as "lived with mother only at age 14" will weaken our results. This means that we may miss some patterns that really exist. But it also means that any patterns we see are likely to be there, and may well be stronger than they appear.

Prospective Longitudinal Data

Asking questions about the past presents major difficulties, since people have trouble recalling for a survey many of the things that happened to them. At times, remembering what happened requires more detailed probing and sorting to establish sequence and timing beyond what surveys normally attempt, and sometimes people have simply forgotten what happened. It is impractical to ask people to remember their attitudes toward working mothers when they were young. Our study only uses retrospective data for childhood family structure, although other studies have been successful at collecting and analyzing data drawn by painstakingly asking people to recount their job, and their residential, marital, and fertility histories (Freedman et al., 1988). Memory, however, is not a problem when a study can return to the same people and find out more about them. In this way, one can see whether attitudes measured at one point in time, when they were current, have an effect on later behavior.[3] For example, do teenagers' opinions about working mothers influence their own marriages, which are often formed many years later?

The people we study are young adults who were exposed to the onset of the divorce revolution as young children in the late 1950s and early 1960s; who came to adulthood in the late 1960s and early 1970s when many were deciding whether to live away from their parents before marriage; and who were making decisions about whether to establish a family by marrying and having children and how to organize that family to complete household tasks up to 1983. By using prospectively collected data, together with some retrospective information, we can examine the unfolding of their lives in close detail. Thus, we can look at the influence of early experiences on later plans and attitudes, and at how those later attitudes affect still later behavior. We can see how childhood family structure influences sex-role attitudes in early adulthood, and turn around and look at how such attitudes in early adulthood influence the decision to divorce or the division of labor in the family. This detailed assessment of one cohort of young people allows us to understand what happened to them, and often why. But it does not provide direct evidence on any other age group. We can and do speculate, however, about the implications of our findings for families in general.

Nonfamily Living: A Problem for Prospective Studies

All the surveys we use collected information on childhood family structure as a retrospective question. However, no question on the timing of leaving home was asked, so to examine the effects of nonfamily living we had to use the listing of all relatives living with the respondent (collected by the NLS in each survey) in order to see whether they were living with parents in any particular year. This allowed us to map young adults' household structure for all survey years and construct a history of "nonfamily" living for young men and women that reflects time spent living independently between leaving the parental home and marriage. (Appendix B includes a detailed description of the construction of this measure.)

To use this information properly, however, we must look only at those respondents who had not yet had the chance at the beginning of the survey to leave their parental household as young adults. Substantial amounts of "nest-leaving" occur around age 18, so we could only look at those aged 14–17 at the first year of the survey, which began in 1966 for young men and in 1968 for young women. By 1983, 15 to 17 years later, this group was still only in its late twenties or early thirties when many had not yet formed families. For those who had started families, most were in their very early stages.

Hence, we can only study the effects of living outside a family setting in early adulthood on the outcomes that occur earliest in adulthood. We can, however, examine how living outside a family setting as young adults affects young adults' plans and attitudes about work and family and we can examine its effect on the transition to marriage. And we can study these processes in considerable detail, disentangling to a great extent whether the effects of non-family living in early adulthood are connected to attending college, living in dormitories, or living more independently, and whether it makes a difference whether this experience occurs early or late in the transition to adulthood. But we cannot see how parents' living outside a family setting as young adults affects whether their teenage sons are included in the household division of labor, because only those who had married and had families at an extremely early age would have had teenage sons by 1983. Any effects that appeared would be on a group too small and unusual to generalize from.

But it turned out in our analyses that our ability to study the effects of nonfamily living early in adulthood on subsequent decisions became even more restricted, and for a very important reason. To study the effect on divorce of living outside a traditional family as a young adult requires that these people get married. But nonfamily living has a negative effect on the likelihood of marriage itself. To study the effects of nonfamily living on sharing household tasks among husbands, wives, and children also requires that those who experienced it not only get married but also have children. But nonfamily living also reduces the chances that young women will have children. For analyses of these later outcomes, then, we could not look at the full detail of living in college dormitories and apartments that we used in the earlier analyses of plans, attitudes, and marriage, and must restrict ourselves to studying whether more or less nonfamily living of any kind influences having children within marriage, and whether it changes how much husbands and children share in household responsibilities.

But families that *are* formed are one of our greatest concerns. The division of household labor is a central factor in our argument, since we see the inclusion of husbands as critical in influencing their sons about the appropriateness of men participating in household tasks, and we see the inclusion of both sons and daughters as essential in giving young people the skills they will need as adults. We also see the inclusion of men and women in the division of household labor as necessary to equalize the burden of the second shift, and thus encourage career-oriented women to marry and have children. Hence, we decided to extend our view of families beyond the early years of marriage, and to include the sample of mature women (age 30–44) in our study of the household division of labor. As a result, we have no information about whether these adult women lived in a nonfamily setting in early adulthood. The only nontraditional family experience we can see reflected in later life is their childhood experience of parental disruption. However, in exchange, these women provide a rich source of information with which to study the immediate effects of remarriage, since we can see how their own marital progress is affecting their children's involvement in household tasks.

Studying Men and Women

In our analyses, we have tried to consider men's lives at the same time we analyze women's. In our view, too many books and articles on the family give short shrift to men's position and contribution. This lack of attention to husbands and fathers results from the traditional view that men act primarily as breadwinners and should do little else, leaving the focus of most data collection efforts on women. Most studies of marriage and virtually all studies of childbearing include only women, although this is beginning to change.

Although we have tried throughout our research to give equal time to men and women, we were often unable to do so because the NLS simply did not ask young men the same questions asked of young women. And when the same questions were asked, the data on young men were often not as carefully cleaned and prepared as they were for young women. Young women were also asked about their sex-role attitudes and the number of children they expected in much greater detail and more frequently than were young men, so our analyses of young people's work- and family-related plans and attitudes are much richer for young women. Young men and young women were asked about their fertility histories, but because unmarried men often give relatively unreliable replies to such questions, the survey organization made the decision not to do the necessary work to make men's replies useful, with the result that it is almost impossible to study even the *marital* fertility of young men. And although both young and mature women were asked to describe the ways in which they shared responsibility for household chores with family members, including children, the version of these questions given young men asked only about how much of each task he did, not whom he shared the task with.

In spite of the limitations of the NLS, we can often include an examination of men's family experiences. We use a series of questions on attitudes toward mothers' working in chapter 4 to study this aspect of attitude formation in men, although we cannot study other aspects. The detailed information on marriage in the NLS allows us to give equal time to men and women in chapter 5, which examines the timing of marriage. We primarily use women's reports of the division of household labor, since the questions asked women provide better information on who shares tasks in the household. These reports include men's role in the division of household labor and we examine it closely in chapters 7, 8, and 10. (Chapter 9 focuses on children.)

Although women were asked many questions about their husbands, including education, earnings, and health status, they provided no information about their husbands' nontraditional family experiences prior to marriage. Therefore, we have supplemented our view of men's role in the household in order to examine the effects of men's experiences of childhood family structure and nonfamily living in young adulthood. This required us to use the relatively limited questions asked young men about their share in the household division of labor. We must ignore men completely only in chapter 6 on fertility and divorce, because of limitations of the NLS data on these topics for males.

Approaching Our
Research Questions

A fundamental premise of our study, and of much social research, is that the decisions people make are influenced by two major categories of factors, which we will call "tastes" and "resources." Many decisions—such as attending college, maintaining a separate household, or having children—are made easier by having money. This is not to say that some very poor people do not manage to do these things, but simply that having resources makes many people more likely to do them. Resources, then, structure people's choices.

But whether people choose to use their resources to attend college, establish a separate residence, or have children is also a matter of "taste." No one has enough resources to have everything he or she might want, so people must consult their own hierarchy of preferences to create priorities, which differ among individuals and social groups. People make these decisions every day: to buy a new car or take a family vacation; to go out for a nice dinner or buy a new snowsuit; or even whether to pay the dentist or the rent.[4]

Measuring Resources and Tastes

In our study we include in each analysis measures of both resources and tastes, in order to be sure that the effect of living independently on, say, marriage is not reflecting these other dimensions. We have worked very hard to tap the appropriate measures of both resources and tastes. But we are most particularly concerned about *the formation* of tastes. We argue here and elsewhere in the volume that although "new families" are increasing partly because changes in the economy have put pressure on married women to work, the major barrier to their full development, and thus the most important factor leading to "no families," is rooted in tastes, specifically the fundamental ideas most people have about the proper relationship between the sexes.

Resources.   The NLS provides detailed information on the resources available to individuals in the sample. For young adults living with their parents, we know their parents' income and the occupation of the head of the family. These two measures provide insight into actual resources (indexed by income) and the life-style requirements that seem to accompany one's occupation in most communities. Parents who are both school teachers may earn as much collectively as a male physician with a wife who works in the home, but the teachers probably do not encounter the pressure from their colleagues and friends that the physician does to drive a Mercedes or send their children to private school. We expect both these dimensions to influence young men's and women's decision to marry, and we study their effects in chapter 5.

Young people's own income also affects their decisions. They may be able to call on their parents' resources, but they cannot command them in the way they can their own. Thus, *whose* money it is must always be considered in looking at the decision making of people in families.[5] And once they have married, the possibility that the family's income comes only from the husband or from a working wife as well is also important, as we shall see in dramatic ways in the analyses of husbands' and children's participation in the household division of labor in chapters 7–10. Unlike many surveys, the NLS allows us to make these distinctions. Details on how we construct these measures can be found in Appendix B.

Tastes, Attitudes, and Preferences.   Our approach to measuring "taste" is to consider factors that influence young people in childhood together with those that might cause them to rethink their attitudes in adulthood. We agree with the many scholars who argue that experiences in childhood are very powerful, which is why we are so concerned not only with children's experiences of divorce but also with the household division of labor, because children watch their mothers and fathers and participate themselves in household tasks. But we also know that many attitudes, even about matters as fundamental as gender roles, can change.

The most critical attitudinal dimension for the study of changes in work and family roles among men, women, and children focuses specifically on the ideas people hold about the "proper" relationship between the sexes, together with their appropriate family roles. In these surveys, both young and mature women were asked a long series of questions about their attitudes toward the appropriate roles for women in the home and in the labor force and about the consequences of those roles. (See Appendix B for a discussion of these items, and how we developed scales from them that tap somewhat separate dimensions of attitudes focusing on men's and women's economic and family roles.) These questions were asked a number of times, allowing us to look at change in attitudes, as we do in chapter 4.

One series of questions that has proved especially valuable for us focuses on young women's plans for employment versus homemaking. In each year of the survey, young women were asked what they would like to be doing when they were 35 years old. We use their answers to shed light on their actual plans and to tell us something about their values and ideals. Young women were also asked about the number of children they thought was ideal for the average American family and the number that they themselves expected to have. Their answers to these questions reflect their underlying views of the centrality of the family in their lives and in the lives of others.

We see sex-role attitudes as developing continuously over the lives of these young adults. In part, this is because many dimensions of adult relationships between the sexes only become salient when young people reach adulthood and come, themselves, to live in or outside families. But the young people we study also came of age in the midst of the gender-role revolution, so that what they were being taught was actually changing—in the media, among their friends, and possibly even in their parents' home—since the revolution hit all marriages. The plasticity of sex-role attitudes among these young people allows us to examine the factors influencing the *development* of these attitudes, which can then be used to predict later adult behaviors, including divorce and the division of household labor.

To look at tastes and attitudes formed in childhood, which lay the foundation for many later choices, we turn to a set of factors normally treated as "taste" variables, but which only measure attitudes indirectly. Blacks, those living in smaller communities or in the South, and the less educated are frequently found to be more traditional on the following dimensions of family life: abortion, on which blacks, southerners, and those in small communities are less likely to indicate support (Henshaw and Martire, 1982); divorce rates, which are higher in large communities and outside the South (but among blacks, not whites) (Glenn and Supancic, 1984); and nonfamily living (Goldscheider and Goldscheider, 1990), which is rarer in the South, as well as among blacks. The general finding for education is that those with more years of schooling are more likely to have developed tastes and interests outside the family, leading to later marriage, fewer children, and less incorporation of other relatives into the household (Rindfuss et al., 1988).

Because of the importance of the context in which young people grow up, those living in the South or in less-educated families are likely to have more traditional sex-role attitudes. But it is also the case that the relationship between people's answers to general questions on sex-role attitudes and their later behavior is influenced to a certain extent by where *they see themselves* along a continuum of liberal and conservative on each issue. And where they place themselves may depend strongly on where they think most people are.

For example, many young Hispanic men, when asked about their views on family issues, will often characterize themselves as quite egalitarian about male-female relationships and quite independent about questions on parent-child relationships. But when their actual behavior is observed, they will appear quite traditional. The solution to this disparity between response and behavior appears in looking at their responses to questions about what *they think* others their age feel, in which case they will give very traditional responses (Moore and Mata, 1982). The South has been an area associated with relatively traditional views on some aspects of gender issues (Mason, Czajka, and Arber, 1976) so that even those southerners who consider themselves relatively liberal, and give liberal responses, might not be very liberal in a national context. Some southern men holding liberal views might feel greater pressure not to act on them, and they can point to what is normal in the neighborhood to counter pressure from their wives. The same processes are likely to be operating for blacks and among those living in more rural areas. These considerations suggest to us that it is important not only to examine measures of sex-role attitudes but also to look closely at the *social contexts* in which people feel they are relatively more or less liberal.

It is also the case that questions on gender roles are fairly abstract, since they refer to general situations or to ideals, and thus can be thought of as measuring more strongly what respondents think *others* ought to do rather than what they do themselves. A classic example of this kind of process is shown when married men are asked about how well women drive. Most will reply close to the low end of whatever scale they are given, suggesting that they have a very poor view of women's driving skills. But when asked about their own wives' driving skills, many more men will reply that their wives are "excellent" or "very good" drivers.

Thus, even people with relatively traditional or stereotyped ideas at a general level may act quite differently in their own lives, based on their judgments about matters they have observed or experienced. As a result, it is important to consider how people's specific experiences might influence their later behavior. We consider nonfamily living in early adulthood an important "taste-forming" experience in this regard, one with the potential to influence later attitudes, plans, and decisions, which we will explore systematically in later chapters.

Studying Families Over the Life Course

Our general strategy throughout this volume is to attempt to explain variation in some outcome among individuals—their attitudes toward family roles, marriage, or division of housework—focusing especially on the impact childhood and young adulthood experiences have on these individual differences. We use the NLS data to predict in a statistical sense what kinds of attitudes young adults hold or whether they marry at a particular age. If we can make better guesses about these outcomes, knowing their family-related experiences, then we can conclude that these experiences "caused" the resulting attitude or behavior, at least to some extent.

Our approach involves estimating a large number of equations that predict individuals' family-related attitudes and behavior. However, we do not present these results in detail in the text; they are relegated to appendixes where they are available for the interested reader. Instead, we use these equations to develop predicted values for, say, sharing housework for individuals who differ on specific characteristics, such as childhood family structure and nonfamily living during young adulthood, but who are otherwise similar to each other on such demographic factors as education, race, community size, and number of children. We can then compare the extent of housework sharing in families of young women who grew up with both natural parents to that among those who lived with their mother only or in a stepfamily. We present these comparisons in the form of graphs that should make understanding and evaluating our results and interpretations clearer for most readers.

We focus on the life course in our analyses in order to see how processes that are influencing the development of "new families" or "no families" in the twenty-first century are working themselves out in people's lives. We first consider the factors influencing young people's plans and attitudes, as they chart their trajectory into adulthood, and then we examine whether they make a series of family-related transitions: to marry; to bear a first child in marriage; or to divorce. Finally, we study families directly, in order to assess those factors that influence husbands' (if the marriage survives) and children's (for those who have them) participation in the tasks primarily thought to be in the province of adult women. Each of these research objectives demands quite different analytic styles.

Studying Changing
Plans and Attitudes

In the data we used, questions on specific work and family plans and on more general sex-role attitudes were asked sporadically, and our analytic strategies vary depending on how often and in which years these questions were asked. The question on plans for working at age 35, which taps whether young women expect their futures to be focused exclusively around family roles, was asked in every survey year. This allowed us to choose the ages we thought best to examine, and we selected ages 20, 22, and 24 to assess how their plans were changing over early adulthood. (These regularly repeated measurements also allowed us to test our strongest proposition that nonfamily living in early adulthood *changes* work and family plans, since we could include in our models for young women the response they gave at age 17, before nonfamily living was possible.)

Other questions, including approval of mothers' working, expected and ideal number of births, and detailed sex-role attitudes, were asked more infrequently. Young women were asked about their attitudes toward mothers' working in 1972, when those aged 14–17 at the original interview were 18–21. Young men were asked this question in 1976, when they were 24–27. Young women also answered questions about their fertility plans and ideals when they were 19–22 and again at 24–27, when they answered questions on global sex-role attitudes.

This variability poses some problems. It is difficult to compare responses to questions asked only once of both men and women since the men were

6 years older than the women when the questions were asked. Men and women's experiences are different because of gender, certainly, but the male respondents were also older and thus were exposed longer to the increasingly positive attitude toward mothers' working that developed during the 1970s. Yet by being able to observe the factors influencing work and family plans and attitudes at different ages, we are able to assess the durability of some experiences over the early adult life course. We can see that durability precisely when we ask the same question, such as one's work plans, over a number of years. But we can also infer durability more generally, as when we see that the effects of nonfamily living on young women's sex-role attitudes persist into the later twenties.

Studying the Transitions to Marriage, Divorce, and Childbearing

Precise measurement is particularly critical in studying transitions, such as those to marriage, divorce, and childbearing, but also to a new job, a child death, or a residential move.[6] The NLS provides information on marital status of the respondent at each interview as well as a complete, annually updated marital history. With these data we can determine exactly when each person married for the first time (the subject of chapter 5) and if and when they ever dissolved that marriage (the subject of chapter 6). The NLS also provides a complete history of childbearing, which we use to study the transition to parenthood (also in chapter 6).

Our approach to studying these three transitions is to use observations of each respondent over several periods of 6 to 18 months.[7] Using marriage, as an example, we begin with people still single when we first observe them. We observe that some marry during the subsequent year, and we use a number of their characteristics to predict, statistically, which people are more likely to do so. Current age then becomes an indicator of duration single. We follow the same strategy for childbearing and divorce, considering for each year of marriage the separate probabilities that a first child is born and that a divorce occurs. In these cases, duration of marriage—not age—is the key dimension over which we observe these processes.

This approach allows us to take into account the fact that the probability of marriage differs substantially by respondent's age (Waite and Spitze, 1981), and the probability of divorce and childbearing vary by duration of marriage. A respondent supplies annual observations until the event being studied occurs or until the survey ends.

For marriage, we selected the ages by sex to include the periods during which most young men and women marry. Since young women begin marrying earlier than young men and are nearly finished at earlier ages, we estimated annual marriage models for young women from age 17 (when 4.7 percent of those eligible marry) to age 27 (when the proportion marrying is again as low as 4.7 percent of those still single). By ages 27 and above, so many women had already married that the unmarried population was virtually eliminated. For young men, we began with age 18 instead of 17 because virtually none of the males married before 18, and we continued observing marriages until age 29, because the marriage market for men tends to extend to these ages. Thus, our analysis includes all ages for each sex at which marriage markets operate actively.

This approach also greatly simplifies the problem of causal direction that other models risk when considering the relationship between two processes both operating over time. For example, for those considering the relationship between nonfamily living and marriage, it is the case that additional years of nonmarriage increase the likelihood of more years of nonfamily living. However, our use of annual segments means that for all individuals in a given regression, variation in the number of years spent in nonfamily living is not the result of variation in age at marriage, since all are the same age and none are married at the beginning of the period.

Studying the Division of Household Labor

Both the NLS young and mature women were asked in various years a series of questions about who in their household took responsibility for each of a series of household tasks. The exact listing of tasks differs slightly for different years but includes the most common household chores: cooking, cleaning, washing dishes, doing laundry, grocery shopping, caring for children, and doing yard work, home maintenance, and family paperwork. Each woman was asked who usually took responsibility for each task, and whether that person had complete or shared responsibility. If someone other than the woman had any responsibility, then she gave the identity of that person— husband, child, hired help, or unidentified "other"—and the proportion of each task that person completed. The woman could also say that her household did not perform a particular task, as in the case of yard work for a family who lived in an apartment.

We analyze women's answers to these questions about the division of household labor. In chapter 7 we look at the impact of married women's experiences outside a traditional family on the extent to which their husbands take responsibility for various chores. In chapter 8 we focus on how other characteristics of the woman and family, especially those reflecting resources and tastes, as we discussed above, affect housework sharing among married couples. We use the same questions in chapter 9 to examine the ways in which women share responsibility for housework with their children, looking carefully at women's experiences outside a traditional family both in childhood and as a single parent. And in chapter 10 we look at the ways in which families with both parents *and* children distribute housework.

In these chapters we focus on particular aspects of families sharing in housework. The question sets inquire about *who* has responsibility for the *performance* of household tasks and *how often*, phrased in terms of "all of the time," "more than half of the time," and so forth. As such, the focus is on the task and getting it done.[8] Our measure of sharing household chores thus does not focus on the amount of *time* spent.

We know what *proportion* of the cooking, say, a wife tends to do and how this changes if she grew up in a mother-only family, but we don't know whether she spends 20 hours a week at it or only 1. We think this is the right approach for a number of reasons. For one, our list of chores includes those that take up the vast majority of housework time (Spitze, 1986). For another, the amount of *time* spent on a task depends on how much needs to be done, certainly, but it also depends on how efficient the person is at the task, how much they want the task to be done, and how much they like or dislike doing the task (which economists refer to as "process utility"). Thus one family may spend a good deal of time on yard and home maintenance because they love to garden, while another spends no time on the yard but a good deal in the kitchen, because they like to cook (or eat well).

We also do not know how *well* a given job is done. One family may spend little time cleaning because they do a good job especially quickly, while another might do very little cleaning because they don't care if the house is dirty. Looking only at the number of hours someone spends on a task doesn't allow a researcher to separate extra time spent because of extra work, an inefficient worker, or enjoyment of the task itself.

A focus on *responsibility* for separate household chores tells us how much work each person does (or at least ensures how much gets done) *of the work that the family has decided that they will do*. We feel that this is the most appropriate approach for our study, where what matters is how families decide on getting the job done and who does it.[9] Nevertheless, we have attempted whenever possible to compare our results that use this measure with those of other studies that use direct measures of time spent on given tasks. Our results appear to be consistent with those using the more tedious data collection methods associated with asking respondents to keep detailed time diaries and the even more difficult challenge of processing those data that result. To date, however, these difficulties have limited the comparisons we could make, since relatively few results relevant to our research questions have appeared. Appendix B presents in detail the way in which we constructed the measures of housework sharing, together with the questions on which those measures are based.

Change Over the Life Course
Versus Change Across Cohorts

This volume examines the process of social change by looking particularly at the effects of marriage and divorce on family lives of the next generation. By studying the factors influencing family life over the life course, we can show that family disruption during childhood can affect the decisions young people themselves make about whether and when to marry and have children as well as how to structure their family lives. Our data allow us to trace the intergenerational links involved in social change. If we are correct that certain experiences outside traditional families appear to affect whether and what kind of families are formed later, then our analysis will suggest that the societal changes that encourage these experiences are likely to have consequences for the future of the family.

But we are also interested in generational changes in the social processes that determine marriage and the nature of the family and in the implications of our analyses for families in the twenty-first century. Our data are much less well suited for the latter question. We approach studying change in family processes over the life course, and we look at *connections* that imply change. If living outside a family early in adulthood influences young men to marry, we infer that the likelihood of marriage should increase, since nonfamily living in early adulthood is increasing. If mothers with more education involve their children less in household tasks, we infer that children's skills in homemaking will continue to deteriorate, since educational levels are still rising among women.

We also attempt to separate the effects of change over the life course from change across cohorts directly. This usually is not possible, since the young adults we focus on spanned only a narrow age range, and they all aged together from the mid– to late–1960s to the mid–1980s. But we do have some ways of looking at change specifically. For marriage, we determine whether women who were youngest when the survey started, and were thus born well into the baby boom, experienced a marriage squeeze, since fewer men several years older than those women were available to marry. Even for data spanning a few ages (for this analysis, we used data spanning 6 years, so that we could follow women who reached age 20 between 1969 and 1974), some short-run changes can be ascertained.

In our studies of the division of household labor, we include the panel of young women and the sample of mature women. This allows us to look at the division of household labor among women who range in age from their mid-twenties to their late-fifties. Although measures of nonfamily living are not available for this analysis, this expanded sample allows us to see whether the factors that influence household functioning among older women, who grew up in homes that experienced the Great Depression and World War II, differ from those influencing younger women, who grew up in the affluent 1950s and came of age in the turbulent 1960s.

In these analyses, however, we can only infer social change, since we look at division of household labor in only one time period. We do not study change in the division of labor, although we think this is an important area for further analysis.

Our results cannot be conclusive despite the very large numbers of people included in the surveys, the long time period that the surveys cover, and the detailed information on many attitudes, plans, and behaviors of the family. We present our interpretations based on ideas we have developed about why and how certain characteristics are connected to certain outcomes; the analyses then give us evidence—that is sometimes overwhelming—about the veracity of our ideas and arguments. But often the evidence is more equivocal, and we must rely on our professional judgment to draw conclusions and often wait for further research on the issue.

But research such as ours often helps individuals, families, and policymakers spot changes underway, in our case in the structure and function of the American family. Then we as a society can decide whether we like the direction in which things are headed, or whether we have to make some effort to redirect the course of events.

4

Planning for New Families

All children form ideas about the kind of life they want to lead as adults. They try on adult roles in various ways and make more or less concrete plans for their later lives, based on experiences in their parents' homes, in school, and in other important parts of their social world. These life plans direct young people's actions, and—although their plans may change—they have important implications both for the decisions young adults make and for the lives they ultimately lead.

Family and work are the two cornerstones of this emerging life plan, with strong effects on each other, as well as on other aspects of life. Work and family roles are typically the most demanding, and both men and women must balance them, so that decisions made early in life affect others later. Those who marry and have children early must often forgo opportunities for employment-related education; those who decide on a demanding career normally defer marriage as a result.

Children's family experiences have perhaps the strongest influence on the families they form. Thus, rigid segregation of roles by sex is reinforced from generation to generation, since adult roles in the family are more differentiated than anywhere else in modern life. In traditional families, women care almost exclusively for home and family, and men earn money to support them. For girls, the traditional view emphasizes the importance of marriage, childrearing, and "keeping house" over employment. For boys, tradition reinforces a disdain for these same activities.

Those with more modern perspectives see both male and female adult lives as requiring a greater balance between work and family roles. Families are headed by a partnership of husband and wife, with each having some responsibility for both the physical and emotional care of family members and for their financial support. These views presume the employment of women, including mothers of young children, and see women's work role as contributing to the family (Mason, Czajka, and Arber, 1976). Women who prefer a less traditional family may choose to obtain job training, delay—or even avoid—marriage and motherhood, and limit their family size to one or two children. These women are likely to seek more equal partnerships, hoping to share in the care of the family and the house, as well as responsibility for financial support.

In contrast, young women who prefer a traditional family life marry earlier and have children sooner, forgoing additional education and preparing instead for adult roles centered on homemaking, expecting only to work outside the home using their spare time and energy, if at all. Although later experiences can change attitudes,[1] research has documented that sex-role norms are strongly associated with marriage, work, and fertility. Women who define themselves in terms of traditional female roles marry earlier, are less likely to be employed full time or to use effective contraception, and expect to bear more children than women holding less traditional views.[2]

Women's traditional roles have been described as "profamily." They emphasize the importance of marriage and motherhood and encourage women to work hard at the difficult task of maintaining family relationships (Blake, 1972; Bumpass, 1987). Many scholars have argued that those women with less traditional perspectives will not put as much effort into keeping family relationships working, leading to poorer family functioning at all levels, more breakdown of relationships, and perhaps a poorer prognosis for the family success of the next generation.

However, it is also the case that traditional sex-role orientations are *antifamily*, in the sense that such attitudes encourage men to put career success ahead of everything else and reinforce the idea that "women's work"—*in other words, family work*—is inappropriate and even demeaning for men to do. Since fewer and fewer wives fill the traditional wife role of working only in the home, many resent their double burden, which increases the chances of marital discord and marital breakdown (Huber and Spitze, 1983). In this situation, traditional male sex-role attitudes weaken the family, because they place demands on women that few can meet. (Those who try are sometimes pejoratively called "superwomen.")

These extreme male sex-role attitudes lead to men and women being disappointed in each other, reducing the likelihood of marriage. And if they do marry, chances are that partners will disagree in fundamental ways about how to run their household, increasing the likelihood of divorce. A shift to more egalitarian views among men, then, may actually strengthen families by giving guidance on appropriate behavior to families with two working heads and by encouraging more active participation by men in the home life of the family. Any factor that influences the views of young people, particularly those of young men, in a more egalitarian direction should, we agree, increase the chances of a future of "new families" rather than "no families." Hence, the life plans that young people make during childhood and early adulthood are important not only for their own lives but also for the direction families will take in the future.

In chapter 2 we showed that dramatic changes are taking place in the structure of American families. Increased marital instability means that more and more children experience parental divorce. And the delay in marriage, together with the increased number of years spent living outside a traditional family, mean that more and more young people are spending an important part of early adulthood developing tastes and skills likely to reduce their orientation toward family roles. Both in childhood and in their transition to adulthood, young people's lives are following distinctly different patterns from those of their parents.

At the same time that these "no families" patterns have developed, "new families" have also emerged, with greater participation by women in men's family support roles, and modest beginnings of greater participation by men in women's family roles. Egalitarian attitudes and behavior are more widespread toward women working outside the home than men working in the home, and people's attitudes are more generally egalitarian than their behavior. Nevertheless, factors that influence young adults' plans for their future work and family lives are extremely important.

What are the consequences of living outside traditional families during childhood and young adulthood? How do these experiences influence young people's attitudes, plans, and expectations about their future work and family roles? If these experiences are affecting both young men and women, they may lead to attitudes and expectations likely to change the kinds of marriages that young adults form. They may become more egalitarian, with a division of responsibility for both financial support and household labor—in other words, "new" families. However, if these nontraditional attitudes and expectations only affect young women, these women may have difficulty finding young men who share their views of marriage and family. This may lead to decreased commitment to the family, resulting in fewer marriages, a decline in parenthood, and greater marital instability—or "no" families.

Measuring Plans, Attitudes, and Expectations

We will consider three types of plans and attitudes: young women's work and family plans; young men's and women's attitudes toward mother's working; and young women's general attitudes toward women's work and family roles.[3] These plans and attitudes are related to each other to a certain degree—relatively few young women planning very large families also plan to work—but each clearly taps different dimensions of young adults' work and family lives.

Plans.   There are two measures of women's plans. Women were asked about their plans to work at age 35 (WORK PLANS), as an indicator of long-run plans for employment,[4] and about how many children they expect to have (PLANNED CHILDREN). They were also asked the number they think is ideal for the average American family (IDEAL CHILDREN).[5]

Taken together, these questions cover the primary roles—mother and worker—that young women must balance during their adult lives. Young women who are not planning to work are clearly planning for very traditional adult lives centered around home and family. Those who plan to work, however, may be planning either not to marry ("no families") or to marry and have no children; although childless couples are certainly "families," too many of them lead to a society unable to produce a new generation.

Since the majority of the young women we study expect to be working at age 35, as well as to marry and have children, it is likely that they are planning for a marriage and family life at least somewhat more egalitarian than that envisioned by their home-oriented sisters. Similarly, those planning many children probably do not expect to have demanding careers (unless they are very optimistic about their husbands' contributions or their own managerial abilities), but those not expecting a large family may expect a small family or no children at all. In each case our analyses of these questions will show which women are planning for traditional lives. But from among those planning nontraditional lives, we want to distinguish those aiming for "no" families from those planning "new" families. For young adults, this requires measures of attitudes.

Attitudes Toward Women's Working.   Both men and women were asked their views on the proper ways that mothers in general should balance work and family roles. Specifically, information was obtained on three conditions under which the respondent thought that a married mother of preschool children may work, given that a trusted relative is available for child care: if she needs the money; if she wants to work and her husband agrees; and if she wants work to but her husband doesn't particularly want her to (see Appendix B). We created a scale by summing their answers, which we call *attitude toward mothers' working*, ranging from low (traditional) to high (modern), since increasingly, both men and women feel that women have a "right" to work.[6]

Sex-Role Attitudes. Young women were asked a third set of questions on their general sex-role attitudes (Appendix B). These questions deal with the impact of women's employment on their families and include value judgments about appropriate roles for men and women. We constructed two scales from these questions.[7] One, which we call FAMILY ROLES, reflects the importance of women's "place" at home to their children and families. The second dimension, JOB ROLES, measures views of the importance of women's employment to their self-esteem and the economic well-being of their families. A higher score indicates greater acceptance of nonfamilial roles for wives and mothers.[8]

The second and third sets of questions—approval of mothers' working and JOB ROLES and FAMILY ROLES—provide some clues about young people's orientation toward "new families" or "no families." Factors that influence JOB ROLES only, and thus speak to young women's orientations toward work and its satisfactions, would seem to be most supportive of a "no families" interpretation. They reinforce women's work orientations but do not support the combination of work and childrearing except when financially necessary.

FAMILY ROLES and the approving mothers' working scale, in contrast, address some dimension of the problem traditional definitions of adulthood are creating for women. The issue of mothers' working is both a narrower version of the general problem and one with particular salience to women with fewer prospects for marrying affluent men, since such women can expect at best to be part of dual worker families, or even to be single mothers. For them, work is likely to be a necessity, whether or not they plan to take total responsibility for the rest of the household. But approval of mothers' working clearly opens the way for more egalitarian marriages, since it allows for the possibility of joint contributions to the family coffers and removes from the husband the responsibility of supporting the family alone. So women who know that they will have to work for financial reasons might also be able to fit in childrearing if their husbands support these more egalitarian views of sex roles.

The FAMILY ROLES scale goes several steps beyond the issue of whether mothers can work, tapping the extent to which family roles and *women's* roles should be coequal. The questions focus not only on womens' responsibility to children, but on the home as women's only source of "happiness," and the general structure of male and female marital roles. (One question asks agreement about whether "it is much better for everyone concerned if the man is the achiever outside the home and the woman takes care of the home and family.") As such, those with more modern views are not only endorsing women's roles outside the family but also men's role in "caring for home and family."

Approval of mothers' working may have a quite different and more general meaning for young men than for young women. Young women have practical concerns of their own to consider, since they normally have custody of children in the event of divorce. When young men answer this question, however, they are likely to think about their future children and the families they are planning, not about the future needs of children whom they might not support after divorcing their wives. Hence, it is likely that although this measure is not a particularly good indicator of a "new families" orientation among young women, requiring the broader FAMILY ROLES measures to interpret factors influencing their attitudes, it is a better indicator of men's willingness to form "new families."

Does Growing Up in a Nontraditional Family Affect Attitudes?

This chapter focuses on ways in which young adults form their attitudes about appropriate roles for men and women, their plans for balancing work and family, and their ideals about family size. We look especially at the impact of having grown up in a family with a nontraditional structure, and the effects of living independently in young adulthood on these important attitudes and plans.[9] We begin by looking at the impact of spending time in childhood in a family that did not include both one's mother and father.[10]

Young people who witnessed the economic and domestic stress and strain of a family headed by a single parent might become less likely to want to form traditional families, which risk the same problems. They may choose egalitarian families, or the experience of divorce and remarriage might even push them away from marriage altogether.[11] We would guess that these experiences would have a more profound effect on young women, making them less likely to invest in marriage and more likely to invest in their own skills and earning power. In fact, some research suggests this to be the case. High school girls who lived in a female-headed household were more likely to say that they wanted to work in an occupation usually held by males, such as engineering or carpentry, than were young women in two-parent families. And those with this nontraditional family experience also chose traditionally female occupations such as nursing or secretarial work less often (Berryman and Waite, 1987).

Living in a nontraditional family might also affect the attitudes of young women indirectly. Mothers who experience a divorce become less traditional and family centered and more work oriented as a result, and communicate these views to their daughters (Thornton and Freedman, 1982; D'Amico, Haurin, and Mott, 1983).

Growing up in a nontraditional family leads young women away from traditional plans and attitudes and increases approval of mothers' working among both young women and young men. The largest effects of this experience are on young women's specific career (work) plans. We show in figure 4.1 that women with this experience are more likely to report at age 20 that they want to be holding a job at age 35 (rather than presumably keeping house and raising a family full time) than those who lived with both biological parents.[12]

Figure 4.1 indicates that, controlling for parental education, region of the country, size of community, and other factors we consider in these analyses, young women who grew up in a family that did not include both biological parents would be more likely to plan to work than 56 percent of the sample—that is, they are in the 56th percentile on this issue. In contrast, those who grew up in two-parent families were in the 48th percentile, with many fewer expecting to work.[13]

Young women who grew up in a nontraditional family also plan to have fewer children than those from families having both biological parents. Young women from an intact family (but otherwise average on other factors) are in the 51st percentile in terms of number of children expected, while those who grew up with a single parent or stepparents are only in the 45th percentile. Thus, young women from intact families expect two children, while those from other homes expect only 1.8 and also think that fewer children are "ideal."

Moreover, young people from nontraditional families see less problem with mothers' working. Although the differences are not great—3 percentage points—the pattern is similar both for young women and young men, perhaps based on having had a working mother when they were growing up.[14]

Having grown up in a nontraditional family does not, however, seem to affect young women's more general attitudes toward work and family roles. This result, coupled with the strong effects of childhood family structure on personal plans for work and childbearing, suggests that the weak increase in approval of mothers' working is the result of young adults' own experiences in a nontraditional family, and their sense that they survived despite their mother's employment. The same effect is likely to influence young men. This suggests to us that young women are planning to work and reduce the number of children they are responsible for not so much to create modern families as to reduce their own (and their children's) vulnerability in the event of a family breakup.

Does Nonfamily Living Affect Family Views?

Although some researchers postulate that family-related norms are laid down early in life (Blake, 1972), other researchers have emphasized how experiences *outside* the family can induce changes in these family-derived

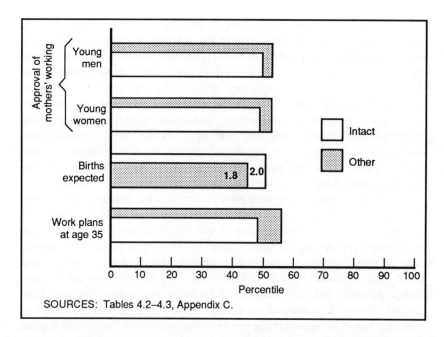

Figure 4.1   Effect of Childhood Family Structure on Work and Family Plans and Attitudes

values and tastes. A "role hiatus" between the traditional role of daughter and those of wife and mother might give young women an opportunity to develop tastes for alternatives to motherhood—especially employment—that alter family formation (Mason, 1974). The rigidity of sex roles in working-class families may result from early marriage and men's lack of experience in living independently from mothers or wives whose role was to care for their physical needs (Rubin, 1976). This suggests that a role hiatus may also affect young men's traditional sex-role attitudes. Hence, not only might family-related norms affect the behavior of individuals but they may also respond to that behavior (Marini, 1984). If so, it is important to establish how such attitudes are formed and altered by experience.

One test of the role hiatus hypothesis, using longitudinal data, found that those women who went to college increased their preference for employment, whereas those who worked and did not attend college increased their preference for full-time work in the home (Spitze, 1978). However, a great many who work or attend college after high school remain in the parental home. Living independently prior to marriage should provide a more complete hiatus, and thus be more likely to lead to changes in young men and women's family-related attitudes, plans, and expectations.

Our measure of nonfamily living in this analysis is the proportion of years that a young person lived away from the parental home between age 17 and first marriage (or the terminal date of the survey). Nonfamily living could include years spent in a college dormitory, military barracks, with roommates of either sex, or living alone.[15] We will discuss each of the results in detail, but we want to emphasize, as shown in figure 4.2, that there is a strikingly consistent picture across the wide range of measures analyzed for young men and women: living away from parents leads young people away from traditional attitudes, expectations, and plans about family roles. The more time that young people spend living independently, the more they depart from traditional family roles, both in attitude and for themselves, planning their own futures around work and smaller families.

Let us begin with young women's preferences for working later in life. The more years that a young woman lives away from parents (or marries, whichever comes first) between age 17 and 22, the more likely she is to plan to be employed at age 35 rather than to be working at home.[16] Our results indicate that otherwise average young women who lived away from parents all the time between 17 and 22 were in the 57th percentile on work plans, compared with a percentile score of 48 for those who never lived away from parents. That is, 65 percent of those who lived wholly away from home before marriage expect to be working at age 35, compared with 53 percent of women who lived at home until marriage.

Experience in living away from home leads young women to expect smaller families. Those who lived away in all years in which they were eligible to do so expected 1.8 children compared with the 2 children expected by those who either moved straight from their parents' home into marriage or were still living with parents at the end of the survey. Nonfamily living, in contrast, has no effect on ideal family size. This makes sense when one thinks about the differences between these two measures. Expected family size refers to a young woman's own views of and preferences for the future, but ideal family size is a more general view of what is good for families, which is likely to be more stable and less affected by nonfamily living.[17]

We also find that nonfamily living increases young people's support of the employment of married mothers of young children, although the effects are considerably greater for young women than young men. An otherwise average young woman who lived away from home all the possible years between age 17 and marriage or Time 2 is in the 64th percentile, while someone who never lived away is in the 48th. For young men, the effect of living on one's own increases approval of mothers' working from the 48th percentile to the 53rd.[18]

Next, we examine our two measures of sex-role attitudes, JOB ROLES and FAMILY ROLES, for effects of nonfamily living experiences. We find that spending time outside a family living situation increases both the extent to which young women define their "place" outside the home (FAMILY ROLES) and their view of the benefits of a woman's employment to her self-esteem and her family's economic position (JOB ROLES). The effects of

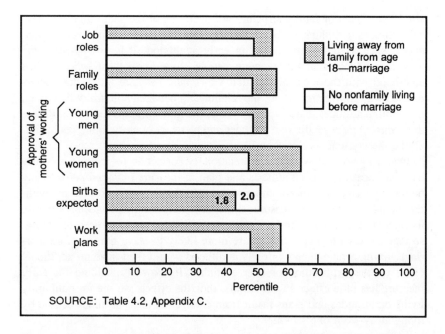

Figure 4.2   Effect of Nonfamily Living on Work and Family Plans and Attitudes

FAMILY ROLES are greater than those for JOB ROLES; living outside a family setting from age 18 until marriage moves young women in a more egalitarian direction by about 8 percentiles (from 48th to 56th), yet only increases their JOB ROLES score by about 6 percentiles.

When we compare the results of sex-role attitudes, which were measured in 1978, with those for approval of working mothers (expressed in 1972), the differences suggest that the effects of nonfamily living are not necessarily short lived. The impact of nonfamily living on these fundamental attitudes toward women's work and family roles persists for at least a decade.[19]

Does Nonfamily Living
Change Attitudes and Plans?

Our analyses of the effects of nontraditional family experiences on young adults' work and family plans and on sex-role attitudes assume that these plans and attitudes are being *altered* by young people's family and nonfamily experiences. Growing up in a mother-only family or stepfamily *causes* young people to form less traditional attitudes toward these issues. Living away from a family-based setting *changes* young people's attitudes and plans by teaching new skills and providing new experiences.

These assumptions seem quite reasonable for experiences in childhood, since the effects of family structure are operating at the same time that sex-role attitudes and plans are being formed. But for more contemporary experiences, such as nonfamily living in early adulthood, it is possible that the attitudes and plans of these young people *came first*—those who reached adulthood with the most nonfamilial views may be more likely than others to live away from home. If so, the relationship between nonfamily living and nonfamilial attitudes that we observe could be reflecting this sequence. Rather than *causing* more egalitarian attitudes and plans, nonfamily living could simply be the consequence of them.

One way to test which interpretation is correct is to include an early baseline measure of each attitude and plan, a measure obtained *prior* to any nonfamily living, and then compare the results for each attitude with and without including the earlier measure. If the basic relationship between nonfamily living and egalitarian attitudes is the reverse of what we have been reporting, so that those with such attitudes are more likely to leave home before marriage, living arrangements in early adulthood would then have no additional effect on the explanation of later attitudes. If, however, adding the early measure has little effect on our results, then the effects we see for nonfamily living on attitudes and plans result from *changes* in these attitudes caused by living away from one's family.

For example, young women in this study were asked in every survey year about their preferences for holding a paid job when they reached age 35. We take the response to this question they gave when they were 17 years old as a baseline before any nonfamily living could occur. We can then look at plans for work at age 35 stated at later ages as a function of nonfamily living.[20]

We find that adding the early baseline measure of work plans makes little difference to our conclusions, and that the same result characterizes our analyses of fertility expectations, approval of mothers' working, and more general sex-role attitudes. Our results for nonfamily living with the baseline measure are slightly weaker than those without them, but these differences are quite small. This test provides strong evidence for the interpretation that nonfamily living moves young women away from traditional family views toward more egalitarian ways of seeing the world.[21] The reverse is not the case. Those with the least traditional views to begin with are not substantially more or less likely to live away from their parents during the transition to adulthood.

Going to College and Nonfamily Living

Living away from a traditional family during young adulthood exposes people to a new set of ideas about the ways in which they can live their lives, thus changing their attitudes as a result. Attending college may have the same effect by giving young people classroom training that might directly change their views, putting them in a youth culture that has often been a hothouse for new and radical ideas about life, and increasing young women's potential wages, thereby making *not* working more costly. In many cases, attending college also takes young adults out of their parents' home and away from the control of an older generation, just as nonfamily living does for those who do not attend college. Can we separate the effects of attending college from those of living away from home? And if both attending college and living away from parents influence young adults, it might be that those who go away to college—and therefore receive the impact of both experiences—may change their views more than those who go to college while living at home, or leave home but do not attend college.

We identified men and women who attended college and lived away from home at some point in young adulthood and those who attended college but never lived away from home before marriage (or the survey date). These make up nearly half (43 percent) of our young adults; the remainder are those who never attended college and never lived away from home before marriage or by the time the survey was taken (46 percent) and those who did not attend college but did live away from home (11 percent). In this analysis, we included the earliest measures of plans and attitudes, since we were particularly concerned that our results not be affected by differences between those who chose whether or not to attend college, as well as between those who do or do not leave home before marriage. (We present the detailed results in table 4.4 of Appendix C.)

Separating the effects of nonfamily living from attending college shows that each makes a contribution, but the effects of college are quite different from those of living independently (fig. 4.3). Attending college seems to be having its greatest effect on longer-range goals and more general issues, while nonfamily living primarily affects more practical concerns. In most cases, however, these effects reinforce each other to produce the overall picture we found in the less detailed analysis.

The strongest influence on young women's plans for future employment is college. Those who attend college, whether living independently or at home, are much more likely to plan to work.[22] Clearly, attending college has a strong influence on young women's personal plans, reducing their orientation toward the most traditional set of female adult roles, which focus exclusively around home and family.

Among women who attended college, those who also lived away are the most likely to plan to work and are in the 61st percentile, whereas those who attended college but did not live away from home are in the 53rd percentile. Hence, living in a nonfamily setting has an additional effect on those with some college education. Since college students who lived away are no more likely to have been employed during that period than those who lived at home,

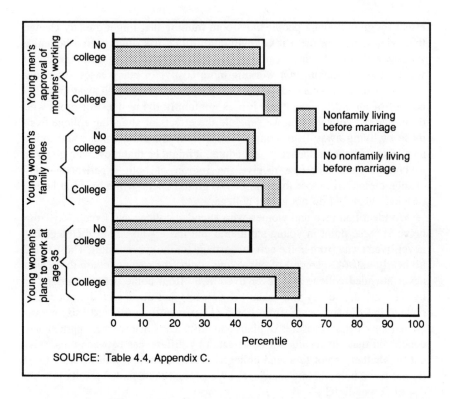

Figure 4.3   Effects of College and Nonfamily Living on Work and Family Plans and Attitudes

the increased likelihood of expecting to work as a result of attending college and living independently probably comes from an increased orientation toward work and independence rather than greater work experience.[23]

Those who lived independently but did not attend college, however, are no more likely to plan to work than others who did not go beyond high school and lived at home. Both groups are at about the 45th percentile in terms of work plans at age 35. Living away from home, then, has no effect among young women with no education beyond high school. This finding is consistent with earlier research showing that working class women who go to work rather than to college are not eager to prolong their work experiences (Spitze, 1978).

Almost all the other effects of nonfamily living on women's plans and attitudes come primarily from the residential component. College attendance, per se, has no influence on the number of children expected, on approval of mothers' working, or on modern job-related attitudes, once living patterns are controlled.[24] The only other "pure college" effect emerges from the FAMILY

ROLES scale, the most general and possibly strongest indicator of egalitarian attitudes. College attendance increases FAMILY ROLES scores by about 5 percentiles.

It is unclear how to interpret this set of results. One should expect college to have some impact on all these issues. Evidently the college experience, while increasing the value of work, is also increasing young women's standards for motherhood and homemaking, which have not yet been challenged by actual experience.

In contrast, the effects of nonfamily living appear strong throughout these more detailed analyses, sometimes reinforced by college attendance and sometimes independent of it. All of the decrease in the number of children these young women expect results from living independently (see table 4.4, Appendix C). Those who lived away, whether or not they attended college, expect fewer children; those who remained at home, either commuting to college or not, expect more children. The same result characterizes approval for mothers' working, at least among women, although not among men.

The pattern resembles one that we found for childhood family structure—those with the nontraditional experience of living away from their family may feel less sure of their financial independence and are therefore trying to ensure their ability to make it on their own, if they have to, by having fewer children and by feeling comfortable working while raising them. But they are no more committed to working, per se, than otherwise comparable women, if work is not necessary. Hence, nonfamily living, even though it increased approval of mothers' working, does not necessarily result in modern families, at least for women. This dimension is being tapped only by the FAMILY ROLES scale, and is thus primarily influenced by exposure to college.

For young men, however, it appears that college attendance is necessary before nonfamily living can have any effect on family-related attitudes. Otherwise average young men who attended college and lived independently are relatively open to the employment of mothers, with an approval level that puts them in the 54th percentile. This is not the case either for those who lived independently without going beyond high school, or for those who attended college while living at home, all of whom register levels of approval no higher than those who neither attended college nor left home before marriage—around the 46th percentile.

Changing family patterns clearly affect young people's plans and attitudes, both in childhood and in young adulthood. The changes in family patterns that have developed so rapidly in the last few decades are continuing to have repercussions, rippling out and creating new forms.

Our results suggest that nontraditional family experiences are leading both men and women away from traditional families, but it is less clear whether they are leading them to "no families" or to "new families." For young men, it seems likely that these experiences are reinforcing greater sharing, increasing the number of men who want families and are willing to spend more time as fathers. For young women, evidence seems to point more equivocally toward "no families," with family sacrificed to work in order to achieve greater independence.

Other Influences on Attitudes and Plans

What other factors are influencing these young adults' family-related plans and attitudes, and do they affect plans differently from general attitudes? Do they influence men and women differently? These questions are particularly important, since we expect that the plans young people make and the attitudes they hold will have consequences for the families they later form—whether they marry and have children and have families that will be stable and sharing (issues we address in the next two chapters). Another important question to consider is whether demographic factors, such as living in small communities or in the South, or having more or less education, actually influence specific family plans and attitudes. Do the answers to these questions provide us with any clues about whether the future is likely to increase the erosion of traditional families, which will lead to "no families" or "new families"? In this section we will examine these questions and consider the extent to which plans and attitudes are influenced by factors originating in childhood or in young adulthood.

We first examine the factors that reinforce specific family attitudes, such as race (black vs. nonblack), living in or out of the South, and community size. These are demographic attributes that proxy the community contexts that influence people's attitudes and plans while they are growing up, which often have a pervasive effect on measures of family traditionalism.

The pattern that emerges for blacks is one emphasizing female employment in the context of high fertility ideals. Young black women are more likely to plan for work from an early age (table 4.2, Appendix C)[25] and to feel that their working is important (JOB ROLES) than are other young women. They also more strongly endorse the idea that a mother's employment is not problematic for her children, as do black men (table 4.3, Appendix C). There is, however, no difference between otherwise comparable young black women and other women in their views of the centrality of women's family roles.

Although black families are more "modern" in their mother-child roles, this is not the case for husband-wife relationships. Evidently, the black family is more centered than the comparable white family around mothers and children, in which black mothers both parent and support their children. Modern relationships between husbands and wives, however, are no more likely to be present in black couples than in others.

The contrast between those living in and outside the South is also complex. Although young southern women do not differ from others in either job- or family-related sex-role attitudes and southern men are not more likely to approve of mothers' working, our results suggest that southern women are more likely to plan to work, to expect *fewer* children, and to approve of working mothers.[26]

Our results for community size, while weak, are consistent with our expectations. Although there are no differences in plans for work or childbearing, those living in larger communities have more modern attitudes toward mothers' working (although only among women). For these attitudes, differences are small but consistent. Those living in cities with 3 million or more are in the 53rd percentile in terms of approving of mothers' working, while those living in rural areas are in the 48th percentile; the percentile scores for urban and rural dwellers on the FAMILY ROLES scale are 56 and 48, respectively.

As measures of modern family plans and attitudes, then, our results generally support those of other studies. Region, race, and size of community represent in some sense real social divisions that are important for family-related issues. However, the patterns are not always fully consistent with a simple "modern-traditional" break.

As a more personal, if indirect, measure of family preferences, educational attainment is much more important for these sex-role attitudes and plans than race, region, or community size, although the patterns of influence vary sharply between males and females. We have three measures of the influence of education: parental education, current education, and whether the young adult is continuing further in school. For young men, the higher the educational attainment for themselves *and* their parents, the more likely they are to approve of mothers' working, by quite substantial amounts. Enrollment, however, has no effect (fig. 4.4).

Parental education has a moderate influence on young men's approval of mothers' working. Otherwise average young men whose parents did not attend high school rank at the 48th percentile on approval; those whose parents completed two years of postgraduate studies rank at the 55th percentile. Differences are even sharper for young men's own education. Those who did not attend high school themselves rank at the 43rd percentile, whereas those who attended school two years beyond college graduation ranked in the 60th percentile. Being enrolled in school at age 20–23 did not significantly increase approval of mothers' working relative to those who were not enrolled.

Education also strongly affects young women's plans and attitudes toward work and family. As has been reported in other research, young women with more education and more educated parents are more likely to plan to work and to have fewer children (table 4.3, Appendix C). However, early influences do not count for sex-role attitudes. Parental education has no effect on

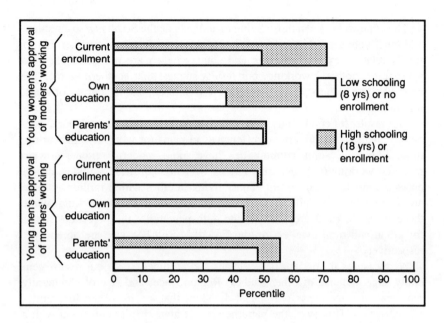

Figure 4.4   Effects of Education on Young Adults' Work- and Family-Related Attitudes

FAMILY ROLES or approval of mothers' working. What does count are current education and, particularly, continuing in school.

Comparing young women whose parents completed 8 and 18 years of education shows no significant difference once the young woman's own education is held constant: 50th versus 51st percentile. But comparable differences in her own education make a much bigger difference. Otherwise average young women who completed only 8 years of schooling rank at the 37th percentile in terms of their attitudes toward women having roles beyond the family. Those who completed 18 years of schooling, in contrast, rank at the 62nd percentile. Relatively few young women (fewer than 3 percent) were enrolled in school when they were asked these questions at ages 24–27. However, this group very strongly rejects home and family as the center of women's lives, ranking in the 71st percentile.

The effects of parents' education, one's own education, and current enrollment suggest that it is most important to impress on young men early—in home and in school—that women need more than traditional family roles in a world with high levels of divorce and female employment. Young men's adult lives will not reinforce this. Women, in contrast, envision roles for themselves beyond the family when they are most involved in the opportunities associated with life outside the family.

Nonfamily living is the only *adult* experience that helps young men learn directly that there are important adult tasks outside the workplace that take time, energy, and knowledge, and that contribute to their quality of life. Living independently in early adulthood also often gives young men some of the skills necessary for making a home. However, other adult experiences, both on the job or as a new husband, do not seem to contradict the strongly held sex-segregated attitudes toward the home and its tasks that they learned while living in their parents' home.

In contrast, some of the strongest effects on women's plans and attitudes involve their experiences in adulthood, as with nonfamily living. This reinforces our view that their parents' home is the primary source of young women's traditional orientations. Continuing in school makes young women's plans and attitudes less focused on traditional family roles. So, too, does employment. Young women who were employed at the time they were asked their views gave a more modern answer to almost all these questions, including their plans for work, their approval of mothers' working, their fertility expectations, and their sex-role attitudes.[27] This result is consistent with a broad range of other research on this issue (Spitze, 1978; Dambrot et al., 1983; Morgan and Walker, 1983).

Interestingly enough, young women's *family* experiences also alter their views in a less traditional direction. Marriage has an important effect on young women's views, and one that depends on *whom* she marries. Otherwise average young single women score at the 45th percentile in viewing a woman's employment as an important contribution to her family. By marrying, young women increase their score to the 53rd percentile. *By remarrying*, they increase their score to the 59th percentile (fig. 4.5). The effect of marriage weakens if her husband's salary is above average.

Becoming a parent also has a strong effect on a young woman's attitudes, depending on whether she is herself an employed mother. Working while raising a young family increases a woman's approval of women working, from the 48th percentile for those with no children to the 56th percentile for those with children.

These results mean that most *unmarried* young women are not yet fully aware of the potential benefits of their own employment to themselves and their families. Most are likely to view marriage in a romantic light, which emphasizes women's homemaking roles and men's "good provider" roles. Marriage evidently makes women more realistic since most of them are working, and they can see that their paychecks make a real difference. But this is less likely to happen if their husband earns a substantial income.

The birth of children also strongly influences young women.[28] For a woman who is not working, becoming a mother centers her more firmly on home and family, making her more traditional in both of our measures of sex-role attitudes. Nonworking women without children rank in the 45th per-

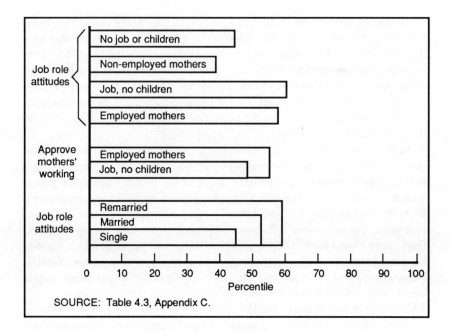

Figure 4.5   Effects of Adult Roles on Young Women's Work and Family Attitudes

centile on the JOB ROLES scale; otherwise similar women with children rank only in the 39th percentile. But among women who are working, the effect of parenthood on JOB ROLES does not appear nearly as strong. Such women value women's work roles nearly as much as do nonparents (dropping only from the 60th percentile among women who are working nonparents to the 58th percentile for women who are working mothers).

Hence, as young women progress into the work and family roles of adulthood, their experiences seem to decrease the traditional nature of their views. And if they have what is an increasingly common family experience—divorce—this also increases women's modernity, although in this case, the effects are strongest on the FAMILY ROLES scale (table 4.3, Appendix C). This result is hardly surprising, considering that divorce may be the most threatening experience a family-centered woman can have, since she is least prepared in terms of work experience to manage on her own.

The cumulative effects of working, marrying, or even remaining in school provide strong evidence that women's sex-role attitudes are not only changing as new groups of young women grow up but as women themselves move away from traditional definitions of their roles. These effects are reinforced by "new" family experiences, such as a divorce in their parents' home or nonfamily living, and by work, marriage, and educational attainment. That this is not happening for men underlines the importance of their childhood experiences.

Planning for New Families or No Families

Young people's plans are changing, not only in response to their own non-traditional family experiences in childhood and young adulthood but also as a result of the typical experiences of young adulthood (at least among young women). More young men approve of mothers' working and more young women are planning their lives around work and fewer children, and to a somewhat lesser extent are changing their views of men's and women's roles in a less traditional direction.

What is less clear is what people will do as a result of these new plans and attitudes. Will a young woman who wants to work and have few or no children be interested in marriage? If she wants to marry, will her standards for an egalitarian relationship doom her search, given that men have more traditional role definitions? And if she does marry, what sort of relationship can she expect? Will it include children, despite the problems children and work cause for women in traditional families? Will her marriage be stable? And above all, will it be egalitarian, providing role models and experiences for children who will start their own families in the twenty-first century?

And what about young men? Will those with less traditional views of gender roles avoid marriage, since they will bear greater burdens of child care and home tasks than their more traditional counterparts? Or might having less traditional views make these men *more* attractive in the marriage market, providing them an advantage over more traditional men? And will they carry out their more egalitarian views, translating them into greater involvement in the home? Or will job pressures and the more traditional men they work with lead them toward more traditional family lives? The chapters that follow try to answer these questions and provide a basis for predicting whether these transformations in young adults' plans and attitudes are leading to "no families" or "new families."

5

The Transition
to Marriage

Marriage is the central institution defining families in almost all societies.[1]
Sex roles in marriage influence male-female relationships elsewhere, even at
school or at work. The roles expected for them in marriage color men's and
women's interactions prior to marriage with "courtship" overtones and influence every relationship between adult males and females, both when they are
unmarried, and when one or the other (or both) is married to other persons.

The extent to which this is so, however, varies. In traditional Muslim
societies, women are symbolically invisible to all but specifically designated
men, and live extremely sex-segregated lives. In contrast, in some modern
societies like the United States, men and women at school, at work, and
sometimes even at play, manage to make issues of gender and marital status
irrelevant.[2]

Hence, although gender differentiation exists everywhere, it appears to be
strongest within marriage. This becomes a problem when men and women
are more nearly equal *outside* the family than within it, as is currently the
case in the United States. Family roles may become associated with the
negative aspects of gender roles. Men worry that to marry, and embark on
the development of a long-term close relationship and possibly parenthood,
necessarily means assuming heavy financial burdens and responsibilities
(since they still feel the requirement to be a "good provider") (Bernard, 1981;
Goode, 1981). Women are also likely to fear that given the experiences of
their mothers and older sisters over the last few decades, marriage and parenthood will require them to assume the double burden of full responsibility for
housework and child care, even while they help support their families and

ensure their own economic independence. As a result, both men and women are increasingly likely to reject marriage and parenthood.[3]

Family roles, however, do not require extreme differentiation by gender, and families may even benefit when men and women take on some portion of each other's traditional family responsibilities. Because men with working wives have more time to spend with their children, they can parent more effectively than in the past, when their burden of total financial responsibility required them to be away from home for too many hours. In contrast, full-time mothers have often felt that they saw too much of their children to appreciate them fully. Spouses may find that communication and close intimacy are enhanced when their worlds are more similar, their spheres less separate. But since family roles are still quite differentiated, the decision to marry normally requires moving into a more gender-segregated life. Being single may have changed for the better, but this is not yet the case for being married.

How have the lives of single people improved? The rise in living away from one's parents' home among the unmarried—in dormitories, barracks, private homes, and apartments—provides a new option that allows young persons the independence and autonomy of adulthood without the responsibilities of marriage and parenthood. Before this option became widely available, many young adults may have married and begun childbearing to acquire adult status.

This growth in privacy, together with the sexual revolution, has fueled the increase in "living together."[4] This has given men greater access to wifelike social and sexual benefits outside of marriage than they have ever had, reducing their incentive to make traditional longer-term commitments of support. The decline in the "double standard" means that an important pressure on men to marry—in order to enjoy a sexual relationship—has decreased.

Men may also now be feeling less pressure from employers to be married. In the past, when marriage was more strongly associated with employee stability among men, research has shown that men tended to receive wage bonuses from marriage (Mortimer, Lorence, and Kumka, 1982). But in the 1990s, marriage often creates problems on the job for men, from the career needs of a working wife (Pfeffer and Ross, 1982) to the traumas of divorce and custody disputes, suggesting that employers may be putting less pressure on men to marry.

Important changes have also occurred that make unmarried women more comfortable. Where once marriage was the only prospect for achieving an adequate level of living, given the scarcity of jobs open to women and the low wages those few who filled them could earn, women have now gained financial options beyond marriage through paid employment and welfare systems. These options have made nonfamily living possible for women, as well, allowing them to live in the privacy and independence of adulthood (Kobrin, 1976; Ellwood and Bane, 1984).

What, meanwhile, is wrong with marriage? And does "his" marriage differ from "her" marriage? Very much so—at least in traditional marriages. In the past, women gained financially in marriage by having access to their husband's income, though they compromised the opportunity to develop their own financial resources. While men have tended to gain promotion prospects by being married, women have received significantly lower wages if they are married rather than single (Treiman and Roos, 1983). This means that a woman's financial investment in marriage is much more problematic in the long run than a man's, and that the loss of a husband's income after divorce is a major blow. Few couples have much marital property to divide, alimony is uncommon, and even child support is rarely adequate or reliable (Weitzman, 1985; Beller and Graham, 1986). The rise in divorce has created a new class of poor. These "displaced homemakers" have few market skills and have been forced to find some means of support after their marriages have ended.

Turning to the noneconomic dimensions of marriage, research has shown that traditionally defined family roles are also very problematic for women. Marriage undoubtedly offers benefits and poses restrictions for both men and women. But women suffer more of the restrictions, giving up more than their husbands in terms of privacy, friends, and control over schedules and lifestyles. In contrast, men gain more than women from marriage on many other dimensions—including survivorship, mental, and physical health—compared to remaining single (Bernard, 1972; Gove, 1972, 1973). Women still do most of the domestic work and take responsibility for household and child management (chapter 7). If one looks beyond the short-run financial gains and losses, "his" marriage is more desirable than "her" marriage in terms of both noneconomic and longer-run economic dimensions.

Research bears this out, showing that men tend to be substantially more satisfied with their marriages than women. Men are also less likely to have thought about divorce or to initiate a breakup of the marriage (Huber and Spitze, 1983; Ross, Mirowsky, and Ulbrich, 1983) suggesting that for young women, and perhaps also for young men, the major barrier to getting married is marriage itself, at least as it has been traditionally defined. For women to enter into a traditional marriage means taking a great financial risk, since traditional marriages require them to give up their careers and take on what has been defined as a subservient role within marriage.

Since the 1950s, however, part of the retreat from marriage has been fueled by changing attitudes toward marriage and family life, in which women have recognized the disadvantages and men have denied the advantages. Although men tend to be more satisfied than women with their own marriage, men have a very negative image of being married, and of long-term human relationships. They contrast the "independence" of being single not with "dependence," as married women do, but with being "tied down."[5]

This moves the establishment and development of long-term relationships out of the realm of important adult choices, such as the choice of an occupation or where to live, and into the trivial and entertaining, such as the choice of a vacation spot. The process of deciding on an occupation or a community requires that one must commit to making *a particular* choice, rather than keeping all options open and developing none. In the 1970s, a major popular psychology magazine prefaced a research report on the lower mortality of married men with a cartoon portraying Woody Allen sitting in a bar with Sigmund Freud. Allen asks Freud, "Is it true that married men live longer?" and Freud replies, "No, it just feels longer."[6]

In this chapter we focus on the transition to marriage for men and women in order to see which factors make marriage more or less likely and to assess what these results imply about the kinds of marriages being formed. Those who do not marry are presumably choosing to remain in the more egalitarian nonfamily world of the unmarried. But for those who do marry, many may be choosing traditional family relationships, while some may be trying to establish more egalitarian ones. We will attempt to distinguish between these two outcomes by relating our results in this analysis to those in chapter 4, in order to see how the factors leading to expectations about more equal gender roles relate to those predicting marriage. But we will only be able to unravel these connections clearly in later chapters, where we analyze the division of household responsibility. There we can see which factors actually lead to more egalitarian behavior in marriage and not simply to egalitarian attitudes.

We ask the following questions: What factors influence the timing of marriage or perhaps the likelihood of getting married at all? Do differences in young people's characteristics and experiences affect their likelihood of marriage? For example, is there any effect of growing up in the South, or with more educated parents? And what about the effect of living in nontraditional families? Are childhood experiences, such as parental divorce, remarriage, or living in a female-headed family more important than those that occur in early adulthood, such as living away from kin in dormitories or in an apartment? And what do these effects tell us about the nature of marriage today and how young people view it?

When Do People Marry?

The ages at which young men and women marry are highly concentrated, particularly for women. Men marry later than women, but most men and women marry during their twenties. Between the 1950s and 1970s, about 75 percent of women had married by age 25, whereas 75 percent of men had married by age 27 (Rodgers and Thornton, 1985)—although both young men and young women are not marrying as early as they did in the 1950s. Hence, we focus our analysis on the likelihood of marriage, starting when young people are 18 (17 for young women) and continuing until they reach 30. At each age, we consider those still single and predict their marriage, assessing the influences that make it more or less likely.[7] During these ages, on average 13 percent of women married every year, compared with about 11 percent of men.

Childhood Family Structure

An important element in marriage is the central relationship between spouses, often characterized by the ideal of romantic, undying love. Yet the rise of divorce has tarnished this ideal and thus may have become an important factor in the increased likelihood that both men and women will delay or avoid marriage. To the extent that building a relationship represents a major invest-ment of time and energy, the increased risk that this investment will be lost could deter many from making the attempt, or perhaps from trying hard enough to make the relationship work.

This risk should be most acute for those who have experienced family change directly. Increasing numbers of young people have felt both the rise in nonmarriage—as more have been born out of wedlock—and the increase in divorce, as they spend less of their childhood with both natural parents than did earlier cohorts. Both sons and daughters have seen in the most immediate and painful way that marriage is not forever, and so may be less willing to risk the emotional commitment of marriage.

We have seen that young men and women who grew up with both biolog-ical parents have less egalitarian attitudes toward mothers' working than those who experienced some other family form during childhood; daughters from these traditional families are also less likely to plan to work at age 35 (chapter 4). Research has also shown that women are more likely to choose a non-traditional occupation if they have experienced family breakup during child-hood (Berryman and Waite, 1987). Such women have experienced the greater poverty of divorced mothers, and this may be an additional incentive for them to avoid not only traditionally low-paid female occupations but that other very low-salaried female occupation—traditional marriage. Is this the case?

Our analysis shows that for most young men and women, growing up in a family that was disrupted at some time before they reached age 14 decreased the likelihood of marriage (fig. 5.1).[8] This effect is much stronger for women, increasing with each additional year they remain single. Family disruption actually increases the probability of very early marriages by about 14 percent among women, suggesting that some portion of teen and other early marriages

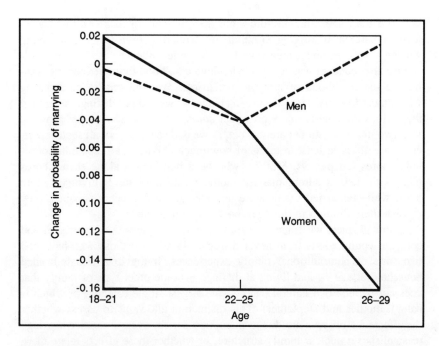

Figure 5.1   Effect of Parental Marital Disruption on the Probability of Marrying at Younger and Older Ages

provides an escape from a difficult home situation.[9] But the effects turn negative quickly, reducing the proportion marrying by 23 percent during the central ages in which most women marry, and are extremely powerful in delaying further or preventing quite late marriages.[10] Our results suggest that if young women from nonnuclear families have not married by age 25, they are extremely unlikely to marry over the next few years.

Growing up in an intact family has less effect on young men. Unlike women, those from broken homes apparently do not face an increased risk of very early marriage. They are significantly less likely to marry than those from nuclear families only at ages 22 to 25, and there is some evidence that this may only represent a deferral of marriage, since men from less traditional families are slightly more likely to marry late than those from nuclear families.

Having parents with a stable marriage, then, may increase young people's likelihood of an orderly entry into marriage, presumably by increasing their preference for marriage relative to remaining single. The effects, however, are much stronger for women. This may reflect the fact that in their experience, it is women who bear more of the financial and child care costs of a high-risk marriage. This reinforces our interpretation in chapter 4 that the effects of parental disruption in childhood primarily serve to increase young women's concern about their own financial independence.

Our next concern was to establish which childhood family experiences influence the likelihood of entry into marriage over the critical ages during which most first marriages occur. In chapter 4, we did not distinguish among the various experiences now prevalent among children who do not grow up with two married natural parents. Yet, as we will see later, not all such experiences are alike, at least in terms of how much children participate in household chores (chapter 9). Mothers who head households alone share chores most with their children, married mothers who have never divorced share least, while remarried mothers are intermediate in the extent to which they involve their children in the household division of labor.

In this chapter, we extend these insights to the question of marriage, and compare young adults from never-disrupted families to those who have had two sorts of nontraditional family experiences: living in a female-headed household at age 14 and living at that age in some other type of family that does not include two natural parents (the largest single category of which is natural mother and stepfather). This distinction allows us to assess whether the effects we observe are due to disruption per se, even if another marriage reestablishes a nuclear family structure, or whether these effects relate more to continuing differences in household structure.

Our three measures all refer to the parental family structure when the young people we study were age 14. We distinguish nuclear families (those that included their natural mother and father) from mother-only families (those that were headed by their mother or another adult female with no adult male present) and stepfamilies (those that include all other family structures, which are primarily stepparent families, but also include a few families headed by the father only and families headed by other relatives). About three-quarters of the young men and women we studied lived in nuclear families during their early teens, and approximately equal proportions lived in mother-only and stepfamilies (10–12 percent).

When we made this comparison, we found that the results of the simpler contrast between nuclear and all other families (already shown in fig. 5.1) appear to be due fairly equally to the effects of mother-only families and stepfamilies. The experience of parental disruption apparently deters marriage, whether or not a remarriage occurs.[11]

Overall, then, the effect of parental marital disruption on the likelihood of marriage is quite substantial. Nevertheless, it is possible that increases in family disruption may have contributed even more to the declines in marriage than this analysis has been able to demonstrate. Not only do we lack information on the timing of any disruption of parents' marriage or their remarriage, we do not know how many parental divorces and remarriages have occurred.

And we do not know how much the child's life was affected by moving, losing contact with one or the other parent, or any other dimension of the divorce experience that can be difficult for children. We need data with more complete parental marital histories, as well as histories of the child's living arrangements, and information on relationships over time to measure more precisely the effects of parental marital disruption on the later marriage of children.

It is also likely that children's experience with disruption may not fully indicate their actual experiences, which are drawn in part from the communities in which they live. For example, the continuing separation between white and black communities (U.S. Riot Commission, 1968; Farley, 1977) and the greater family instability experienced by blacks mean that black children have earlier and more intimate experience with family disruption, even if the experience was not in their own family. This is probably also the case for many subgroups. Data that include information on the extent of divorce in young peoples' family and community networks are needed to test this possibility.

Nonfamily Living in Young Adulthood

Another group of young adults may have gained increased perspective on traditional marriage, simply because they have had more time to think about it. We saw in chapter 4 that nonfamily living during early adulthood was shaping young people's plans and attitudes, making young women in particular less family-oriented on a variety of dimensions. Young men who have experienced nonfamily living early in adulthood are somewhat more likely to take an egalitarian attitude toward mothers' working.

Nonfamily living could also influence the marriage process. It should make any marriage less *necessary*, since the independence of adulthood is to a large extent already achieved. We know from chapter 4 that nonfamily living increases young women's plans to be working at age 35, so that the financial pressure on them to marry is less as well. Consistent with this result, residential independence should reduce the need to enter into traditional marriages, although it would not necessarily make an egalitarian marriage less desirable. Nonfamily living should lead to the development of skills traditionally viewed as the specialty of the opposite sex. Some speculate that the rigidity of sex roles in working-class families may result from early marriage and men's lack of experience in living independently from either their mother or wife, whose role was to care for their physical needs (Rubin, 1976). If so, then nonfamily living might increase men's likelihood of marriage by making them more desirable as spouses than more traditional men, since they are likely to be less dependent on women for their domestic needs and more likely to have developed some homemaking skills while living alone. This experience might also increase young men's awareness of the sheer volume of work necessary to keep a family clothed and fed.

Our first estimates of the effects of nonfamily living on the probability of marriage appear in figure 5.2, showing overall results for each sex. We find strong effects of nonfamily living on the likelihood of marriage for both sexes, but in opposite directions. Women who experienced nonfamily living at some point are less likely to marry at a given age, but comparable males are more likely to marry. The effects are nearly as strong as that of parental marital disruption. Women who had lived away from the parental home were only about 80 percent as likely to marry in a given year as those who had never lived away from the parental home—with annual rates of 11.1 percent compared to 13.5 percent. The difference for men is also about 2 percentage points, but in the opposite direction. Since about 10 percent of those still single at the beginning of a year marry during the next 12 months, these differences are large enough to be important.[12]

Clearly, then, living away from a family situation in these critical years of young adulthood has an influence on marriage, although the effect for males is quite different from that for females. Women become more independent of families, deferring marriage (or perhaps forgoing it altogether). For men, however, nonfamily living in early adulthood does not increase the trend toward "no families," nor is it neutral. Rather, it appears to be a strong "pro-family" experience. If living independently has made young men more appreciative of the amount of work involved in carrying full responsibility for making a home, this would give them a wider choice of mates than young men who have had more traditional experiences, since there are more young women who want to share work and family roles with their future husbands than there are young men who are willing to share both roles with their future wives. Traditional men would be more likely to insist on a traditional spouse. In contrast, those who have lived independently, though perhaps still quite happy to marry a traditional woman, would be more open to a wife who wants to share responsibility for household tasks.

Does it make any difference what type of nonfamily experience young people have? Does living in a dormitory as opposed to more independent quarters, which we saw had different effects on attitudes about traditional male-female roles (chapter 4), carry over into behavior, as we just discovered was the case for childhood family structure? And are there sex *differences* in their effects on marriage, as there were for young men's and young women's approval of mothers' working?

To test this notion, we created two other measures of independent living, in order to reflect both the duration and type of nonfamily living. The first counts years lived in a college dormitory. We reasoned that this type of non-

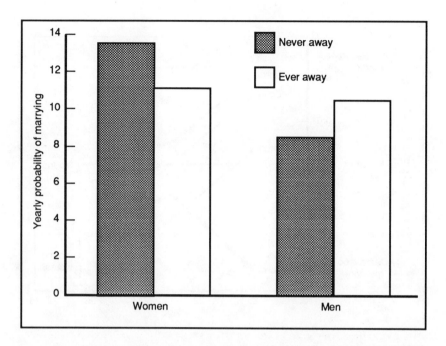

Figure 5.2   Effect of Ever Living Away from Home on the Probability of Marrying

family living offers less separation from parents or parent surrogates, less independence, and less responsibility than other types of living away. It confers some independence (since living in dormitories and other group quarters provides social, emotional, and physical separation from the parents' home), but it does not involve the responsibilities of apartment living (particularly those related to food preparation), much less those of a new home. In addition, residence in group quarters often involves some type of adult supervision. To test this reasoning, we also created a measure of years living away in more independent and responsible situations, including living alone, with nonrelatives, or with own children.

We are also interested in seeing whether it makes a difference *how long* young people live away from family, and at what age they do it. Socialization theory suggests that early experiences normally have more impact than later ones on such fundamental attitudes and behavioral orientations as those relating to family formation. Further, a longer experience of such independence should have greater effects, although it is possible that most of the impact could occur quite quickly.

In order to examine the effects of type and timing of nonfamily living experiences, figure 5.3 summarizes the results separately for each age grouping, varying how living arrangements is measured in order to show the effects

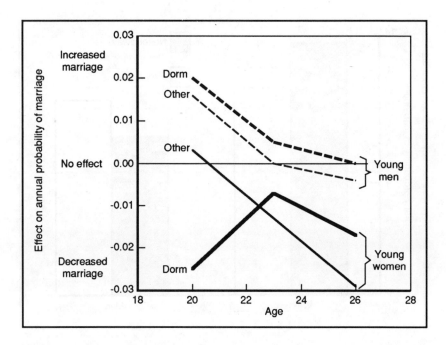

Figure 5.3   Effects of Type and Timing of Nonfamily Living on the Transition to Marriage

of timing and duration of nonfamily living. Evidently, the negative effects of nonfamily living for females at younger ages are due to the effects of living in dormitories; living independently among very young women seems to increase the likelihood of marriage. But the effects of having lived in a dormitory wear off at older ages, while living independently begins to have a much greater effect on deterring marriage.

Except for the youngest ages, then, the results for women support our reasoning that the effect of nonfamily living on marriage would be greater for those living arrangements offering the most separation and independence from family. For boys, on the other hand, the increase in marriage chances that results from ever having lived away seems to result about equally from years spent in a dormitory and from years spent more independently. To achieve the strongest effect for boys, then, requires living away from home during the college years, whether in a dormitory or more independently— exactly the same result that we saw in chapter 4. It took both the experience of college and residential independence to significantly increase young men's approval of mothers' working.

For women, the picture is more complicated. The negative effect of dormitory living on marriage is felt primarily during the years of actual college enrollment, usually between 18 and 21. Having lived in a dorm does not appear to affect the chances for marriage much at later ages, with some tendency to concentrate marriage in the few years after college normally ends. (These are consistently negative effects, whose influence is over and above the negative effect of college enrollment, which is controlled.)

In contrast, the effects of years spent in more independent living arrangements seem to display a reversed life-cycle pattern. Those young women living away from parents during the early years after high school, and who are primarily not attending college, appear to be slightly more likely to marry than those who remain with their parents. This pattern resembles the one we saw for childhood family structure, in which those who did not grow up in a nuclear family were also likely to make a very early marriage. Beginning in the twenties, however, just when the effects of dormitory living are wearing off, the effects of more independent living abruptly turn negative and intensify with age, so that by age 24 or so, both experiences are working together to reduce the likelihood of marriage. The negative impact on marriage is thus greatest among young women who both went away to school and remained away from the parental home after finishing school, as we found in chapter 4.

For young men, the effects of considering type and timing of nonfamily living are simpler, although their meaning is less clear. Both types of living arrangement experiences strongly increase the chances of marriage at the youngest ages and then vanish, so that nonfamily living at later ages no longer has any effect on the likelihood of marriage. This result seems puzzling, and suggests that continuing into adulthood unmarried leads to an accumulation of experiences that offset the early experience of nonfamily living. Clearly, much more research is needed on young men's experience of family roles, and the extent to which unmarried men are managing on their own or living with a woman to care for their domestic needs, before we can fully untangle the relationship between living away from parents and living with a spouse.

Overall, these results indicate that nonfamily living is having an effect on marriage. For men, learning to manage their domestic needs and perhaps to respect women's economic independence seems to lead to marriage, suggesting to us that the marriages they are forming are likely to be more egalitarian, at least among those marrying in their early twenties. This is consistent with the results we found on the effect of nonfamily living on young men's sex-role attitudes, which became somewhat more egalitarian. Women, in contrast, by learning to support themselves, or simply by being introduced to options beyond the family, are avoiding marriage, or at least traditional marriage.

Clearly, then, experiencing one of these new family forms, whether by growing up for some period outside a two-natural-parent family or by living away from one's family in early adulthood, is contributing to the delay or avoidance of marriage, at least among young women. The effects of each experience are the same for young women, suggesting that whatever happened in childhood has led them to distrust traditional marriage and that their experiences in young adulthood provide them alternatives to it. The results are more complex for young men. The emotional blow from childhood does deter their own marriage (although not so strongly as it does for women), but the experience of independence from family roles actually increases the odds of marriage.

These results are consistent with an argument that sees traditional marriage as becoming less attractive for both men and women, as it has become increasingly fragile, while the costs of divorce are more problematic for women. Hence, any experience that exposes young people reaching marriageable age to these new truths will have a more sobering effect on women than on men. If so, then there may be other situations in which some women might see that marriage is not a great bargain for them. But this same characteristic might make it easier for males to search successfully for a mate, by giving them a wider market. For example, women who have greater earning powers, perhaps because they are more educated, give up more by assuming traditional marital roles than highly educated men, whereas more educated, and hence, more egalitarian men would not be as affected. We will examine whether those who are avoiding or delaying marriage have the most to lose by traditional definitions of marriage, and are thus moving toward "no families" as well as whether those more likely to marry are candidates for "new families."

Influences on the Desirability of Traditional Marriage

Our approach to studying variation in the desirability of traditional marriage focuses on how *attitudes* and *resources* affect the probability of marriage. As we discuss in chapter 3, we consider education (here measured by educational attainment of young adults' parents),[13] race, region, and city size as factors that influence family attitudes. For each young woman, we have a measure of plans for a traditional or more egalitarian female life course— whether she expects to be working at age 35 (the middle of the childrearing years).[14] We reason that women with more modern attitudes are likely to prefer not to marry, while men might well be more *able* to marry.

Attitudes and Traditional Marriage

Our one direct indicator of orientation toward more egalitarian marriage— young women's plans for working at age 35—has a strong effect on reducing their likelihood of marriage (see table 5.2 in Appendix C). This result poses the "new families" or "no families" dilemma most clearly—women who reject traditional marriage are also rejecting marriage generally, at least during the most common ages of marriage—and is consistent with the patterns we have seen so far, whereby new family experiences make young women both more modern in their work and family attitudes (chapter 4) and less likely to marry. That this is less the case for young men, given the differences in effects of the experiences of nonfamily living and of parental marital disruption, suggests to us that this equation between modern attitudes and "no families" is not a necessary one. Indeed, some factors can increase the likelihood of egalitarian marriages, or "new families." To the extent possible, then, we will refer back to the results of chapter 4 as we examine influences on marriage, to see whether these marriages are likely to be more traditional or more egalitarian.

Turning to our indirect measures of family values, we see that young men and women living in the South are more likely to marry, and marry younger, than those in other parts of the United States (see table 5.2 in Appendix C). The effect is particularly marked for young southern women. This difference between the two sexes is likely to mean that southern women are particularly likely to be marrying men considerably older than themselves, rather than marrying the younger southern men who are in our sample. This combination—high marriage rates, early marriage, and large age differences between spouses—is associated with relatively traditional marriages, even though young southern men and women did not appear be particularly traditional in their attitudes and plans (chapter 4).

Here is a situation in which context is affecting how one should interpret opinion responses. Southerners respond to attitude questions in a relatively nontraditional way, but appear very traditional in their behavior. This result will arise again among southerners when we consider the extent to which husbands and children share in the household division of labor (chapters 8 and 9).

Attitudes and behavior are somewhat more consistent when community size is considered. The likelihood of a young adult's marrying is greater in rural areas and smaller towns than it is in large cities, with about equal effects for women and men. Community size only affected approval of mothers' working among young women, however, not among young men. This suggests that traditional attitudes deter marriage among young women, but the higher marriage rate of rural men is not related to their attitudes on this issue.

Young black adults, like those in large cities, are also very unlikely to marry (see table 5.2 in Appendix C). The difference is particularly dramatic for women, with by far the strongest effects in the analysis.[15] Yet we know that black women think more positively about raising larger families than other women, and expect to be (and approve of) working while doing so (chapter 4). This focusing of the black family around mothers and children, then, represents a realistic response to the likelihood of marriage, rather than a rejection of it, either in its traditional or modern form.

We expect parents' education to affect their children's attitudes toward marriage, since many have argued that those with more education frequently are less tied to traditional family roles. Increasing education is an important factor in the decline in fertility, since educated people tend to have fewer children, and it is associated with more egalitarian sex roles, particularly among men, as we saw in chapter 4. Our results, presented in figure 5.4, show that the more years of schooling a young person's parents completed, the less likely he or she is to marry at a young age. However, this effect is much stronger for women. The negative effect for females is consistent at all ages of marriage, and the overall effect of parental education is much more strongly negative for women than for men. In contrast, the effect of parental education on the marriage probabilities of males weakens and becomes positive at older ages. This suggests that parental education produces a timing effect for males, primarily leading young men to defer marriage for a while. It may also mean that the marriages they eventually contract will be more egalitarian, given the effect of parental education on increasing young men's approval of mothers' working. For young women, parental education appears to reduce the probability of marriage by reinforcing young women's preferences for alternatives to traditional family roles.

The Effects of Parental Income and Occupation

In addition to factors that influence young people's preferences directly, we are also interested in the effects of parental resources on their children's decisions, and what these decisions tell us directly about young people's preferences, whatever their parents' preferences might be. Given that most parents make some portion of their resources available to their children, one way or another, children making decisions about marriage are reflecting their own preferences, by using their parental-origin resources to buy into or out of marriage. We use two direct indicators of parental resources—family income and father's occupational prestige—measured close to the ages at which their children were beginning the transition to adulthood.

Variation in parental income and occupational prestige should have different effects for men and women, since access to more resources increases women's option not to marry, while it broadens men's marriage market to include both modern and traditional women. This approach to tastes and resources follows from exchange theory and the central tenets of consumer choice theory of economists. Put simply, the indicator of the desirability of a given option is whether consumers elect to consume more or less of it as their income rises.

Including a resource dimension in the analysis of marriage raises some complex analytic issues. The first problem is causality, since married women

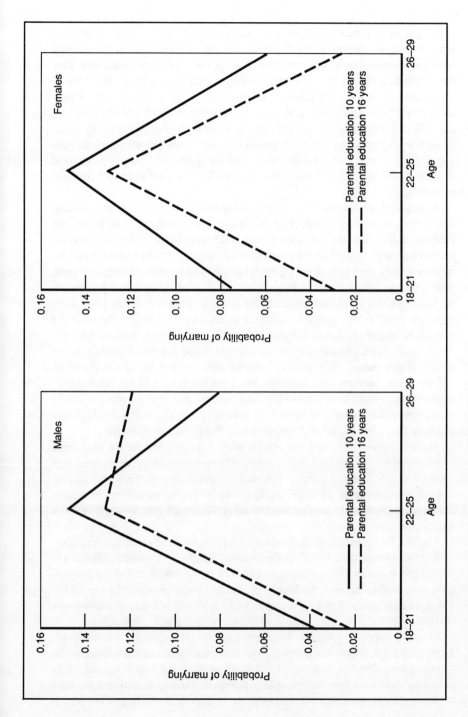

Figure 5.4   Effects of Parental Education on the Probability of Marriage

make less money than single women and with men it is the reverse. Women who remain unmarried generally must support themselves, while married women can expect to be supported by their spouses. Similarly, men who support families normally work harder and longer than those who do not.[16] These differences arise as a consequence of marriage, so how can we tell if they are a cause? Our analysis was designed to resolve the problem of causal order. We are able to eliminate the reverse effects of marriage on men's and women's economic resources in two ways. We consider only persons single at a given age, and examine the relationship of their resources to their probability of marriage in that year, and we focus on measures of parental resources.

A second issue derives from the mutuality of the decision to marry: Whose decision is being explained? Factors that can be interpreted as indicating preference for marriage can also reflect "marriageability." Marriage market analyses attempt to explain the positive relationship between marriage and resources among men as a result of the relatively greater attractiveness of more wealthy men, rather than as an indicator of an underlying male preference for marriage that increased resources allow them to realize. These interpretations are reinforcing, and thus difficult to separate. However, the case for women is clearer. It seems unlikely that having access to resources through, for example, greater parental income, would make a women less attractive to potential spouses. With second incomes now characterizing a majority of all marriages, women with access to more resources should be, other things equal, more attractive as wives, get better offers, and thus be more likely to marry than other women. If women do not marry, we argue that this logically suggests that they are using their resources to buy out of marriage.

Figures 5.5 and 5.6 show the effects of these two factors on the likelihood of marriage for young men and women. These results show an unusual and strongly sex-differential pattern. Parental income decreases the probability of a woman marrying at all marriage ages, while having no effect for males. Father's occupational prestige significantly decreases the probability of a man's marrying, but not of a woman's.

The results for males are consistent with prior research relating occupation to fertility (Freedman, 1963; Oppenheimer, 1982). Occupations define expected life-styles, which sociologists call "reference groups." Among families with comparable income, the higher the occupational prestige, the higher the life-style requirements, which are apparently achieved not only at the expense of fertility but also at the expense of marriage in the next generation.

However, opposing results characterize females. Despite its "life-style" effects, father's occupational prestige does not deter a woman's marriage, while family income makes marriage less likely at most ages and overall. This seems to suggest a very different interpretation. Among traditional families in the American occupational structure, the resources associated with father's

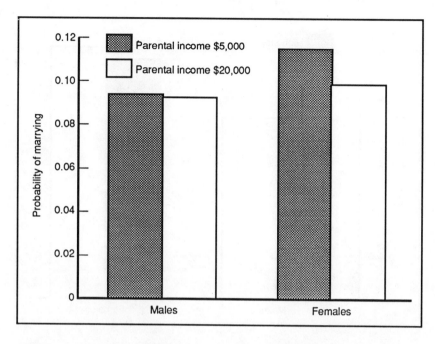

Figure 5.5   Effect of Parental Income on the Probability of Marrying, Ages 18–29

occupation are much more transferable to sons-in-law than to daughters, since these resources can involve sponsorship for trade school admittance, union membership, or jobs, as well as access to the network of business contacts that produces clients, capital, and customers, which increase in value with increases in socioeconomic status. To realize these resources, daughters must marry, and thus, as economic status increases, the "cost" of nonmarriage (in terms of opportunities forgone) increases, as well. These effects would offset the effects of the life-style requirements of father's occupation. Family income, by contrast, can be transferred directly to daughters, and to the extent that this is the case, may be used by young women to buy out of marriage.

These results are very difficult to explain in terms of reverse causality. Unmarried women certainly have to earn more than married ones. It is even plausible that those who are more likely to remain single for other reasons might be more likely to plan for supporting themselves by increasing their own education.[17] However, it is hard to argue that in the United States in the twentieth century, *parents* who expect that their daughters might eventually have difficulty in the marriage market would have been able to increase their family income in time to meet this contingency. It is more reasonable to conclude that young women with more parental resources are using them as an option that allows them to avoid traditional marriages, much as young women

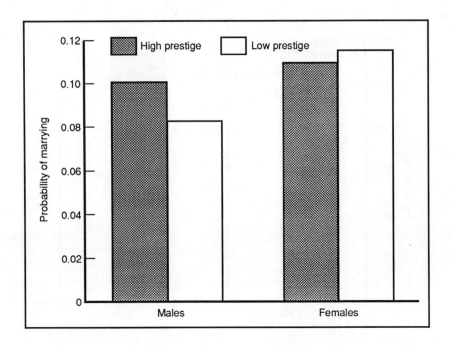

Figure 5.6   Effect of Parental Occupational Prestige on the Probability of Marrying, Ages 18–29

are doing who have experienced nonfamily living, or who have more educated parents.

Taken together, these results—both those reflecting the effects of directly experiencing new family patterns and those that focus our attention on other differences among and between men and women in American society— suggest to us a basis for understanding the decline in the marriage rates that has characterized the recent past, and can be interpreted not simply as a rejection of marriage but as a rejection particularly of traditional marriage. But in our view our analyses also show that the recent declines in the likelihood of marriage reflect more than these issues. Other factors have created barriers to young people's access to both traditional and more egalitarian marriages.

Barriers to Marriage

Many scholars concerned about the recent trend in marriage rates have ignored the issue of traditional versus egalitarian marriage because they are concerned that specific problems have emerged in recent years that pose barriers to all types of marriages. Two barriers have been discussed. The first directs our concern to economic hardships among young people. Young adults have been in an economic squeeze for most of the 1970s and 1980s, leading to higher unemployment rates for young people and slower ascent for many on their chosen career path (Easterlin, 1978; Oppenheimer, 1988). This has made it difficult for traditional young men to marry (although presumably it would be less of a barrier for men expecting to share financial responsibility with their wives).

The second barrier is thought to be the "marriage squeeze"—an imbalance in the sex composition of the marriage market that has characterized the 1960s and 1970s as a result of the baby boom of the 1940s and 1950s, limiting the marriage options of young women (Heer and Grossbard-Shechtman, 1981). The numbers of men and women of marriageable ages became unbalanced as a result of rapid swings in fertility. Since women traditionally marry men several years older than themselves (and rarely marry younger men), periods in which fertility has risen rapidly, like those that occurred during the baby boom, are followed in 25 years or so by a shortage of older men for women to marry, since there were fewer men born just before the baby boom who are available for the increased number of younger women. This demographic squeeze has been operating against women throughout the 1970s and most of the 1980s.

These two arguments disagree on which sex should be the focus of analysis, but share the view that marriage for both remains the most desirable state; short-term changes occur when marriage becomes more or less difficult to attain. These particular barriers to marriage can be considered temporary, irrelevant to later-born persons who come to adulthood and thus to marriageable ages in different economic and demographic circumstances.[18]

We tested for the effects of the marriage squeeze by examining whether it made any difference when young people reached their prime marriage ages. The data we use span 6 single-year birth cohorts, including young people born between the mid–1940s and mid–1950s (1947 to 1952 for males and 1949 to 1954 for females). The later part of this period included years of rapidly increasing births as the baby boom gathered momentum, which peaked in 1957. According to marriage squeeze theory, females born later should have experienced a much less favorable market than those born earlier, because of their large numbers relative to non-baby-boom males a few years older. For males, the large cohorts of baby-boom females should give those born in the later years a greater advantage in finding a mate, compared with males born earlier.

Our results, shown in figure 5.7, however, are quite similar in direction and in age pattern for men and women, showing declining probabilities of marrying over time. The effects are much stronger for women than for men, suggesting that the squeeze on women is adding to the decline in their likelihood of marriage. But it seems unlikely that the decrease in probability of women's marrying primarily reflects the shortage of eligible males, since

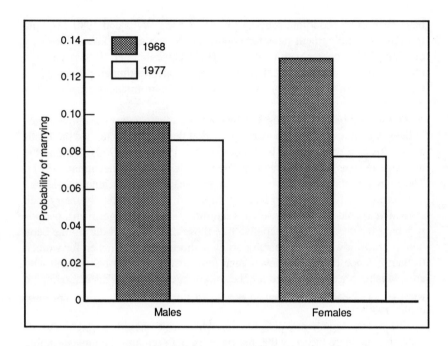

Figure 5.7   Effect of Time Period on the Probability of Marrying, Ages 18–29

young men did not respond to the increase in the number of eligible females by increasing their marriage rate. Other factors not measured in our data, such as the greater experience of the divorce of friends' parents, changing attitudes toward marriage and remaining single, made young people of both sexes increasingly unlikely to marry.

We measured the barriers to marriage posed by the lack of employment opportunities by looking at whether young people were actually employed at the beginning of the year (controlling, of course, for whether they were still in school). Employment facilitates marriage by providing the resources needed for forming and maintaining an independent household, and this effect should be particularly important for males, given traditional definitions of marriage. It also indicates, at least for men, the beginning of a lifetime of essentially continuous employment, since men are much less likely than women to exit from the labor force before retirement, once they have entered it.

Figure 5.8 shows that this factor is operating, since employment is an extremely strong predictor of marriage for men. Relatively few are willing to enter marriage while not employed. Evidently, difficulties in becoming employed continue to affect the marriage chances of young men, and have probably contributed to the decline in both traditional and egalitarian mar-

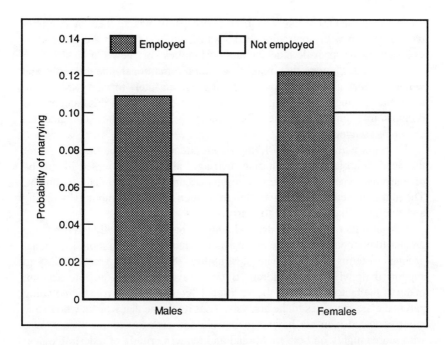

Figure 5.8   Effect of Current Employment on the Probability of Marrying, Ages 18–29

riages over the period. But the effects of current employment are consistently positive for women as well, although the effects are not as strong. This suggests that the economic dimension of the marriage decline is affecting modern couples, as well, since it is clear that young women ready to assume some of the economic responsibilities of marriage together with their husbands are more likely to marry—if they are successful at getting a job. So if modern young couples need *two* jobs in order to begin their married life, the economy is a problem for them, as well.

New Marriages or Traditional Marriages

We will summarize these results by placing them in the context of factors influencing young adults' work and family plans and attitudes. We pointed out some of the most dramatic parallels between the two analyses—that the experience of parental disruption during childhood led both to more modern attitudes and *away* from marriage. And we noted some of the differences that appeared—particularly the way in which nonfamily living in young adulthood made young men more likely to marry, perhaps by making them more attractive to women with nontraditional views of family life. But are there other experiences that provide clues about "no families" or "new families"?

In general, factors that make men more traditional about men's and women's work and family roles make them more likely to marry. Men who are white, southern, and from small communities all fit into this category, as do those from unbroken homes. But some of the results of these two analyses are more equivocal.

To begin with, nonfamily living in adulthood may not be the only factor that leads both to more egalitarian marriages and to an increased likelihood of marriage. The same pattern of results occurs for educational attainment. The higher the educational level, the more men approve of mothers' working and the more likely they are to marry.

Research literature on the determinants of marriage normally interprets the greater likelihood of marriage among more educated men on more traditional grounds in terms of their greater desirability—that is, their greater ability to support their wives and children. But we have already taken into account many of the factors linked to the traditional "good provider" role by including parental class measures in the analysis. Thus it may be that women who marry more educated men are having their cake and eating it too, with a spouse who scores highly on both traditional and modern criteria of a desirable husband. To the extent that male educational levels are continuing to increase, we think this creates pressures for the growth of "new families."

However, there is a larger complex of factors operating in men's lives that separately or together might make "no families" more likely. Men who are comfortable with mothers' working but are themselves unlikely to marry for some reason or another may also be more likely to divorce should they marry, or otherwise father children whom they later feel little responsibility to support. This combination is found in larger communities, among those from broken families, and among blacks, as well as among those with higher parental education.

The first three of these factors—large communities, disrupted parental family, and being black—are often seen together, reinforcing their separate effects in combination with one another. It is less clear how to interpret the comparable finding for parental education. It may simply represent a timing effect, leading to increases in marriage among men in their thirties to balance or offset their low rates of marriage while they are in their twenties. Or it may be the consequence of the very low involvement of *children* in the household economy that characterizes the most educated families (chapter 9), so that when those children grow up, they are uncomfortable in family roles. This is clearly an important issue that should challenge later research.

Among women, the equation of "traditional" and "marriage-oriented" also holds to a certain extent, but again not fully, with some basis for expecting growth in "new families." As we just saw for young men, a young woman's educational attainment increases both her orientation toward modern work and family roles (particularly as indicated by the FAMILY ROLES scale) and her likelihood of marriage. At young ages, the effect of education on marriage may simply reflect grade advancement, in which young women aged 18 who have completed high school are more likely to marry than those who have not yet finished school,[19] together with a piling up of marriages as young women finishing school (which we saw much more fully inhibited marriage for young women than young men) enter the marriage market. But since most women complete their education by age 20, the continued positive effect of educational attainment on marriage may reflect the greater optimism young educated women may feel toward an egalitarian marriage, based on their long-term association with the highly educated men with whom they attended school.

Employed women are also more likely both to approve of mothers' working and to marry. This suggests that while young men may expect to share financial responsibilities *before* children are born, and choose wives who will do so, their wives probably expect to continue to work after the children are born. Although we sometimes think that the links between egalitarian gender roles in the workplace and the home are extraordinarily weak, one is likely to lead to the other as working wives turn into working mothers.

Conclusion

Comparing the results of this chapter with those of chapter 4 reinforces our argument that one of the most important challenges to marriage is traditional marriage, especially in an era of high employment for wives and mothers. When both sexes are analyzed comparatively, in a format that separates the effects that differentiate earlier from later marriage, patterned sex differences in the determinants of marriage emerge that together paint a consistent picture.

Some support, to be sure, was found for traditional interpretations of the decline in marriage rates. Male employment is clearly an important factor encouraging marriage, and the difficulties young men have increasingly faced in the job market must have had some influence. The fact that the decline in marriage rates over time was greater for women than for men suggests that the marriage squeeze was acting as a further brake on women's transition to marriage relative to the men in their cohort. But men's rates were going down, too, even controlling for their employment difficulties, and despite their advantage in the marriage market based on relative numbers. These factors, which assume that people want to get married, but are unable to, are clearly only partial explanations of the overall trend in marriage, and our fuller analyses suggest that there are also many new reasons why people, and particularly young women, might be less willing to marry now than they were in the past.

For men, it is clear that the experience of parental marital disruption reduces their interest in marriage, since it undermines the foundations of marriage as a long-term relationship, whether in its traditional form or in a more egalitarian version. For such men to marry, they would need greater than average reassurance of commitment. Women, however, seem to need more than that, such as some assurance of a more equal relationship. This is especially true for those with the most attractive alternatives to marriage. Not only are the effects of parental disruption much stronger for women, but the option-enhancing situations, such as experiencing nonfamily living and having parents with more education and income, also reduce women's likelihood of marriage.

Whether these changes in the desirability of marriage relative to remaining single will turn out only to be a short-run barrier depends on whether young people, particularly young women, can either accept traditional roles within marriage, or can fashion new, less traditional marriages, with roles that equalize the burdens within marriage and the risks that accompany breakup. For those unwilling to accept traditional definitions of marriage or unable to find a partner with whom to create a more egalitarian one, our results suggest that the likely response, at least in the short run, is nonmarriage.

It seems to us, then, that pressure to find alternatives to traditional marriages can be expected to increase as a result of these combined experiences. For some, this may mean nonmarriage, at least for a while. However, some of the pressure is likely to be felt on the institution of marriage itself, pressure that may reduce its dependence on the traditional division of labor, and thus increase sharing in all aspects of traditional male and female family roles. To the extent that marriages are becoming less traditional, with men increasingly involved in the home and wives more involved in nonfamily activities, we would expect these pressures to weaken on women to delay or avoid marriage. Indeed, the generally positive effects of female short-term employment on marriage suggest that men choose wives who can share some economic responsibility. If further research can show that men who are less traditional in their sex-role orientations are also more likely to marry—for example, those who expect fewer children, or who are willing to assume a greater role in child care—this would support our argument that we are observing not simply a decline, but rather a restructuring and transformation of the role of marriage in men's and women's transition to adulthood.

6

Transitions in the Early Years of Marriage: Parenthood and Divorce

The Early Years of Marriage

The early years are a critical time in the development of a marriage. Whether the bride and groom are modern or traditional in their approach to women's and men's roles within marriage, all expect the relationship to be both emotionally close and personally rewarding, goals that produce tensions in all marriages. Closeness often appears to compete with personal autonomy, as the marriage takes on a life of its own and sometimes seems to threaten a young and often fragile sense of self. There is also a struggle between partners to find a comfortable balance for both as each tries to meet the partner's needs together with those of his or her own.

The emotional peaks of the honeymoon period need to be routinized and integrated with their ongoing lives. This process takes time and energy and often quite considerable interpersonal skills. Young adults learn that even the most loving partner is not a mind reader and begin to try to communicate clearly. The difficulties of this process are reflected in the level of divorce rates, which are higher in the early years of marriage than at any other time.[1]

How successfully these tensions are resolved has a continuing impact on the strength and development of the couple relationship. The competing demands on their time and energy usually multiply over these years and can severely threaten their ability to maintain emotional closeness. New career and family roles may prove unsuccessful—or very successful—unsettling each partner's sense of self. New tasks and needs emerge, and how these are met may well challenge their sense of equity. If the early years of marriage have not produced a relationship strong enough to meet these continuing challenges of adulthood, divorce remains an option, even in later years.

The early years of marriage normally include an even greater challenge: integrating the stresses of parenthood with the development of the couple relationship. Babies demand time and attention when they need it, not when their parents are best able to provide it. This leaves new parents little opportunity or energy for intimacy. Thus, as the couple shifts their energies from each other to the new child, each is likely to feel that the couple relationship is less satisfying for them (Rossi, 1968). Issues of equity become particularly salient; both may feel deprived, given the shrinking amount of energy their spouse has left over after caring for the baby. The question of equity becomes particularly problematic for women, since the extra demands of caring for the child are likely to be felt disproportionately by them. Social expectations about who should provide primary care are powerful, and the contours of the mother role are much more detailed and specific than are those of the father role (Russell, 1986; Hoffman, 1988).

These early years of marriage are likely to have become particularly problematic in an era of changing sex-role expectations. Marriages that began as explicitly egalitarian come up against strong social (and often internal) pressures to conform to a more conventional definition of parental roles. Both men and women tend to become more traditional in their views of appropriate roles for the sexes when their first child is born (Morgan and Waite, 1987), so that even if the young wife's family role becomes more demanding and stressful, the young husband may feel less involved, even shut out, from an adequate relationship with the new infant.

Couples with a strongly established relationship are likely to be more able to weather these challenges. Couples who delay the arrival of the first child for at least a period after marriage give themselves time to establish this relationship and their respective roles in the marriage. Those who have children very quickly may have more trouble laying the groundwork for the dyad because it is a triad so soon. This reasoning suggests that couples who wait several years before becoming parents stand the best chance of a satisfying (and lasting) relationship over the long run.

There is increasing concern, however, that many modern marriages will be childless—that children delayed will become children never born (Neal, Groat, and Wicks, 1989). According to this interpretation, parenthood is a wrenching experience whenever it happens, and those who have invested the most in their own relationship, developing settled patterns and expectations for shared time and responsibility, may have the most to lose by the addition of a child. In this view, it is better to add the challenges of parenthood to marriage at an early stage, before such patterns have developed, forcing young couples to integrate marital and parental roles more fully. Couples who have children early in life often also seem to end up with larger families (Dyer, 1963; Rossi, 1968).

In many ways, this argument about parenthood timing parallels that for marriage. While research has shown consistently that very early marriages are at high risk for divorce, continued postponement makes observers—both among scholars and among family and friends—increasingly nervous, since continued delay may reduce the chances of ever marrying or having children. Recent changes in the ages women are bearing children are consistent with delay. Those in their teens are much less likely to have a child and those in their thirties are much more likely to have a child now than at any time in the recent past (National Center for Health Statistics, 1988), but changes in the age pattern of childbearing are also consistent with an overall increase in the proportion childless. Although most young women (9 out of 10), and even more young wives (19 out of 20), say that they expect to become mothers (U.S. Bureau of the Census, 1989a), one study, which took into account both delayed marriage and delayed parenthood within marriage, has predicted that 25 percent of young women now in the childbearing years may never have children (Bloom, 1982).

Hence, although a couple can have an egalitarian relationship and yet remain childless, someone must have children—and raise them successfully—for the human species to continue. In fact, bearing, rearing, and educating children for participation in society have been the main function of the family. One could envisage a world in which "new families" often consisted of only a couple, with all children born to and raised in traditional families with a breadwinner father and homemaker mother—or in mother-only families. But this scenario flounders on the reality that the number of such traditional couples is shrinking dramatically, and on the fact that women in single-parent families raise few children and often under straitened economic circumstances (Rank, 1989). So for modern American society to produce enough children to make up the next generation, most of these children will have to be born into "new families" in which the parents share both breadwinner and home-tending roles and in which they *stay together*, at least long enough to raise the children. Hence, in this chapter we examine the factors that lead to two transitions in young marriages: parenthood and divorce.

The Transition to Parenthood

We saw in the last chapter that a broad range of factors led to delayed marriage among young people coming to adulthood in the late 1960s and 1970s. The general pattern is that those whose characteristics link with more traditional values (chapter 4) are more likely to marry early. This was not wholly the case for young men. Among men who were unmarried at a given age, those who had experienced nonfamily living early in adulthood, together with men with higher levels of education, were each *more likely to marry*, suggesting that men with more egalitarian attitudes may have become more desirable to women in the marriage market—but there was little evidence that factors reinforcing an egalitarian view of the family did anything but delay marriage for young women.[2] Further, the experience of a nontraditional family form in childhood slowed the transition to marriage for both young men and young women, suggesting that for each of them, the primary issue is that marriage itself is the problem, with less concern over finely distinguishing *what kind* of marriage is the more problematic.

The number of children expected was one of the major indicators of women's orientation toward more egalitarian roles (chapter 4), since young women with traditional sex-role attitudes would be more likely to expect very large families. And in fact, the factors that decreased the number of children young women expected were very much the same as those that also decreased their approval of mothers' working and their level of egalitarian responses to questions on women's roles in the workplace and in the home.

In this chapter, we examine whether the factors that affect sex-role attitudes, marriage, and expected family size continue to operate during the next step in the process of forming and maintaining families: the choice to have a first child after marriage. We are particularly interested in the factors that lead to early childbearing in marriage, which is the more traditional pattern, as compared with those that might lead couples who have delayed childbearing in the earliest years to finally have a child.

Despite the differences we found between men and women in what affects marriage, we must restrict our attention to women for the analysis of the transition to parenthood. The information available in the NLS on family matters for young men is skimpy and unreliable, preventing a detailed analysis of fatherhood or of male divorce (chapter 3). The information on the childbearing and marital histories of young women, however, is complete and of very high quality. This will force us, again, to study the prospects for "new families" only through the behavior of women and thus we will not be able to assess whether the same factors that make young men with egalitarian attitudes enter marriage more rapidly also lead to modern fatherhood.

Although most recent research on the transition to parenthood includes never married women, we focus our analysis on the childbearing of *married* women.[3] This reflects our concern about the prospects for "new families," in which men and women build homes and families together, sharing not only in the financial responsibilities but also in their care.[4] It is also the case that the decisions to marry and become a parent are closely intertwined. Some women might marry at least in part because they wanted to have children, and some might have children at least in part because it is one of the things married people do. And despite the rise in actual unwed childbearing, the vast majority of young white women and most young black women do not expect to have a child at an earlier age than the age they expect to marry, and affirm that they would not consider having a baby if they were not married (Abrahamse, Morrison, and Waite, 1988).

This approach allows us to separate the effects that lead to early parenthood from those that lead only to early marriage. It is possible that some factors have a strong influence on marriage timing, but might have no—or even reversed—effects on the timing of parenthood *within* marriage. We saw earlier that women living in the South marry earlier but expect fewer children than those living in other regions (chapters 4 and 5). Southern women may also be planning to delay having those children, since they were more likely to be planning to work.

Our focus on married women also provides us with simplicity and conceptual clarity. We know for each of the women we observe that any experiences outside traditional families occurred before she married. And marriage gives us an easily identified starting point for looking at the transition to parenthood. Thus we can look at the chances that young married women have a first child beginning with the date of their marriage.

This approach forces us, however, to restrict our focus to women who married either at normal ages or relatively early. Given that we are studying women who were aged 14–17 in 1968 whose marital and parenthood status was last observed in 1983, to be able to examine factors influencing parenthood 3 or 4 years *after* marriage, these women had to have married by age 28 or so in order to be in the survey and married that long. Since many of the most egalitarian couples delay marriage, our picture of the process of the transition to parenthood within marriage may be incomplete.

Although we do not include young women who had a first birth when they were unmarried, we *do* include those who had a child within 6 months of the wedding, indicating that they were pregnant at marriage and may have wed because they were expecting.[5] These marriages begin with the greatest pressure, in the sense that the stresses of parenthood begin even before the honeymoon year has ended.

Then, for those who had not conceived a child premaritally, we look at the chances of an early first birth (between the 7th and the 18th month of marriage). Among couples with no desire to postpone childbearing, this is the most common period for a first birth, since the typical delay of conception is between 4 and 9 months among couples not using contraception (Bongaarts and Potter, 1983). We then predict having a first birth in the next 12 months (from the 19th to the 30th month after marriage) and continue with those still childless, stopping at the 4th anniversary.[6] Most couples have begun a family by this time, so that we have too few cases to continue the analysis.[7]

New Family
Experiences and Parenthood

Young women with some sort of nontraditional family experience have been in the forefront of the family revolution leading to "no families" or "new families." Those who experienced a mother-only or stepparent family in childhood are more properly the victims of this revolution, while those who lived outside a family prior to marriage are more likely to have decided upon their course.[8] In both cases, however, traditional family formation patterns are likely to be weaker. Each experience results in greater plans to work at age 35 and expectations for fewer children. Hence, many of those who experienced new family forms either in childhood or in young adulthood might be particularly resistant to adding children to their marriage, and might particularly resist planning to have children early in the marriage, since this would increase the pressure on them to stop working and to move their relationship in a more traditional direction.

Childhood Family Structure.   We saw in chapter 5 that the effect on marriage for young women who experienced a nontraditional family during childhood depended on *the age* we looked at them. When considering only teenagers (those aged 18 and 19), the chances of marriage were greater among those who did not grow up with two natural parents, but this pattern ended quickly, so that among those who had not married by age 20, and particularly among those who had not married until their late twenties, young women with nontraditional family experiences were *less* likely to marry. Thus, it is difficult to conclude whether these experiences facilitate or retard marriage without taking into account where young women are in the transition to adulthood.

The pattern we observed for marriage could emerge if the "nontraditional" family pattern during adolescence involves more sexual experimentation, while during adulthood, when marriage has become the traditional pattern, to be "nontraditional" implies nonmarriage. For example, a mother raising children alone or with a new husband may have less time to supervise the activities of the children, allowing them to experiment with sexual activity at earlier ages than they might if they had two parents keeping track of their comings and goings. In addition, a single parent might—in the process of dating—act as a role model for sexual activity outside marriage. And divorced mothers become more accepting of sex without marriage both for themselves and for their children (Thornton and Freedman, 1982), perhaps implicitly or explicitly giving their children the freedom to experiment with sex earlier than the parents might have encouraged if they had remained married.

It is likely that this pattern leads in many cases to early pregnancy and motherhood (McLanahan and Bumpass, 1988). Many of these births would occur out of wedlock, but some may precipitate a marriage. This would increase the likelihood that young women who did not live with both parents during childhood would experience parenthood very early in marriage.

But for marriages formed at later ages, it is less clear that early parenthood should be expected. These are young women who are delaying marriage as a result of their childhood experiences. It may be that among those who survived adolescence without bearing a child, the experience of childhood family disruption is not only delaying marriage but also childbearing *within* marriage, in order to minimize the risks of having their children experience the pain they felt themselves.

Figure 6.1 shows the chances that a young woman will have a first birth within the first 6 months of marriage, and if she does not, the chances that she will become a mother in the later periods.[9] One bar on the graph shows the chances of becoming a mother for those young women who grew up in a household with both their natural parents but were otherwise average in terms of their personal and background characteristics. The other shows the chances for otherwise similar young women who grew up in a family with a nontraditional structure. This figure shows that young women who grew up in an intact family are much less likely to enter marriage already pregnant than are young women who grew up in another type of family. A young woman who did not live with both parents was nearly twice as likely to be pregnant when she married compared with one who grew up with both parents (14 percent versus 8 percent). We cannot tell whether this results from one or more of the mechanisms we suggested above that might delay the onset of sexual activity among daughters in two-parent families; we can only say that the differences shown in figure 6.1 are striking.

After the first 6 months of marriage we see a change in the effect of childhood family structure on the transition to motherhood. Coming from a traditional two-parent family *increases* the chances that a young woman will have a first birth by about one-third compared with similar young women from a family of another type (26 percent versus 19 percent). We can speculate that those young women whose parents divorced might be somewhat reluctant to rush into motherhood until after they see how happy their own marriage is. Perhaps having witnessed the struggles of a single mother trying to raise a family, they are reluctant to make themselves vulnerable to the same situation by having a child quickly after marriage. Young women from intact families may just be more confident that their marriage will prosper—or be more family-oriented in general—than young women with experience in a nontraditional family.

Whatever the reason, it is clear that, as with marriage, the effects of childhood family experiences on the timing of parenthood depend on the circumstances being considered. Although some young women who experienced a mother-only or stepfamily may have a child out of wedlock or marry as teenagers and become parents early in marriage, most will avoid that outcome. Our results suggest that these young women enter adulthood wary of marriage, and are reluctant to risk the additional stresses of parenthood when they do marry.

Since couples that begin marriage already expecting a birth face substantial

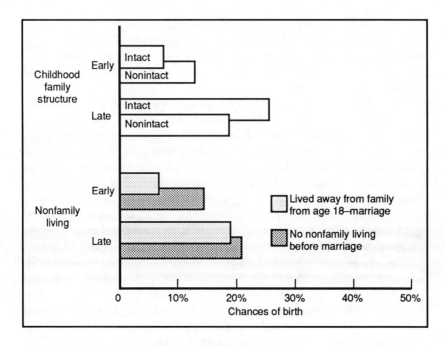

Figure 6.1   Effect of Childhood Family Structure and Nonfamily Living on Chances of a First Birth, Early in Marriage and Later

obstacles to the success of their marriage (Thornton and Freedman, 1982), growing up in a family with a nontraditional structure makes building a family riskier and probably more difficult for young women, at least in part because it increases the chances that they are pregnant at marriage. And for those who avoid a premarital pregnancy, a childhood family structure that does not include both of one's own parents propels young women toward "no families" by reducing the chances that they will have a child, at least in the first 4 years of marriage.

Nonfamily Living in Early Adulthood.   Young women's experiences of independent living in early adulthood lead them to reduce the number of children they expect to have themselves (chapter 4). Those who lived away from home from age 17 until marriage reduced their expected family size by nearly 15 percent compared with the number wanted prior to any independent living. This change is part of a general move among these young women away from traditional family patterns. Their priorities may have shifted so that getting established in their careers takes precedence; having children right away is probably a less important component of their sense of being an adult woman.

However, as with the effects of childhood family structure, it is possible that living independently could *increase* the likelihood of a young woman's being pregnant at marriage. Living away from home provides privacy—and opportunity—for sexually risky behavior. Parents often think they will have a greater opportunity to serve as chaperons if their daughter lives at home. Further, it is also likely that some of the young women living independently of their parents are cohabiting in marriagelike relationships. A common observation of such relationships is that they are more likely to become formal when a birth is impending, since the social and legal problems of maintaining a committed relationship increase when a child is involved.

Figure 6.1 shows chances of having a first birth for the first 6 months, and later through the first 4 years of marriage, comparing young women who lived away from home all of the available years between age 17 and their first marriage with otherwise similar young women who lived at home until marriage. We see from this figure that living independently during early adulthood has a dramatic effect on the likelihood of entering marriage pregnant, but not in the way we expected. Those who have lived on their own are less than half as likely to marry under the shadow of a shotgun than are those who were living with their parents until their wedding (7 percent versus 15 percent). In the later months of marriage, although independent living appears to continue to delay motherhood, the effect is small (19 percent versus 21 percent) and not significant.

Thus, independent living in young adulthood appears to provide considerable protection against a hasty or ill-considered marriage. If young women who have had this experience begin their sexual lives earlier than those living with their parents, they evidently also use their greater privacy to contracept more effectively before marriage, and may also continue to delay childbearing within marriage. To the extent that early parenthood disrupts young women's career progress, delay increases the likelihood of "new families." Independent living in early adulthood, then, may be increasing such an outcome for women.

What Else Affects Early Motherhood?

Many other factors affect the timing of the transition to parenthood after marriage. We have tried to take these factors into account throughout these analyses for two reasons. Omitting them might bias our view of the effects that are influencing family-related attitudes and transitions, which could occur if, for example, those with nontraditional family experiences differ in other ways that might make them more likely to marry, or to have children early in marriage. But these factors also provide us with a clearer view of the broad range of forces that we argue create pressures toward "no families" or "new families." Many other factors in addition to individual experiences of nontraditional families in childhood or young adulthood might influence young women's preferences or "tastes" for building their lives primarily around family as opposed to nonfamily roles (which often conflict, at least for women), and not all have the resources to indulge their preferences.

Family-Centered Preferences.   Our analysis of factors that should either reflect or influence preferring traditional women's roles include two direct measures of her sex-role attitudes: her views of appropriate roles for the sexes within the family (FAMILY ROLES) and her attitudes toward the importance of women's work roles for themselves and for their families (JOB ROLES). (These scales are described in more detail in Appendix B.) As indirect measures that might tap differences in family-centered preferences and values, we include a measure of whether the young woman is black, to take into account the earlier family-building patterns black women often show (Michael and Tuma, 1985) as well as the characteristics of the place where she lives (community size and whether she lives in the South). In addition, we consider the number of siblings the young woman had, the amount of schooling her parents completed, her plans for working in the future,[10] and her educational level, since highly educated women tend to have their children somewhat later than do those with less schooling (Kiernan and Diamond, 1983). We decided not to include measures of other roles, such as student or worker, that a young woman might have held during the early years of marriage. For those women in school or employed we could not be sure that these activities did not result from their plans not to have children soon.

A young woman holding quite traditional ideas about women's place in the home is substantially more likely to have a first child in any period than a comparable woman who thinks that a mother can work without neglecting her family. Evidently, young women who see their proper job as raising children are eager to get on with this phase of their lives, having a first baby and taking on the role of mother relatively soon after marriage, while women with egalitarian views about women's roles in the family have reasons for delay. They may be working, or they may simply be less eager to move on to motherhood. Women with more egalitarian views tend to have an "ideal age" at which a woman should become a mother that is older than the ideal age given by women with more traditional views.[11]

In contrast, holding more modern views on job-related dimensions of women's roles has no impact on the speed with which a woman has a first child. This is also the case for plans for long-run work in the labor market. These results reinforce our view that the critical dimension for the development of "new families" focuses on women's roles *in the home*. Those who have only thought through work-related issues, whether in terms of their own specific plans or in terms of more general attitudes relating to women's work, but have not thought through how these plans and attitudes might affect women's family roles, are evidently planning to be supermothers, and do not delay childbearing as a result.

As we expected, black women and those from larger families enter parenthood earlier than otherwise comparable women (see table 6.2, Appendix C). The young black wives in our sample begin their families at a somewhat faster pace than others, are more often pregnant at marriage, but even in later periods remain more likely to have a first birth. The effect of coming from a large family is strongest in the 2d and 3d year of marriage. Young women from larger families may simply be repeating the patterns they have observed most closely, but it may also be the case that they want to become parents because they had closer bonds with their own parents (Lawton, 1990), and hence view parenthood more positively than those from smaller families. The number of siblings does not influence premarital pregnancy, and its effects appear to attenuate in the 4th year.

The size of the community in which these young families live has no apparent effect on the speed of the transition to parenthood within marriage. Although those in rural areas have more traditional attitudes toward women's roles (chapter 4) and marry earlier (chapter 5), once married, they are no longer distinctive in their family-building behavior. However, southern families are more complex. Both young men and women marry younger than otherwise comparable young people, but southern women are *more likely* to plan to work and also expect fewer children. These expectations are evidently acted on promptly. Southern women delay childbearing within marriage, even if their early marriage leads them, overall, to early parenthood. We will see that southern women also tend not to involve their children as much in domestic tasks as other women (chapter 9), suggesting at least one reason to defer having them.

It is interesting that neither a young wife's own education nor that of her parents influences her transition to motherhood after marriage. Parental education had a strong influence on the timing of marriage, and young women who were still in school were very unlikely to marry. Apparently, studies that have found education to delay parenthood were simply reflecting these effects on marriage delay; in our results, they have no effect on the timing of parenthood within marriage.

Family Resources and the Transition to Parenthood.   Children cost money. How much a couple might want to spend on them probably differs, with relatively comfortable families feeling that they need to be ready to provide expensive baby equipment, private schooling, and any necessary orthodontia, while working-class families are more concerned about snowsuits and space. But in all cases, families are likely to feel that children will compete with other needs for resources. So we expect that the higher a family's income (which, because of the problems of separating out women's work and earnings from her plans for pregnancy, we use the husband's income as the measure), the greater the chances that a couple childless at some early point in the marriage will become parents in the near future. This is in fact the case. The higher the income of the husband, the greater the chances that a young couple will add a 3d member in the near future.

Husband's Education.   Unlike our findings on the lack of effect of the education of the wife and her parents, our results show that husbands become fathers more slowly the more education they have. We have treated this result somewhat separately because our theorizing and the research literature suggest that education could affect two different dimensions of choices about family building. More educated men generally show more egalitarian attitudes toward family issues (chapter 4) and share more in household tasks (chapter 8), which could affect the timing of parenthood; but they are also usually in occupations that place high demands on them early in their careers, requiring a great deal of time—both in terms of formal schooling and later, on the job. Couples in which the husband works in these relatively demanding occupations might not feel ready to begin raising children early in the marriage and may delay their first birth as a result.[12]

It is our view that the slower transition to parenthood among more educated husbands primarily reflects a timing effect, rather than plans to have smaller families among more educated men. We will show later that such men have every reason to prefer smaller families, since what happens to the family economy among the more educated is that husbands perform household chores that their children would otherwise do (chapter 10). Nevertheless, an analysis of data in which *young men* were asked about their fertility expectations showed that the most highly educated, while slow to begin their families, were likely to expect as many or more children than the less educated.[13]

Since our analysis looks at the timing of the first birth after marriage, it only allows us to say that those young women who lived independently before marriage, as well as those with more modern attitudes about women's roles in the home, together with those married to more educated husbands, begin their families more slowly than their opposites. We cannot answer the other obvious question: Do these factors also cause young women to have smaller families than they would have had otherwise? They may well not.

Nevertheless, we feel that despite the concern over long-term childlessness, this constellation of factors implies that couples who do enter parenthood later will be considerably more mature, not only in terms of their marriage but also in terms of their knowledge of the world outside the family, which women evidently gain from independent living and men from education. This should allow them to parent much more effectively and encourage the growth of stable and egalitarian families in the next generation. Whether they will have enough children for egalitarian families to increase in the future, however, requires us to continue to observe them until they can no longer have children. Since these young women have a considerable period of time to enter motherhood, or to have more children (they were last observed in their late twenties to early thirties), it is very possible that they will.

Dissolving a Marriage

The early years of marriage not only produce children; they are also a "sorting-out" time, as the newlyweds attempt to establish themselves as members of an ongoing couple. Some succeed and some fail. In the first few years after marriage, they rapidly gather information about their mate and about themselves *within the marriage*. This information may match their often idealized views of what marriage was going to be like or the kind of spouse they thought they were getting, but often it does not. If the disagreements about how life should be lived become basic enough, or if the spouse does not live up to expectations in some important ways, then the marriage may dissolve.

If marriages seem to be especially unstable during their early years, they become especially stable later. The longer a couple remains married the lower the chances that they will divorce or separate. The possibility of unpleasant surprises declines over time and couples accumulate many things that belong to them as a pair rather than to either one as individuals. These often include a house and furniture, but children, friends, and relationships with extended family also belong to them both, at least to some degree. And many couples develop shared skills and interests that hold them together, with one perhaps perfecting a tennis game because the other likes tennis or learning to cook a favorite dish.

But couples are not all equally likely to divorce. As a relatively new phenomenon, divorce is particularly anathema to those with traditional family orientations, often reinforced by religious commitment. In this view, marriage is a responsibility as well as a pleasure—one not so easily given up in difficult times. These values are often embedded in differentials by region, ethnicity, and religion.[14]

Divorce is also more likely among those with fewer interpersonal coping skills inside the marriage or with better opportunities outside the marriage, either for self-support or for remarriage, as well as among those who are likely not to have searched long or chosen their spouse well in the first place. For example, couples who enter matrimony at very young ages are likely to combine all these characteristics: they have had less time to search and are often not sufficiently mature to make an appropriate choice of a spouse or to do the interpersonal work of building a new relationship. They also are much more likely than those who married at a relatively late age to feel that they have plenty of time to "try again." For these reasons, a youthful age at marriage is one of the most consistent predictors of divorce (Martin and Bumpass, 1989).

But the risks of divorce have been rising for everyone as the divorce revolution has roared on through the 1970s and 1980s. The sex-role revolution has increased the problems couples have to face within marriage, as the rules underlying men's and women's roles in marriage have become less clear. Women's opportunities for supporting themselves outside marriage have greatly increased their option to leave not only an alcoholic or abusive marriage, but also simply a troubled one, and men may feel less guilt over leaving. These changes appear to be affecting nearly all couples, overwhelming historical differences in levels of divorce by region and among some ethnic groups. There are now almost no regional differences, or differences between Hispanic and non-Hispanic whites.[15] But couples with relatively low levels of education have become increasingly likely to dissolve their relationship since 1970, relative to the more educated (Martin and Bumpass, 1989), suggesting that those with more education may be having less difficulty with the sex-role revolution. And as the ages at which people marry have risen and the ages at which young people begin to search for partners in a serious way have as well, what actually is an "early" marriage may also have changed, so that young women who married in their early twenties face divorce risks much closer to those of teenagers, compared with brides of the same age from an earlier generation.

Nontraditional Family Experiences and Divorce

We are particularly concerned about the effects of nontraditional family experiences, whether in childhood or young adulthood, on the pressures that the future holds toward "no families" or "new families." Does the experience of parental divorce reduce the stability of marriages as it delays the entry into marriage for many? Does living independently from parents and other relatives prior to marriage weaken young people's commitment to family roles?

Childhood Family Structure.   Children of divorce may be at particular risk of repeating in their own marriages the process they experienced in childhood (McLanahan and Bumpass, 1988). The apparent effect of parental marital disruption on children's own marriages is quite modest (Pope and Mueller, 1979); most children apparently learn something from their parents' mistakes and avoid repeating them. Nevertheless, this experience with a nontraditional family may well increase the risk of "no families."

It is unclear what factors account for this phenomenon, or whether they are growing or decreasing in importance. We know that young women who did not grow up with two biological parents are more likely to approve of mothers' working, so despite their negative experience with the stresses on a mother-only family, they may be more willing to divorce and try to support their own families than women with traditional family experiences. Children of divorce may also see less stigma in ending a marriage and so leave troubled relationships more quickly. If these factors are responsible for the effect of parental divorce on the likelihood their children's marriages will not succeed, the effect is likely to weaken over time, since approval of mothers' working has become nearly universal among the youngest generation (Thornton, 1989) and the stigma of divorce has been decreasing for everyone.

Children from disrupted homes, however, are particularly likely to marry very young (chapter 5) and, as we just saw above, were more likely to be pregnant at marriage; they may have chosen less wisely as a result. And children whose parents divorced may fail to learn—or learn less well—the interpersonal skills necessary for successful relationships. If these are the factors primarily responsible for the effects of childhood family structure, then the contribution of parental divorce to the growth of "no families" through divorce among their children is likely to continue in each generation.

Our analyses of divorce and separation during the first five years of marriage (presented in full in table 6.3, Appendix C) show very little effect of childhood experiences of parental breakup on the dissolution of their own marriage.[16] Young wives raised in two-parent families are less likely to disrupt their marriages than others, but this effect is too small to be statistically reliable. We looked separately at chances of disruption during each year of marriage from the 1st through the 5th. In no year did childhood family structure influence the stability of these women's marriages.

It is possible that the effects of childhood family structure are too weak to observe over the relatively short period we look at here, but might show up later during the lives of these marriages. But given the small size of the effect, it seems more likely that as divorce has become more pervasive in American society, its impact on the later lives of children has declined. The divorces of these young women's parents are likely to have occurred after the divorce revolution had already begun, unlike in previous studies, and have no more effect on their own children than the reality of divorce has had on the entire generation.

Independent Living During Early Adulthood.   Experiences of young adults with independent living could also affect the chances that they end a marriage later in life. As we saw in the previous two chapters, as well as earlier in the present one, young women who live independently become more individualistic and less oriented toward family in general, less likely to marry, and less oriented either toward having many children or toward early motherhood within marriage. They may have developed skills required for living alone—such as balancing a checkbook or doing the laundry—that make the prospect of a return to single life somewhat less daunting. The knowledge that they lived independently before might make them less reluctant to disrupt an unsatisfactory relationship, since they know that they could manage to keep a household running on their own.

But the experience of living independently could lead young people to choose a spouse more carefully and more wisely than they might have if they remained in their parents' house. Young adults living away are free to form friendships, to date and to have sexual relationships without parental supervision or restrictions, and so may be less likely to marry to escape an unhappy home situation. They have escaped already, by moving out on their own.

In fact, our analyses found no effect of independent living during young adulthood on the chances of disruption, overall or in any individual year of marriage. Again, this may reflect the short duration over which we are observing these marriages; it may also have resulted from our inability to distinguish among *types* of independent living among married women, given the few who had married at all among those with this experience.[17] However, it may simply be that the conflicting effects we anticipated of living independently before marriage actually do balance each other out so that the net effect is neutral. Young women who lived independently may be less reluctant to leave their marriage, but since they were more likely to have picked an appropriate spouse, they less often find themselves in relationships that they want to leave. Although we cannot test this reasoning directly, we find it persuasive.

What Else Matters
for Dissolving a Marriage?

In our analysis, we also included indicators of other factors that should influence the likelihood that couples divorce, measuring to the extent possible: resources and coping skills inside marriage as well as opportunities outside the marriage; the likelihood that couples have made a wise choice in the first place; and particularly differences in traditional attitudes that might affect commitment to marriage. Unfortunately, the data we use, which are generally highly suited for our analyses, do not contain ideal measures of many of these dimensions.[18] However, many of the characteristics that we can measure are likely to be related to these factors, so we will estimate their effects as well as we can.

Coping Skills and Family Resources.   We measure coping skills with the wife's age at marriage. Given the importance of women's interpersonal skills in family matters, we felt that *her* age was the more important indicator,[19] but we know that simple age is not an ideal indicator of interpersonal skills, and may also be measuring the results of young couples' shorter exposure to the marriage market and consequently foreshortened search for a suitable spouse. It is also likely that educational level taps communication skills, to a certain extent. We discuss these effects below.

We measure family resources using the husband's income. Given the frequent movement of women into and out of the work force early in marriage, we felt that his earnings were the best long-term indicator of their financial well-being within the marriage. Marital stability of the couple should increase with financial well-being, in part because money is a chronic problem in most marriages, and because having a higher income increases the amount of their common property, such as a home—and even children—as we saw above.

We found that women who marry at a young age are considerably more likely to separate than women who married at an older age (table 6.3, Appendix C). And the higher the husband's earnings, the lower the likelihood of divorce or separation. These results suggest that as the age at marriage has increased, families should become more stable. They also suggest that the difficulties that young people have experienced in the labor market in recent years (Easterlin, 1978) have also wreaked havoc with the stability of their marriages, providing another boost to "no families." Apparently, not all the recent increase in divorce is the result of new attitudes toward married life.

Traditional Family Values and Preferences. Our most direct measures of traditional family values are those that focus on gender differences in family roles. These measures distinguish two dimensions of gender differentiation: in the family (FAMILY ROLES), measuring the extent to which young women think family roles are central in their lives; and at work (JOB ROLES), indicating how important a woman's work might be for herself and her family. In addition, we include even less direct measures of differences in family values, including a young woman's plans for working at age 35, community size, region of the country, race, and education.

Of course, conventional sex-role attitude questions do not provide ideal indicators of willingness to divorce, despite popular opinion. They do not distinguish between attitudes that should lead to a rejection of marriage per se, decreasing young women's willingness to marry and likely increasing their willingness to divorce, from attitudes that simply tap a preference for a more egalitarian marriage, which could well be coupled with a willingness to work hard to preserve it. More modern attitudes also could lead to a marriage with a young man with a modern sex-role orientation. Wives whose husbands help relatively little with housework were more likely to have considered divorce than were wives whose husbands did a greater share of the work (Huber and Spitze, 1983). Similarly, young women planning a life-time career may still be committed to having a marriage and a family, much as most men are.

Nevertheless, as women with more traditional attitudes have children fairly quickly after marriage, presumably because they are eager to assume the mother role, such women should be less likely to leave a marriage than less traditional women, because they are more reluctant to give up the wife role. And women who plan to work are accumulating the credentials in the job market that would allow them to support themselves and any children after separation.

Our results show no differences between the wives with the most traditional views and those with the most liberal views in the likelihood of ending their marriage during its first 5 years (table 6.3, Appendix C). Neither views of women's roles in the labor market nor views of women's roles in the home affect the stability of the marriage. We also find that young wives who plan to work later in their lives are no more likely to end their marriage than those who plan to be housewives. Young women with liberal views of men's and women's roles probably do not marry men with very traditional views, or at least men unwilling to compromise them for the sake of the marriage. And women who plan on careers in the labor market are likely to have chosen spouses who support them in this plan and to value this quality enough in their husbands to offset the greater economic security their work experience provides them after separation, relative to women with no work orientation.

Young black couples are more likely than those of other races to divorce or separate, even after one takes into account their other characteristics. Our results match differentials in rates of divorce reported nationally, and remain a challenge to students of the black family. We will see later (chapters 9 and 10) that the mother-child bond appears tighter than the husband-wife bond in the ongoing activities of black families than in white families. To the extent that this means that black men feel they have less invested in their marriages, they may feel less constrained to leave them.

Consistent with other research finding that regional differences in divorce have dwindled, we find no differences across regions in the stability of the marriages of our young couples. The size of the community these young families are living in also has no apparent effect on the chances that young women will dissolve their marriages. Although those in rural areas have more traditional attitudes toward women's roles (chapter 4) and marry earlier (chapter 5), they are not less (or more) likely to remain married, all else equal. These differences have evidently dwindled, as well.

Education.   We measured three dimensions of education: the young wife's education, the education of her parents, and the young husband's education. The relationship between education and divorce has been shown in other research to be particularly complex, depending on whose education is being measured, which dimension of family life is being considered, and *for what period* the relationship is being tested (Martin and Bumpass, 1989). For women, measures of education seem to tap the complex of values that decrease the centrality of family in their lives, increasing their approval of modern work and family roles (chapter 4) and reducing their likelihood of marrying before age 30 (chapter 5). Among young men, their own education and that of their parents increases their approval of mothers' working (chapter 5) but only delays, not reduces, their likelihood of marriage (chapter 6). Education also increases men's participation in household tasks (chapter 8). We cannot tell how these factors affect men's likelihood of divorce directly, since we cannot measure divorce for men adequately; however, we can include the education of the husband (but not of his parents) in our analyses of separation and divorce for women.

It is also the case that the more highly educated tend to be trend leaders. They may have led the divorce revolution in the 1960s and 1970s. During that period, divorce rates rose the most for men with some college, narrowing the differences in the chances of disruption for educated and less well educated men (Glick and Norton, 1977). In the 1970s and 1980s, however, differences in the probability of divorce by educational level (measured for the wife) have widened again substantially, with the continuing increases in divorce wholly accounted for by those with less education (Martin and Bumpass, 1989). This pattern led us not to classify education as an indicator of skills in interpersonal communication, although it is a strong indicator of that dimension of marital life, but to use it more as a measure of sex-role attitudes, particularly for men.

As in other studies, we find that measures related to the wife's educational level and background have a complex relationship with marital separation. Figure 6.2 shows that *parents' education* increases the likelihood of divorce, consistent with its effect on marriage for young women. Daughters with highly educated parents are less likely than other young women to marry, and among those who do, are evidently more likely to regret the decision. Young women whose parents had a postgraduate education were 70 percent more likely to divorce than those whose parents never reached high school (4.4 percent per year versus 2.6 percent per year). However, we find no effect of *the wife's* education on the stability of the marriage. Highly educated wives are less likely to disrupt their relationship but the effect is so small that it is quite unimportant.

But the most important effect of education is for men. An additional year of a husband's education is "worth" nearly twice as much in terms of marital stability as an additional year of wife's age, making husband's education both the most powerful and most statistically stable indicator of the durability of marriage in the 1970s and 1980s. Women married to men with a postgraduate education are less than half as likely to divorce as those whose husbands never reached high school (2 percent per year versus 4.5 percent per year).

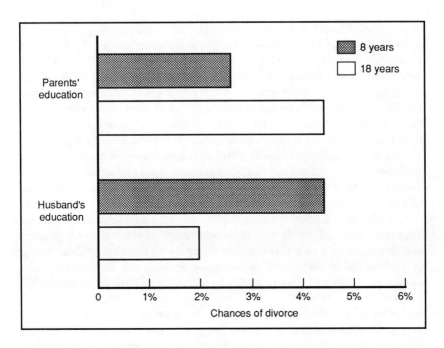

Figure 6.2   Effect of Parents' Education and Husband's Education on Divorce

The fact that men with more education have more modern attitudes and help more around the house makes this some of the strongest evidence we have that the divorce revolution may end, and that "new families" could eventually help stabilize family life. As an indicator of modern male attitudes toward family life, it tells us that wives married to more modern husbands are happier with the relationship and that the time spent together by these couples in performing or organizing household chores is strengthening, not weakening, their relationship.

Conclusion

Many pressures are building in the homes young people live in and those they form that are influencing the chances that the future will hold "no families" or "new families." However, it is clear that we are not seeing a pattern of simple inheritance of "no families"; those who have experienced new family forms are not doomed to repeat them. Neither experiencing a non-traditional family in childhood nor living independently in young adulthood has simple effects on the pace with which young women build their own families and their likelihood of divorce.

Young women who grew up in a family headed by their mother face heightened chances of entering marriage already pregnant. Since premarital pregnancy may propel a couple into matrimony before they are ready, it increases the risks that the marriage will end in divorce. Yet among those who do not have a child in the 1st year or so of marriage, women with this family experience are *less* likely than young wives from intact families to have a birth in the next 2 or 3 years, increasing stability in the early years of marriage. It is likely, then, that our finding that childhood family structure had no effect on divorce reflects a balance of these two effects. Some young people *learn* from their childhood experiences of marital instability and the difficulties of being a single mother and attempt to lower their risks by postponing childbearing; others may simply repeat their childhood pattern. Which outcome results is likely to depend on whether a premarital pregnancy intervenes.

Living independently before marriage has even less impact on the families young people later form, perhaps because they *chose* to live at home or away from home when they reached adulthood. There is no effect on divorce risks, and while those young women who lived independently are less likely to have a child quickly after marriage, by the 2d or 3d year of marriage they are no more or less likely than other young wives to become mothers.

Thus, there is no strong "inheritance" of nontraditional family experiences either through divorce or early parenthood. It may be that as these new experiences have become more commonplace, they are less traumatizing; it is already less stigmatizing to children to have divorced parents. We need to keep in mind, however, that we look only at the early years of marriage, and the effects of these experiences may need time to accumulate.

But in fact, many of the effects on parenthood and divorce that we found did not date from childhood or early adulthood, but related more to these young adults' marriages themselves. Some clearly come from childhood, such as the effect of having more siblings on the early timing of parenthood and of parental education on the likelihood of divorce. Young women whose own parents were highly educated were also less likely to marry than those from less-educated backgrounds. Perhaps these young women find the alternatives to marriage more attractive than do others; perhaps they have higher standards for marriage and have difficulty finding a marriage that meets their expectations. Results we present later (chapter 10) suggest that *their* parents shared the responsibilities of home and family more equally than families with less schooling, and may have passed on ideals about sharing of power and responsibility to the daughters.

But equally important are their experiences in their new marriage. A critical factor is the husband's earnings, which hasten the transition to parenthood and decrease divorce. It is clear that the economic difficulties faced by young people are an important part of the constellation of forces leading to "no families." But also important in protecting against divorce (and perhaps against too early childbearing) is finding a well-educated spouse. Since we saw in chapter 4 that male education is associated with more modern sex-role attitudes, and we will see later that highly educated men share more housework than those with less schooling (chapter 8), this suggests to us that highly educated men are attractive spouses not just because of their earning capacity—we take that into account—but also because these men share more housework and decision-making power with their wives. As these characteristics become more widely spread among all men, rather than being concentrated only among more educated men, our results suggest family stability could increase dramatically, and that "new families" could be even more stable than traditional families.

7

Family Structure and Husbands' Share in Household Tasks

The keystone of traditional marriage is the division of labor in the home. Even though women have become increasingly involved in the world of work, with goals that often include a successful career, the "ideal" home still centers around women, and is their task. Men have very little place there, except as providers of resources and consumers of services. There is a vast array of books and magazines that provide information about issues of family and domestic management, from recipes and decorator tips to current theories of child development and adult aging. But they are aimed at women, and few men have ever looked at them. When men are encouraged by the popular press to learn about some essentials of domestic life, it is assumed that they are unmarried—still single or newly divorced—with no woman in residence to provide them a home.

It was not always so. Before urban and industrial jobs drew men away during the daytime, all work was based in the home, which served as a center for industry, politics, education, and religion, as well as domesticity. Men chopped the wood for the fires women cooked with; broke the ground for the gardens women tended; made the frames for the chairs women covered. Men also took an active role in one of the most time-consuming tasks of the home—supervising and instructing the children their wives washed clothes for and fed (Rotundo, 1985; Demos, 1986). Men's and women's tasks in the home were certainly segregated, as they have been in all traditional societies, but they worked together to make their homes, and to live in them in health and comfort.

But the nineteenth century changed men's work, taking it out of the household to factories and offices, leaving the home women's exclusive domain.

Family roles were restructured in dramatic ways in response to these changes in the *location* of men's work. As the home became increasingly a "sanctum" separate from the stresses of business and industry, women's roles broadened to include the moral responsibility for children (and, during the Temperance crusade, for the world, as well). Meanwhile, men yielded much of their patriarchal power as they lost the opportunity to see directly what was really going on in the household, since they were no longer there much of the time. A cult of domesticity developed, enshrining married women as "angels on the hearth" (Matthews, 1987).

Although industrial development lightened women's burdens, particularly replacing the heavy tasks traditionally done by men, their responsibility for making the home became total. And since it was now their exclusive task, any *new* tasks associated with home and children that emerged got assigned to them, as well. Thus the move to the suburbs turned mothers into chauffeurs, and the development of new, powerful but unreliable homemaking "gadgets" forced the women who used them to master a new intricate realm of appliance servicing (Cowan, 1983).

Now, new changes are drawing women into employment. Many of the jobs that economic growth generated in the twentieth century seemed to employers to be especially suitable for women (Oppenheimer, 1970) and with increased education and work experience, women have begun to compete successfully with men for a broader array of positions, so that they could support themselves (and often others) on their own. Also, men's salaries have not kept pace during the last quarter century with the rising costs of maintaining a family, increasing the pressure on wives and mothers to join their husbands in providing financially, and changing women's lives and their families in the process. More and more, women are sharing with men the traditionally male task of supporting the family. Approximately two-thirds of women in the prime working ages (25 to 55) are in the labor force, making a substantial financial contribution. In fact, employed women earn about 30 percent of the total family income (U.S. Department of Labor, 1990).

So far, the family seems to have adjusted to this massive influx of wives and mothers into the labor force by simply adding hours of paid employment to wives' existing responsibility for maintaining the home and family. Few women socialized with the traditional attitudes of the 1950s would have been likely to have expected any other outcome. This has resulted in what Arlie Hochschild (1989) calls "the second shift," since a generation of married women, when they were also employed, carried the burden both of traditional female roles and of some substantial portion of the most central traditional male role. But we feel that this adjustment is likely to be only temporary, since it is less appealing to younger generations of women socialized in the more "liberated" 1970s and 1980s. This makes "no families" more likely, since unlike the past, women no longer need to marry for their own support, but can live as independent adults.

Thus, the availability of the "no families" option, together with the burden of both earning and housekeeping faced by most married women, may mean that more women will avoid marriage unless conditions change to make it more attractive to them. This, we argue, will require a transformation of men's family roles, increasing their involvement in more of the tasks and responsibilities for making the homes and maintaining the relationships that enrich human life.

Are men taking over some responsibility for the performance of these roles? All the early evidence on men's roles in the home suggested very little involvement (Walker and Woods, 1976). But recent evidence suggests that the family may be continuing to change and adapt, despite the severe shocks that it has taken, and that men are beginning to assume a greater share of domestic responsibilities.

The next two chapters focus on the role of husbands in the division of household labor, and on how much they share in the domestic tasks that must be done to keep families functioning. In this chapter, we are especially interested in the ways husbands' and wives' childhood experiences of family life—as well as their experiences in independent living as young adults—affect the division of housework within their current marriages. We will consider, as well, the effects of current family structure: Are there differences between couples in first and later marriages? Or between those who have not yet had children and those whose children have left the nest? After answering these questions, we will go on in chapter 8 to look in detail at many other factors influencing husbands' roles in household responsibility. Then, after focusing for a chapter on children's roles in the household (chapter 9), we bring the analyses of husbands, children, and wives together to see how the family role system is operating, and how it might be changing (chapter 10).

The Nature of Housework

In most societies, the family is responsible not only for producing and socializing the next generation but for those tasks that need to be done to keep family members housed, clothed, fed, and otherwise prepared to meet the world—housework. Even in modern societies, characterized by few children and many labor-saving devices, housework takes a lot of time. Families spend on average about 10 hours per day on cooking, cleaning, shopping, caring for children and other household tasks, as much or more than most families spend at paid employment (Sanik, 1981).

Despite the similarity in the amount of time spent on household chores and on paid employment, the two types of work are viewed very differently.

Today, most productive work outside the home is salaried, yet housework is almost entirely unpaid. It carries no vacation or sick leave, no raises or pension benefits—at least not directly. People generally feel that almost any able-bodied adult can do it, since although some people are clearly better cooks, or shoppers, or financial managers than others, there are no raises and few prizes for superior performance, and often little recognition. As a result, housework, which was once dignified as a craft, has very low prestige.

The tasks themselves do not compare well with working conditions for many jobs performed outside the home. Housework is repetitive and often characterized as dull (Oakley, 1974a). The housewife (or househusband) typically feels isolated, with little sense of working as part of a team. Housewives often feel that they have totally lost control over their own time and their own lives, since so many household responsibilities have to be done when the need arises—particularly when children are young. But it is also true that many paid jobs have these negative characteristics, whereas particularly when the children are older, the housewife is pretty much her own boss, gaining vicarious rewards from caring for others and experiencing the satisfaction of a skilled job well done.

In most families today, responsibility for various tasks is divided clearly by sex, with the wife responsible for most home-based tasks. She cares for the children, makes sure that the house (and everything in it) is clean, sees that the family is fed, and maintains contact with most of their friends and relatives (di Leonardo, 1987; Robinson, 1988). The husband's major contribution to the family economy is to support it through his waged labor. In some families, he may, in addition, make household repairs, maintain the car, take care of the yard, do the paperwork, and take out the trash, but in other families, wives also carry these responsibilities.

This traditional division of labor is maintained and reinforced in a myriad of ways. Families strongly replicate this sex-linked division of labor in the allocation of chores to children (White and Brinkerhoff, 1981a). Mothers teach teenage daughters to cook, but not their sons; sons learn, usually from their fathers, skills needed for traditionally male chores. As a result, at an early age girls and boys learn separate skills and become generally more efficient at them. Hence they feel more satisfaction and less frustration with their sex-linked tasks, leading to the development of tastes and preferences for those tasks that they learned in their parents' home and feel that they do well. The traditional tastes and preferences normally created in the parental home are further reinforced by the responses of friends, family, and neighbors.

Overall, time budget studies show that the traditional division of labor is "fair" in traditional families in that it requires approximately equal numbers of hours of "work" from the breadwinner husband and housewife, if one counts as "work" both time on the job (including commuting) and time in household tasks (Stafford, 1980). But even when it is "not fair" in terms of hours, as when the wife is also employed outside the home, the effects of family experiences, personal satisfaction, and the responses of friends and neighbors combine to increase the likelihood that many women will still spend much larger amounts of time in housework than men and yet still feel satisfied with this allocation (Berk, 1985).

But the often unequal division of household work in families can be a source of conflict. Numerous studies show that the traditional division is no longer "fair" for dual-earner couples, since employed women work substantially more hours—at their job and at home—than the vast majority of men or housewives.[1] This inequality is exacerbated by the presence of young children. Employed mothers of young children appear to meet their responsibilities to job and children chiefly by taking time out of their own sleep and passive leisure, such as reading or watching television (Stafford, 1980; Gershuny and Robinson, 1988).

What these studies make clear is that husbands do not step into the breach very often, if at all; employed wives seem simply to add the demands of a job to their traditional responsibilities of running a household. These women do cut down on the number of hours that they spend on housework and their husbands increase very modestly the time that they spend on such tasks, so that husbands' *share* of housework increases when wives work (Spitze, 1986), but women, whether or not employed outside the home, continue to be responsible for most household tasks.[2]

What factors, then, influence the division of labor in the families in our study? Are new family experiences in childhood or young adulthood of one generation leading to changes in the household division of labor in the next generation? Will the "double burden" of employed wives and mothers be eased by their husbands' greater sharing? Before we can look at the answers to these questions, we need to assess what kind of information we have, and how it should be organized.

Responsibility for Household Tasks

Since we are particularly concerned about whether a family's division of household labor is more or less equal, our attention should focus on the *share* done by each party. This has the advantage of combining the amount of housework done by the husband and wife into a single indicator: the amount each does *of the total amount that they actually do*. This approach has the additional advantage of not being influenced by the standards of order and cleanliness households choose for themselves, but only by how they achieve them.

Other studies have focused on precise measurement of hours spent on household tasks. Our measure does not reflect hours, since one's share is affected not only by how much one does but also by how much others do. For example, in a family that eats at home every night, if the husband cooks 1 dinner a week, he prepares 14 percent of the dinners. But if the family began eating out 3 nights a week and the husband continued to cook 1 dinner, his share of dinner preparation would jump to 25 percent. On the one hand, his effort did not increase at all. On the other hand, this measure accurately reflects the way the couple now divides between them the amount of housework that they do, and allows us to focus directly on their *division* of household labor.[3]

Measuring Husbands' Share in the Division of Household Labor

For our analysis, we examined information on sharing tasks with husbands for all married women in the young and mature women's samples.[4] The questions on household sharing that we used were obtained in 1982 for the mature women, 1983 for the young women, and 1981 for the young men. For most analyses, we pooled the responses of the young and mature women, since the questions were asked at approximately the same time. We also examined separately a sample of the young women who were aged 14–17 at the original interview in 1968 and married by 1983, in order to be able to examine the effects of their experiences with independent living prior to marriage. Older girls and women were not asked questions about their history of living arrangements prior to the survey's beginning, so we could only study those who entered the survey before they were at risk of leaving home as adults.

The men and women included in the National Longitudinal Studies of Young Men, Young Women, and Mature Women answered a series of questions about a variety of household chores, including cooking, cleaning, laundry, child care, dishes, yard work, grocery shopping, and paperwork. Most of our analyses are based on answers the women gave, since the questions were asked in much more detail than those asked of young men.

From the answers to these questions, we created an overall scale, using all the tasks for the young men, but using only the 5 most "female" tasks for women. Appendix B shows how the scales were constructed for sharing tasks between husbands and wives. For women, the scale takes on values from 0 to 20, depending on whether husbands share nothing on any of the 5 tasks or take full responsibility for all of them. For men, the scale was constructed quite similarly.

How Much Do These Husbands Share?

Most women retain primary responsibility for the household tasks on which we have information, but the list of tasks includes some that families frequently assign to the husband and some that he virtually never does. Thus, husbands' participation in household tasks depends very much on *which* task.

Figure 7.1 indicates that on the 4 thoroughly female domestic tasks—laundry, housecleaning, cooking, and dishwashing—husbands are reported by their wives as sharing relatively little overall, taking responsibility for less than 25 percent of the task (and much less responsibility for laundry).[5] Husbands share somewhat more in grocery shopping (just over one-quarter) and in the paperwork associated with the family's finances. Among standard household tasks, men only take significantly more than a quarter of the burden for yard and home maintenance, but even here, wives do not report much relief from this task, since their husbands' average share is about 40 percent.

Interestingly, the "task" that wives in these families report their husbands to share most is parenthood—caring for children. From other evidence, we know that this usually means interacting with older children, rather than changing infants' diapers and staying home with sick schoolchildren (Hill, 1988). Even so, wives are indicating that more fathers take some share in child care than share in the most traditional male household tasks, yard and home maintenance. This suggests that on an important dimension of family care, men are achieving close to equal involvement.

Nevertheless, on other tasks, even traditionally male tasks, there is a lot of room for men to share more. Do they have time? Do they not want to? Do their work responsibilities preclude greater sharing in household responsibility?

Most of the evidence on the division of household work between married couples suggests that families have a lot of discretion in how they divide up the chores of daily living in the household. Most couples, even when both are employed, report significant numbers of leisure hours (although in the case of employed wives, most of the leisure is enjoyed by the husband). Hence, there is scope for a wide range of divisions. Given that there are many cases in which employed wives nevertheless do almost all the household tasks, presumably the range can run from this extreme to its opposite, in which husbands both work full time and take responsibility for most of the chores around the house, which might occur, for example, if the wife were disabled.

How they in fact divide up these responsibilities, then, reflects what mix of tasks and responsibilities fits their needs best, balancing in some fashion their joint and personal preferences, their ideas of equity and social appropriateness, as well as their skills and the need to get the work done (at least at some minimal level). What factors, then, influence this mix?

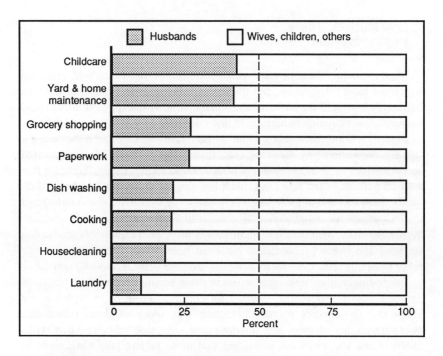

Figure 7.1   Husbands' Share of Responsibility for Household Tasks

New Family Experiences and the Division of Household Labor

Sociologists and psychologists agree that couples will tend to replicate the families that they experienced as children. Those who grew up in households where tasks were rigidly divided by sex will show more traditional allocations of household tasks in the families that they form themselves.[6] But those who spend some time as children in a single-parent family may have been pressed into service to perform chores usually done by the other sex because the family desperately needed their labor. Single-parent families tend to be short of the mother's time at home because most unmarried women must work to support themselves and their families, and they also do not have the household time of the absent male parent. These families more often enlist their adolescent sons to do traditional female tasks such as cooking, laundry, and cleaning and their daughters to do yard work and home maintenance than do two-parent families, as we see in chapter 9. So spouses whose experiences as children led them to perform a wide range of household chores, not just those traditional for their sex, as well as those who watched their opposite-sex siblings cook and clean or mow the lawn, may carry some of this more flexible division of labor into their own families after they marry.

This argument extends to experiences in independent living during young adulthood. Young men or women who lived away from home—in a dormitory while in school, in an apartment alone or with a roommate, or in some other independent situation—had to perform both traditionally male and female chores. So the young men living on their own had to shop, cook, clean, do laundry, and wash dishes—or at least had to arrange for food, clean clothing, and clean sheets. The young women had to maintain their own car, pay bills, and take out the garbage. These experiences in performing household tasks usually done by the other sex could give young adults the skills and self-confidence to take over some nontraditional chores themselves, or to negotiate with a spouse to take over some of "their" (sex-traditional) chores. Hence, experiences in childhood and young adulthood should influence the division of labor in the next generation.

In earlier chapters, we saw that nontraditional family experiences often have considerable effects. For women, growing up in a disrupted or mother-only family and experiencing independent living in young adulthood both have a liberalizing impact on attitudes about male and female roles and reduce the likelihood of marriage and childbearing. It follows that such experiences will also influence the kinds of families young adults eventually form.

It is also possible, however, that experiencing family disruption in childhood has very different effects on young women's attitudes toward *getting* married and *having* children than on their behavior, once they have a family. As we will see in chapter 9, if these women grew up in female-headed households, they are even more accustomed than traditional women to having the household work done by women and children, not by husbands. And experiencing a stepfather may not be helpful in breaking up this pattern, since stepfathers tend to be less involved in many household chores than biological fathers. In fact, women who have lived as children through family breakup may *overcompensate*, becoming less willing to fight for an egalitarian division of labor. If so, we may not see greater sharing in the marriages of women who have experienced family disruption as children. Further, we know from other studies that the husband's attitudes matter much more than the wife's in reaching a more egalitarian division of household labor. Hence, it is likely that the wife's experiences would have little effect, while factors making the husband more egalitarian are critical.

For young men, however, nonfamily experiences have not necessarily moved them in an egalitarian direction. Experiences of living in a nontraditional family in childhood reduce the likelihood of marriage, but living away from home actually increases it. It is possible, therefore, that those who experienced parental disruption are only avoiding *traditional* marriages, while those who lived independently before marriage are more attractive as mates in more egalitarian marriages, hence their increased likelihood of marrying. If this speculation is correct, then these young men's more liberal attitudes and stock of household skills should carry over to their behavior, once they have married and perhaps become fathers. What do our results show?

Women's Nontraditional Family Experiences

Women's experiences in a nontraditional family affect sharing between spouses in complex ways (see fig. 7.2).[7] First, among women as a whole, those who grew up in a one-parent or reconstituted family share less with husbands by about one-third of a chore than those raised by two natural parents, although the effect is only significant among those with no children at home. Apparently, wives with experience in a nontraditional family try to "do it all," by taking responsibility for more chores themselves.

However, there is some sign that this pattern may be changing. Among the youngest women, experience of childhood disruption came at a time when such experiences were becoming increasingly common. Since their families were less deviant, living in a one-parent family at age 14 (although not living with a stepfather), does result in greater rather than less sharing.

Our other nontraditional family experience, living separately from parents prior to marriage, however, does not seem to be having this effect, at least among women. Our evidence is that the experience of "doing it all" for themselves, while living outside a family setting, carries over in later household tasks, so that the greater the proportion of time young women live outside a family setting, the *less* they share domestic responsibilities later with their spouse. Figure 7.3 shows that young women who lived away from their parental home continuously from the time they were age 18 until marriage shared less with their husbands after marriage than those who never lived away from home. This is the case for most chores.

However, some of the strongest effects of this "independent" experience are felt on the *least* stereotypical female chores. Wives with a history of residential independence share only half as much responsibility for grocery shopping with their husbands as wives with none, although this may simply reflect their greater experience with driving. Similarly, such women share less with their husbands in yard and home maintenance by more than 15 percent, which may also reflect greater experience with plumbing and electrical problems acquired in their days of living independently. In contrast, only weak and statistically insignificant effects emerge for washing dishes and clothes. So rather than leading to greater sharing of home-based tasks, independent living seems to be leading to greater sharing of responsibility *by women* of what are often traditionally male chores. The only exception to this pattern

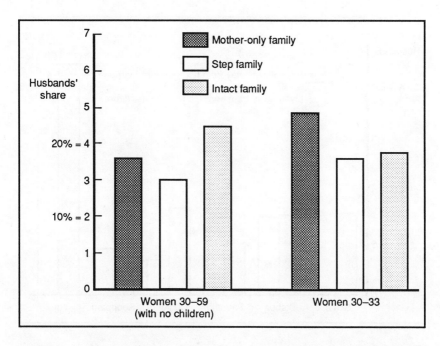

Figure 7.2   Effect of Women's Childhood Family Structure on Husbands' Share of Household Tasks

is the result for cooking, since independent living also appears to lead women to take 12 percent more responsibility for this quintessentially female task.

~~One explanation for this unexpected relationship between living on one's own and later division of housework may be that women who have kept house for themselves are simply better at it, so that their husbands feel less need to join in to make sure that household tasks get done in a reasonable way.~~ Many women who live with their mothers until marriage may not be as skilled in household tasks as those who live on their own for a while. If so, these results suggest that when confronted with a wife whose domestic needs have previously been met by her mother, men are more likely to take over the cooking than the laundry.

An alternative explanation is that women living alone before marriage may have become less used to sharing such tasks than those who remained at home, sharing tasks with their parents and siblings. After marriage, such young women tend to continue to do them alone, and share less with their husbands. But whatever the explanation, it is not at all clear that experiencing nontraditional family structures in childhood or young adulthood is contributing to making modern marriages more egalitarian, at least when the experience is the woman's.

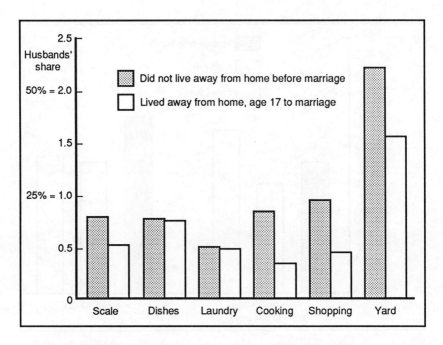

Figure 7.3   Effect of Living Away from Home Before Marriage on Husbands' Share of Household Tasks

Men's Nontraditional Family Experiences

Nearly as many of the children involved in divorce are boys as girls.[8] And our results in figure 7.4 show that experiencing parental disruption in childhood has a small but statistically significant effect for boys, increasing their sharing in household tasks from 31 percent to 33 percent. Although all men reduce the extent to which they share household tasks with their wives when there are children present (as we will see below, in more detail), this is less the case for men who have experienced parental marital disruption. These men are particularly likely to pitch in when there are children in the household. Evidently, since boys greatly increase their responsibility for the most stereotypically female household tasks when their mother is managing a household on her own (chapter 10), this experience carries over when these sons form their own families. Many may be used to teaming up with younger siblings, and seem able to transfer this experience into teamwork with their own children.

We would like to explore this relationship further, but we are again limited by the weakness of the measures for young men; few multipurpose social

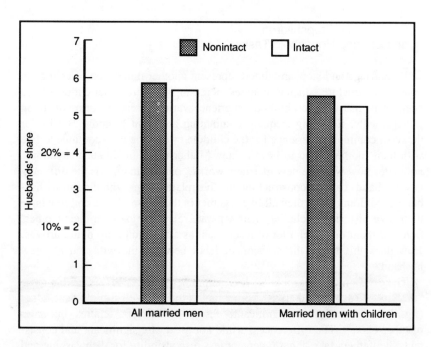

Figure 7.4 Effect of Parental Marital Disruption on Husbands' Share of Household Chores

science data sets ask *men* any questions about sharing in household tasks, and if they do, the questions are not in the kind of detail that we have found useful in our analyses of sharing household tasks based on the questions asked of women. Nevertheless, the result is provocative, and serves as a challenge to further research to explore it more fully.

Clearly, experiencing new family (or nonfamily) forms in childhood and young adulthood is having an effect on the families that young men and women later form. However, these effects are not the same for men and women, and depend on whether the experience is living in a female-headed family, living with a stepfather, or living outside a family altogether in young adulthood. The effects of independent nonfamily living seem to be to reduce cohesion in the family, as measured by sharing household chores, but parental divorce is increasing sharing among the young men and women who experienced it.

It is also possible that divorce can influence the division of responsibility between husband and wife in their current marriages. Remarried partners may take a less traditional approach to family roles. How do "later" husbands compare with first husbands? How do stepfathers who join a family that has already been formed compare with biological fathers?

Remarriage, Stepchildren, and Sharing Household Tasks

Remarriage and stepparenthood represent another dimension of change in household structure, since as couples increasingly divorce after children have been born, many more children experience various creative forms of living arrangements, including frequent commuting and joint custody. But by far the most common experience for the children of divorce is to continue to live with their mothers, and to have a "new" father move in. In such situations, no matter how well the new marriage works,[9] one strain on it is the difficulty new husbands have of constructing positive relationships with the former husband's children, while they all live together in the house. These children have their own histories, including their separate relationships with their mother. Some of them may feel a lot of resentment as a new authority figure arrives. How does this affect the division of labor between the wife and her new husband?

The division of household labor in stepfather families[10] is somewhat more "traditional" than in otherwise comparable families with a biological father (fig. 7.5). Stepfathers do significantly fewer "female-type" chores, but more of other chores. The differences, while not great, are significant and consistent. Stepfathers take about 6 percent less responsibility for dishwashing and child care and about 3 percent less responsibility for housecleaning and cooking; yet they take 4 percent more responsibility for both paperwork and for yard and home maintenance. One interpretation of this pattern is that stepfathers may feel that they need to establish themselves as the new "man of the house," forcing them to a certain extent into more stereotypically masculine positions than they might otherwise be comfortable with.

There may also be a spirit of competition between stepfather and stepchildren, particularly with older children. Teenage children normally relieve both their fathers and their mothers of some household responsibility (chapter 10). Figure 7.6 shows that this is particularly the case for teenage stepchildren, who "replace" their stepfathers to a significantly greater extent than do natural children.

This may also reflect the pattern of mother and children working together that developed while they lived in a one-parent family, which remains after the remarriage. The domestic "team," then, apparently does not accommodate a stepfather as easily as a biological father. In fact, as we will see in chapter 8, fathers actually join more in household responsibilities when there are boys between the ages of 12 and 18 in the household (compared with having younger children only). This reinforces the idea that many households do their work as teams, and that fathers feel most comfortable joining a team with other "men." In contrast, stepfathers are less likely to share responsibility when there are teenage boys in the household than when there are younger

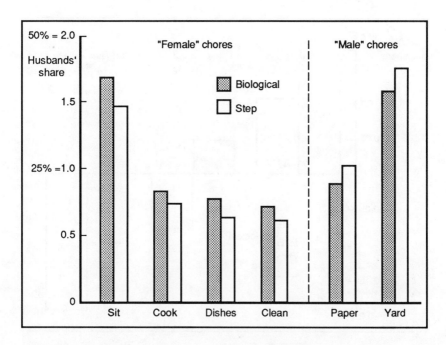

Figure 7.5   Sharing Chores: Biological Fathers and Stepfathers

children, suggesting that they find it more difficult to become part of the "team."

Similarly, while all fathers reduce their sharing in household tasks when there is a teenage daughter in the household, perhaps in order to allow her greater opportunities to learn these tasks, stepfathers reduce their contribution even more when such substitutes are available. Cinderella's problem was a stepmother, but it may be the case that a stepfather would have increased her housework burden just as much.

In most cases, the teenage girls and teenage boys in stepfather families are these men's stepchildren. However, we also found that very young children create an unusual effect on household sharing in stepfamilies, even though they are likely to be the children of the *new* husband. We will see in chapter 8 that husbands generally help more with the housework when there are babies or toddlers in the household, reflecting the enormous time such children take. But figure 7.6 indicates that later husbands respond less than first husbands to this pressure. Evidently, since these wives had worked together on many tasks with their older children prior to her remarriage, they enlist them in this task, as well. Overall, then, the basic response in later marriages is for the husbands to reduce their household involvement when there are both much older children and very young children in the household.

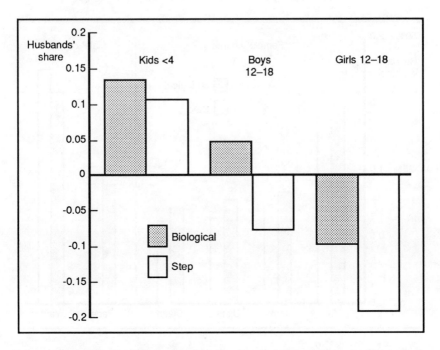

Figure 7.6   Children's Effects on Husbands' Share of Household Tasks: Biological Fathers and Stepfathers

Given our results on the reduced sharing with husbands of women who grew up in a stepparent household (fig. 7.2), this pattern seems to carry over between generations.

The Consequences of New Family Experiences

We have examined the effects of varying dimensions of family change on the division of household labor, looking to see whether they are leading us to greater closeness in more egalitarian families or even further away. What we have found is that both trends are in evidence, and it is not at all clear how they will balance themselves in the future.

The experience of divorce and remarriage leads to *less* sharing between husbands and wives in their new marriages, decreasing the likelihood that they will build close bonds as they make their new home together. The experience of independent living in adulthood, while leading to more egalitarian *attitudes* among young women, seems to translate in their marriages into a form of independence based on separation of tasks, as they assume more responsibility both for traditionally male and traditionally female tasks.

Nevertheless, the experience of parental divorce during childhood appears to lead young men toward greater involvement in household work, particularly when there are children. This suggests that these households may share a high degree of close interaction, working together to get the necessary jobs done and to make one another's lives cleaner and more pleasant. Parental divorce makes husbands less traditional, and it is *their* attitudes that matter most. Increasingly, however, these effects appear for younger women.

We conclude from this that the experience of working together gets reinforced over the generations, as does the experience of working alone. If we are correct, then the greatest impact of the general trend toward husband-wife sharing will be felt on the next generation, as children see their fathers taking on more domestic roles. In the next chapter, we will assess whether this trend seems likely to continue. If it does, then change could accelerate very rapidly through the intergenerational mechanism. Modern families, then, could be reinforced among those experiencing parental divorce, or diluted among those who have opted out of family living in early adulthood. But whatever special experiences children have, the overall more egalitarian experiences of sharing household tasks should be reinforced with each later generation.

8

Change in Husbands' Share in Household Tasks?

Stated briefly, family changes in one generation appear to influence family life in the next generation. Women who grew up in a stepparent family, who are remarried, or who lived away from home before marriage appear to be moving in the direction of "no families," because they are not marrying or having children. And those who do marry share less time and energy with their husbands in making their home together, reinforcing "old"—or traditional—families, with a more sex-segregated division of labor in the families they do form. Although there is evidence that young men, and perhaps younger women as well, move toward more joint activities when exposed to these experiences, it would seem that in most cases the feedback effects of family change have been negative, weakening family sharing in the next generation. As more couples contain members who have had these new experiences, then, one might think that husbands would become less involved in household tasks over time.

We saw, however, in chapter 2 that the opposite is happening—couples are becoming more egalitarian in their approach to household tasks. In order to assess whether the recent trend toward a more egalitarian division of household labor is likely to persist, we need to look beyond the effects of new family experiences, to see what other factors seem to influence couples' levels of sharing these responsibilities. Are there other exercises, attitudes, or situations that are becoming more prevalent—as divorce and independent living are—that would lead to increased sharing? Do couples with more modern attitudes share more? In this chapter, we look beyond the various effects of divorce and independent living to see whether the other factors we included in our models present clues about the trends we are likely to find as the twentieth century yields to the twenty-first.

We included several categories of explanatory factors that researchers who study the division of household labor between husbands and wives have found to be important, all other things being equal: the attitudes and values of the spouses toward domestic roles; the amount of work required; the relative power of the husband and wife; and their availability for domestic work. We review evidence for each of these dimensions in turn.

Attitudes and the Family

Sex-Role Attitudes.   Those men and women who believe in the equality of the sexes and hold liberal views of sex roles might put their ideas into practice in deciding on their own division of household labor. If so, men with nontraditional sex-role attitudes should be more willing than otherwise comparable men to cook or clean or shop. And women with liberal views would more often attempt to enlist their spouse in these activities and would more often manage the finances or mow the lawn themselves than other wives. Such couples are also likely to have family and friends with similar ideas.

Other research has usually found that egalitarian sex-role attitudes *of husbands* increase husbands' contribution to domestic labor, but their wives' attitudes have little or no effect.[1] This suggests that men take a role in domestic labor only if *they* want to. Women who think that men should share housework have little success in achieving this sharing unless their husbands agree with them.

As we have seen, women have been changing their sex-role attitudes in an egalitarian direction more rapidly than men, so it is not surprising that change in the division of household labor has been slow (chapter 2). Nevertheless, men have been changing their attitudes as well. If such attitudes do have a strong influence on sharing household tasks, this would be an important predictor of accelerating change in the home life of adult men, and hence, a key influence on their sons and daughters, who will be forming families and making homes near the end of the century.

Our first approach to the question of measuring "modern" egalitarian attitudes was to take the measures used in chapter 4 of sex-role attitudes, and to see whether more egalitarian attitudes would decrease the extent to which couples worked out a segregated, traditional division of household labor. There were two such measures. One seemed to reflect less traditionally sex-typed ideas about women's roles in the workplace, emphasizing the importance of women's pay to her family and the satisfactions that she might derive from working (JOB ROLES). This is constructed so that high values on the scale indicate more nontraditional (or modern) attitudes on these issues, while low values indicate that the respondent was unaware of or uncomfortable with work as an important role for women.

The other measure has a more idealistic component, and strongly evokes a vision of traditional women's roles in the home (FAMILY ROLES). The questions focus on mothers' obligations to children at home (whether they suffer if their mothers are not home full time); on husbands' needs in the home (the importance of his being "king" in his "castle"); and on the importance of home-based roles for women (whether women's "greatest satisfactions" should come from their domestic roles). We also scaled these questions so that higher values mean a less traditional response. Those with high values on this scale are rejecting the double burden, and might be willing and even eager to have others perform tasks that do not, after all, give them their "greatest satisfaction."[2]

We reasoned that our two measures might have very different effects on how couples decide to divide up the responsibilities for household chores. Many women (and couples) with modern attitudes toward a woman's role in the workplace may nevertheless feel that her *first* priority is to her home and family, and that she should not work unless she can continue to meet her family obligations. But if she holds modern attitudes about her roles in the family, this means that she is less concerned about "neglecting" her family, since she does not feel it is her exclusive responsibility, and since she does not gain great satisfaction from her household tasks, she may feel more justified in calling on her husband to share in household chores. But if she feels that a wife should really stay home even if she is working, this may translate into a sex-segregated division of labor.

In fact, this is what the results show. Husbands in couples in which the wife expresses strong agreement with nontraditional definitions of FAMILY ROLES share significantly more in *all* the traditionally female tasks. In figure 8.1, we compare the husband's share in families with a scale score of 2.0 (very egalitarian) with those with a score of −1.5 (quite traditional). In more liberal households, the husband's share of grocery shopping is 25 percent greater, his share of cooking is nearly double, and he does nearly 3 times as much household cleaning as do otherwise comparable husbands in traditional families.[3] In contrast, these attitudes do not significantly affect the balance of sharing for the male on such neutral tasks as yard and home maintenance or paperwork.

In contrast, having either a very traditional or very nontraditional orientation toward women's roles in the workplace had no effect on the extent of overall sharing, and those with more "modern" attitudes actually showed *lower* levels of sharing responsibility with their husbands for washing dishes, household cleaning, and child care (tables 7.2 and 7.3 in Appendix C provide these details).

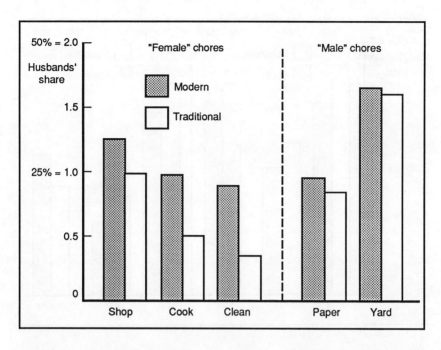

Figure 8.1   Effect of Modern Family Attitudes on Husbands' Share of Household Tasks

Indirect Attitude Measures.   As we discuss in chapter 3, JOB ROLES and FAMILY ROLES are direct measures of ideas about men's and women's roles, but they do not tap all the dimensions that reflect preferences, particularly how reported tastes affect behavior. Demographic indicators reflecting people's social contexts, such as race, region, community, and educational attainment, shape people's attitudes as well. This is clearly the case for our analysis of the extent to which husbands share in household tasks, since even after one takes into account their general attitudes toward men's and women's roles at work and in the family, measures of these social contexts generally have an impact. Figure 8.2 indicates that southern men share slightly less than men in other parts of the country, although differences are not great on any particular chore (they share 13 percent less in child care than nonsouthern men, and 12 percent less in grocery shopping). Interestingly, southern men also share about 9 percent less in yard work. It is possible, however, that this reflects the greater availability of low-wage labor in the South, allowing the employment of nonfamily members for this task, rather than a nontraditional male-female division of labor.

Differences between black and white couples in figure 8.2 are generally

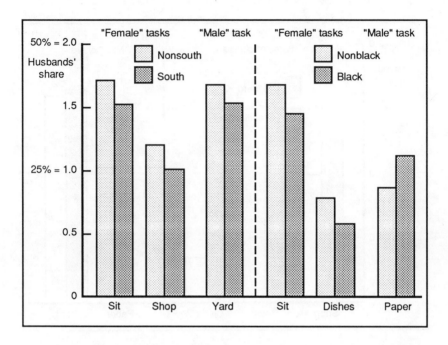

Figure 8.2   Regional and Racial Differences in Husbands' Share of Household Tasks

larger than those between southern and other couples, and the pattern is more complex. On the one hand, there is some tendency for black men to take a more traditional approach to the division of household labor. Like southerners of all races, they avoid child care (nonblacks do 15 percent more) and also another chore commonly shared with husbands—dishwashing (nonblacks do 39 percent more). On the other hand, black men assume 29 percent more responsibility for paperwork than otherwise comparable men, suggesting more willingness to contribute to the nonpaid tasks of the household. In contrast, there are no noticeable differences between couples in the largest metropolitan areas and those in the most rural. Apparently once one considers the other characteristics of such couples, those living in large cities or on farms divide household tasks between husbands and wives in about the same way.

The most dramatic effect of social context appears for education, particularly the husband's. Married men with more education share significantly more in every chore—with the single exception of yard and household maintenance—than men with less education. In figure 8.3 we compare the amount of sharing husbands do for two levels of husbands' education, grammar school graduates and college graduates.

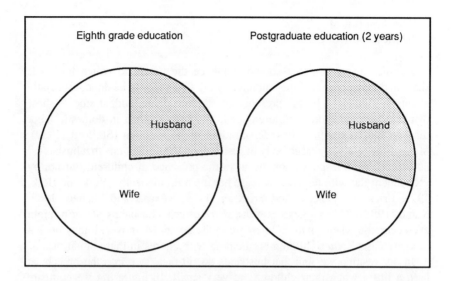

Figure 8.3   Effect of Husbands' Education on Husbands' Share of Household Tasks

The most highly educated husbands take almost a third more responsibility for household tasks compared with those with little education (30 percent compared to 23 percent). They take 30 to 50 percent more responsibility for dishwashing, child care, shopping, housecleaning, and laundry, with smaller but still substantial differences in cooking and yard and home maintenance.

The education of wives also has a separate effect, increasing husbands' responsibility further for child care and dishwashing. However, there is an interesting difference in the effects of education between families with children and those without. The wife's higher education only influences husbands to help with household tasks when children are present (table 8.1, Appendix C). The man's education increases his sharing for all couples, even those without children, but the woman's education only has an additional effect when there are children. This finding suggests that more educated people not only prefer husbands to do more around the house in order to achieve a more equal division of household labor between husband and wife, but will enlist husbands *to substitute* for the work of children around the house. We will develop this theme further when we examine children's roles in the household division of labor (chapters 9 and 10). More educated couples see childhood as a time for children to prepare for their adult tasks in the workplace (Zelizer, 1985), encouraging them in their homework, outside school lessons, and even sports to a greater extent than less educated parents. They may also see less value in household tasks—for children or anyone.

The Amount of
Work to be Done

Another dimension that should influence the extent to which husbands share in domestic work is the amount of work that needs to be done, especially as this is influenced by the presence of children. Time budget studies show that families with young children spend much more time in domestic labor than do families with only older children or no children (Stafford, 1980). Most of the relatively large body of research on this topic finds that husbands' housework time responds somewhat to the presence of children, but not by very much; the wife tends to increase her input dramatically (Berk and Berk, 1979; Ericksen, Yancey, and Ericksen, 1979; Rexroat and Shehan, 1987; Kamo, 1988). This suggests that the *share* of tasks husbands perform might even decrease when small children are in the home. Moreover, it may be that in many cases, *other* children are helping with chores in these situations.

In our results, we find that husbands do, in fact, step into the breach, at least a little, when their children are very small. In figure 8.4 we compare families with and without toddlers (aged 4 or under) and find that husbands share more on household tasks when there are toddlers present than when there are only older children. But by and large, they take on chores that are not directly related to these small children. They share 25 percent more on dishwashing, 22 percent more on household cleaning, and 26 percent more on paperwork than husbands with no children that age. But husbands do no more laundry, which is the task that often increases most when children are born, and are not significantly more likely to share in child care, which is most demanding at this age. This suggests that husbands pick up on tasks that otherwise would not get done promptly while their wives care for these very small children, instead of sharing child care with them, directly.

Time Available

Who does the household work should also be influenced by the availability of each spouse. How do the husband's hours of work, the wife's employment status, and her hours of work constrain the amount of time that each spouse *can* spend shopping, cleaning, cooking, or caring for children? Previous research shows that when wives work, husbands increase their *share*, although this is primarily because their wives' response is to decrease their own hours of housework when they take a job. Nevertheless, husbands do relatively few more actual hours of housework when their wives are employed. However, husbands participate more in housework if they work relatively few hours, suggesting the importance of availability (Coverman and Sheley, 1986; Gershuny and Robinson, 1988).

These analyses generally examine the effect of the wife's *employment* on

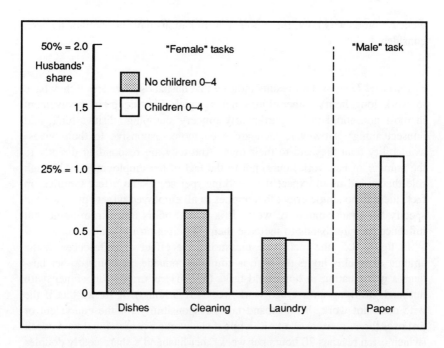

Figure 8.4   Effect of Children 0–4 on Husbands' Share of Household Tasks

husband's sharing, as if it made no difference how much the wife actually worked. This approach reflects the view that there are really two kinds of families: those in which the wife is not employed, in which case she should manage her "own" tasks in the traditional division of labor; and those in which the wife is employed (no matter how much), in which case husbands should take over some of the chores. If she worked more hours, he might or might not expand his responsibilities commensurately. If this is the case, then the simple fact that the wife is employed should have an independent effect on her husband's participation, with perhaps some additional effect on his sharing if she works many hours.

These studies of the division of labor between husbands and wives have rarely looked beyond the amount of time husbands and wives spend on paid employment to see that children can also spend some of their time on household tasks.[4] But older children, and particularly the older daughters in more traditional families, can take over a substantial amount of responsibility for many household tasks. In our analysis, we consider not only the spouses' time, as indicated by their employment obligations, but also whether the family has others available to help. Finally, we consider the effects of a wife's disability, which might make her less able to do household chores, and for symmetry, consider the effect of the husband's being disabled as well. As far as we know, these potential limitations have not previously been considered.

Parental Time.   Our results indicate that husbands share less if they have to work long hours, other things being equal, limiting their involvement in most household tasks (particularly grocery shopping, dishwashing, and housecleaning). However, men are even more responsive to their wives' availability than they are to their own. And they are responding directly to the number of her work hours, not to the fact of her employment. Although role theory led us to expect that working, per se, would affect families, in fact, there is no single effect that applies to all employed wives, once we can specify her exact amount of work. It is wives' hours away from home that influence their husbands to increase their participation in domestic tasks.

In figure 8.5, the main line measuring the effect of differences in the amount of weekly hours the wife is employed outside the home on her husband's participation in household tasks (WIFE1) is drawn for women with husbands working an average work week (37.5 hours). It shows that if the wife does not work, her husband takes responsibility for the equivalent of just over three-quarters of a task, while if she works a professional work week (which often reaches 70 hours per week), her husband's share nearly doubles (although the absolute increase is only about three-quarters of a task to 1 and one-half tasks out of the set of 5).

The main line measuring the effect of differences in the amount of weekly hours *the husband* is employed outside the home (HUSBAND1) is drawn for husbands whose wives are working an average work week for wives in this sample (17 hours). A change of one hour of his employment has less impact than a change of one hour of hers. This suggests that while husbands' work hours limit their involvement, other factors, such as traditional attitudes about how much men should be involved in household tasks, limit their involvement as well, so that the marginal effect of their employment hours, while consistent and statistically significant, cannot be large.

We also compare two extreme role possibilities: very traditional couples in which the wife does not work outside the home while the husband works long hours (point B on the line labeled HUSBAND'S WORK 2); and "role reversal" couples in which the husband stays home and the wife works long hours (point A on the line labeled WIFE'S WORK 2). In this case the difference is greater. Nevertheless, the difference between points A and B is still not very large. Our results project a difference in the extent to which husbands share in household tasks between very traditional and role reversal couples of only a little more than one task.

These results clarify that the effects of the wife's employment on her husband's sharing in household tasks depend on the number of hours she works

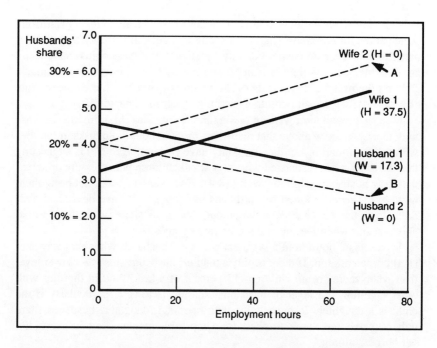

Figure 8.5   Effect of Employment Hours on Husbands' Share of Household Tasks

outside the home. If she works outside the home only on a part-time basis, her spouse increases his contribution relatively little; if she works more, most husbands increase their sharing. There is no evidence that assuming the role of "working wife" has any separate effect, which might have been more likely during earlier decades when work of any sort for married women was much rarer.

The Availability of Children.   One of our central arguments in this book is that children are members of families. Both sons and daughters need to feel that they contribute to the well-being of their family *and* to learn how to make a home in adulthood. And children can contribute considerably to household maintenance (chapter 9). How does the arrival of children affect how husbands share household tasks? And when children leave home do husbands and wives revert to the patterns of the "honeymoon period," or have the long years raising children left their mark? And how much do the gender and age of children matter?

Our results indicate that children have a powerful influence on how much husbands share household responsibilities. At this point in the analysis we cannot tell whether it is the children themselves who are substituting for their fathers or whether perhaps others are being hired, but it is clear, even from these results for husbands' sharing, that children generally *reduce* their fathers participation in the domestic economy,[5] particularly if these children are teenage daughters. We will address in chapter 9 what factors influence how much children themselves share, and consider factors that affect the whole system of husbands, wives, and children (and hired help) in chapter 10.

Men share with their wives more in families with no children, than in those with them.[6] We saw above that men share more in household tasks in families with toddlers than in families that only have children aged 6–11, suggesting that the extra work associated with very small children puts pressure on wives that their husbands help relieve (fig. 8.4). However, this does not bring them quite to the level reported for husbands in couples that have never had children. In figure 8.6, we show the amount husbands share when there are no children and when there is a child at various ages.

Wives share household tasks most with their husbands when they have not (yet) borne children. If there is only a toddler, husbands share at a lower level than when there are no children (13 percent of a task), and in families with older children, the level of husbands' sharing is lowest, particularly if the child is a daughter. In households with one adult daughter, husbands share only 60 percent as much as otherwise comparable men whose wives have not yet borne children.

We examined the separate tasks, to see which areas differed most for families at various stages of childraising. In families who have not (yet) had children, husbands share more on several tasks compared to when children are available as substitutes. Children reduce their fathers' responsibilities for grocery shopping and dishwashing, in particular, but they have no effect on fathers' responsibilities for laundry, housecleaning, cooking (already low), or yard and home maintenance (which are quite high). Perhaps the new (and frequent) food requirements of small children lead mothers to take on more shopping and dishwashing for the child, and as a result, for the family as a whole.

In families with teenage girls, husbands take less responsibility for the female tasks of dishes, laundry, housecleaning, and, in families with young adult daughters, cooking. Both types of older daughters also *decrease* fathers' responsibilities for yard and home maintenance, while teenage boys only reduce their fathers' responsibility for the yard.

Since parents of daughters show somewhat higher chances of divorce than do parents of sons (Morgan, Lye, and Condran, 1988), it seems unlikely that increased involvement of fathers with household chores increases the likelihood of divorce. Perhaps the lower divorce risks of parents of sons result not only from the special relationships fathers have with their sons but also from men's increased involvement with *their wives* in making a home. If so, then

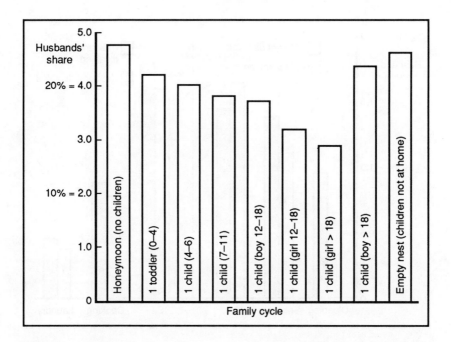

Figure 8.6   Effect of the Family Cycle on Husbands' Share of Household Tasks

the traditional mother-daughter pattern of home maintenance increases men's detachment from the household.

In the later years of marriage, there is again the opportunity to share more tasks together, as they become less onerous after the departure of the children. There is some evidence that marriages become emotionally closer during this period (Glenn and Weaver, 1979). This is often interpreted as being the result of the diminution of the frictions associated with rearing adolescents, but it could also result from simply being able to spend more time together. Our evidence suggests that part of the increased time that couples have together is spent sharing housework, since husbands increase their responsibility almost to the level of the "honeymoon" period, with more sharing for all relevant tasks except paperwork.

Our final measure of the constraints on couples' sharing in household chores is disability—both the husband's and the wife's. In general, men whose wives report a disabling condition share substantially more in household tasks than otherwise comparable men with able wives (fig. 8.7). In particular, they take nearly 50 percent more responsibility for household cleaning and 25 percent more responsibility for grocery shopping. However, when the wife is disabled, men do *fewer* of the tasks related to yard and home mainte-

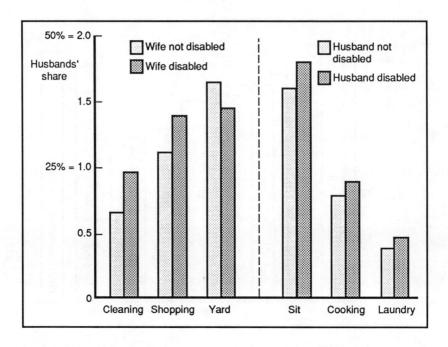

Figure 8.7   Effect of Disability on Husbands' Share of Household Tasks

nance, reducing their share slightly to about 88 percent of the level of men with wives not so limited, although these are the tasks for which men traditionally have had the most responsibility. Perhaps this is a task that couples normally do together, so that if she cannot join him, they hire someone else to do it all, thus reducing his (as well as her) responsibility.

Interestingly, the effect of the husband's disability does not parallel that of the wife. Husbands with a disabling condition share *more—not less*—responsibility for household tasks. Such men take a significantly greater share in cooking (13 percent), child care (12 percent), and laundry (21 percent). We interpret this to mean that disability is serving to keep men at home, and involving them more in many ways in what goes on there, with the result that they share more in its tasks.

Evidently, there are many situations that draw men into involvement with household chores or repel them from such involvement. We first saw this process operate with stepfathers and then again, with the fathers of daughters, each of whom systematically shares less in household affairs. Now we see another instance. Whereas able husbands are fairly peripherally involved in running the home, disabled husbands evidently stay home more, perhaps reducing their social activities outside the home, and getting involved instead in household tasks. Hence, although their disability presumably makes these tasks more difficult for them and should reduce their household sharing for that reason, in fact, the overall effect is the reverse.

Power

A final feature of marriages that may affect who does the housework is the relative power of each partner in the relationship. Research in this tradition assumes that power derives from command over resources and hence, particularly for women, the existence of alternatives to the current marriage.[7] The implicit assumption underlying the notion of marital power and division of household labor is that housework is undesirable and low status, and therefore performed mostly by those who cannot enforce a more equitable division of labor.[8] However, if neither cares particularly, or if the spouses agree on the appropriate division of labor, then who is the boss will never come into the decision-making process.

Increasingly, however, who does household tasks has become an issue, with men holding very different attitudes than women toward the appropriateness of their doing such chores (Berk, 1985). The question of power seems even more salient in two-career families, since the evidence is that wives continue to perform most household tasks. In some cases, no doubt, wives are using their marital power to retain control over household management, even when their husbands are willing to share more equally (though apparently not likely to insist). But in most cases, men are using their greater power in the relationship to get out of cleaning bathrooms, vacuuming the floors, or doing other chores necessary for the household to run smoothly.

The most common way to measure the power of the spouses in a marriage is through financial resources. Researchers reason that the wife's earnings give her an independent power base that she can use to influence decision making in the marriage and even to leave it if she chooses. And the higher the husband's earnings the more power he has, according to this perspective.[9] This literature seems to point to the earnings of the husband and wife as key determinants of the way they allocate home chores.

Our study does find that earning money matters, and that husbands use their earnings to "buy" out of sharing in household tasks, while wives use their earnings to "buy" increased participation by their husbands. As in the results for hours of employment, however, the effects are very small. In fact, the patterns are so similar that a graph of the effects of husbands' and wives' earnings could essentially be superimposed on figure 8.5. Again, the differences within a normal range of incomes suggest that at most, responsibility for a single chore would change hands, and that her earnings matter more than his. (An additional $68,000 of wives' earnings leads husbands to increase their sharing by a full chore, and it takes an additional $150,000 of husbands' earnings to reduce his sharing to that small extent.) Of course, these are not realistic estimates, since we observe almost no couples with husbands or wives earning that much. The major point is that our measures are powerful enough to detect such very small differences (differences that are, after all, in the direction hypothesized); but we should not look to increases in wife's earnings to cause any transformation in the division of household labor between husbands and wives. Husbands with low earnings are not "demeaned" into doing women's work, and wives with high earnings do not demand relief from household work. The roots of the current division lie elsewhere.

How are Families Changing?

This section considers two types of changes in men's experience of sharing in household responsibilities. First, do men change their patterns of sharing as they age, becoming either more or less egalitarian than in the early days of marriage? Second, is there any evidence that new husbands are more egalitarian than husbands who started their married life several decades ago? Is the sex-role revolution having an effect, so that marriages are starting out on a more even footing in terms of the work to be done around the house?

As marriages change over time, two processes can operate. On the one hand, role segregated male-female relationships often become more egalitarian over time, since dating couples are most bound by general social expectations and ideals for each sex. After marriage, they begin "playing house," full of traditional expectations and eager to follow them. Eventually, however, the realities of his poor checkbook balancing ability and her toast burning predilections become evident, at which point they move toward a reality within their relationship that takes their separate skills into account. Many quite traditional men find that they like cooking and that they eat better when their wives do not cook; some quite traditional couples have apparently learned that bills are more likely to get paid and complex financial forms filled out with less hassle if she does them.

But a second process is also operating, which is particularly important for more egalitarian couples. For these newly married couples, before children are born and there are fewer tasks (and perhaps time together is particularly valuable), they can be "true" to their egalitarian ideals. When they are young, idealistic, and egalitarian, they can start off sharing, wrapped up in each other and their common tasks. But such couples usually find themselves becoming less egalitarian when children are born, since they can no longer afford the time to shop or cook or run errands together—one must watch the infant while the other accomplishes the needed tasks. And at the same time, the family is under increased economic pressure, since children cost money, and the income lost if she reduces her work hours to care for them puts added pressure on young fathers to work longer hours and to work harder. Hence, the diminishing hours husbands have to spend with their families become more necessary for rest and the release from tension (and her "power" is reduced, if only slightly). As time becomes rarer, and tasks more pressing, the time cost of learning new tasks becomes greater, and thus specialization also becomes more efficient.[10] Couples also become more traditional in their sex-role attitudes with the birth of their first child (Morgan and Waite, 1987).

If both patterns occur, the experiences of couples whose attitudes were originally very different may lead them to increasingly similar patterns of sharing over time. However, our data do not lend themselves easily to answering questions about change over time. We have seen that many of the factors that influence husbands' participation in the domestic sphere are themselves changing. We interpret this to mean that as education increases, as sex-role attitudes become more modern, and as women increasingly work and earn salaries, their families will become more egalitarian. And as young people grow up in more egalitarian households "new families" will be reinforced.

Nevertheless, we were interested in seeing if we could test these inferences more directly (without waiting the decades needed for more data to be collected), and we decided to use the wife's age as a proxy for change over time. We reasoned that younger wives, whose marriages have been formed during a period in which employment for women has become the rule, are more representative of the future relationship between work and family, while older wives, who established their household patterns in a more traditional era in which women who worked were an exception, would represent the patterns of the past. Hence, we asked: How does holding modern attitudes toward women's JOB ROLES among young wives affect how much they share household tasks with their husbands? Does it differ from the patterns of older women?

Figure 8.8 shows what we found. Consistent with a scenario of convergence over the life course, sex-role attitudes make the biggest difference for young wives. Among those with very traditional sex-role attitudes,[11] aging from 27 to 47 increases sharing with husbands (from point A to point B), while among women with very modern attitudes, aging from 27 to 47 decreases sharing with husbands (from point C to point D).

But reading the lines of the figure reveals another interesting and important result. For younger women, holding modern attitudes with regard to JOB and FAMILY ROLES leads to a great deal of sharing with their husbands. But the effects of sex-role attitudes are weaker among older wives (particularly for JOB ROLES), so that wives born before World War II actually share less if they hold modern sex-role attitudes than if they do not.

This may result from the very different life-cycle work patterns of women in these two cohorts: those born before the war normally did not work when their children were young, and "returned to work" when they were older,

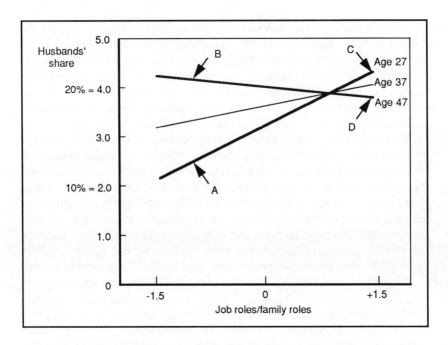

Figure 8.8   Effect of Wives' Sex Role Attitudes on Husbands' Share of Household Tasks by Age of Wife

while younger women have been much more likely to work even when they have small children. Hence, the older wives seem to be attempting to maintain *their own* patterns of home maintenance, created when they were at home all day, even though they have gone back to work, while wives who have never worked exclusively in the home build patterns that integrate the two dimensions of their lives more completely. This would explain a stronger effect for younger compared with older women.

But our results show that among older women, the effects of modern sex-role attitudes are not simply weak, they are reversed. This suggests that many older working wives not only attempt to carry out all their household chores but also perhaps feel "guilty" about getting satisfaction from work, and bend over backwards to make sure that their husbands and do not suffer as a result. They end up sharing even less with their husbands than wives with more negative attitudes toward the employment of women.

This result explains a great deal of what has been puzzling in studies of change in the division of labor. The relatively little change that occurred during the early years women were entering the labor force now appears to be the product not only of resistance by husbands to taking up much of the burden but also the outcome of wives struggling to maintain their traditional responsibilities. And the result we will show in chapter 9, in which mothers' employment has little effect on the participation in household chores of *their children*, also makes sense in this context. The more satisfaction middle- and older-aged women felt from their work (in a period when women were "not supposed" to work), the more they needed to compensate their families for their working. And so a whole generation—the baby boom—has grown up seeing relatively little change in their own families, even though their mothers were working, with homes very much like those of children who grew up in days when few mothers worked outside the home.

If these results can be projected into the future and the baby-boom couples themselves age into their prime years, then the "guilt" effect should no longer be operating. Couples with modern attitudes toward both women's work outside and inside the family will create more egalitarian families in which children can grow up and later emulate.

9

Children's Share in Household Tasks

Children growing up in America learn early that the home is not a very egalitarian place, far less even than the world of work. The roles of males and females in the home differ sharply. Although most mothers are working, like fathers, it is mothers who are primarily responsible for running the household, with few fathers taking more than a secondary role. Further, the tasks children do are still rigidly divided by gender in most families, with girls doing different and *more* tasks around the house than boys.

Sex typing of children's household tasks begins very early, so that sharp differences have crystalized by adolescence. Girls tend to spend about twice as much time on housework as their brothers, mirroring the different levels of contribution by their mothers and fathers (Thrall, 1978; White and Brinkerhoff, 1981a). However, their schools have relatively gender-free curricula (at least in theory) and they have working-mother role models, so that most girls are being prepared for adult roles both in the workplace and in the home. In contrast, boys in most families receive almost no preparation for competence in any aspect of making a home.

It is often the case, however, that neither boys nor girls gain much experience doing household tasks, because in many families their mothers do almost all of them. As men's productive efforts were being withdrawn from the home with the growth of new urban, industrial jobs, children were also increasingly diverted from home tasks by a new definition of childhood that emphasized the importance of preparation for adult roles only in the workplace, not in the home. The old view that children should help their parents (and eventually support them in their old age) has given way to an expectation that parents must exert themselves to the utmost to ensure that their children grow up to be successes. As a result, the ideal American child has been transformed from a "useful child" to a "useless child."[1] Few children would agree that their childhoods totally fit this new stereotype, thinking of the many onerous and resented tasks that diverted them from play; in fact, children do almost as much household work as their fathers. But young people learn early that claiming heavy school assignments will nearly always serve as an adequate excuse for the room uncleaned or the lawn unmowed. What has happened?

Children's Work in the Household

A relatively small literature focuses on children's participation in household labor. It virtually ignores the ways in which families balance the labor of the father, mother, and children to arrive at a *household* division of housework,[2] a process that we examine in detail in the next chapter. Nevertheless, some important clues suggest that the potential for children's work in the household as preparation for "new families" is still largely unrealized.

When mothers and fathers are asked *why* they expect their children to share some responsibility for household tasks, they give a variety of reasons, revealing the strong ambivalence parents in the United States feel about children's role in the household economy.[3] Most parents respond that performing household work builds character and develops a sense of responsibility.[4] Only a few report that they require the child's labor in running the house, and even fewer indicate that they view "chores" as a way to prepare the child for the performance of household tasks they will need as adults—learning to cook, do laundry, and clean up one's room—and this answer is most often given by families with daughters. Another minority response, most commonly given in large families, is that parents want children to feel they have a responsibility to participate in the work of the household enterprise. (Of course, since more than a third of parents *pay* children for work around the house, they are really reinforcing a view that such work is optional.)

Our premise in this study is that the experiences children have in childhood and early adulthood are extremely important for the families they later form. And it is clear that the experiences children have even in relatively modern families reinforce a traditional division of labor in the next generation. If children, particularly boys, have little experience with the tasks associated with maintaining a home, it is difficult to expect them to feel comfortable taking them on as adults.

This is a critical area for our understanding of future family trends: Will egalitarian roles be achieved only through a complete abandonment of family-centered activities, or can men and women achieve a redefined and more egalitarian combination of work and family life? However, systematic research on children's roles in the family that would help us understand how children are being prepared for future family roles is even more dramatically lacking than it is for men. For example, although we have learned in the last decade or so that married men are increasing their contribution to domestic tasks, we have no direct evidence for trends in the extent to which children have participated in household tasks, or trends in the proportions of boys and girls performing these tasks.[5] There have been studies showing that youths growing up on farms have numerous duties that often require substantial numbers of hours (Light, Hertsgaard, and Martin, 1985). We have also learned that families in urban areas depend less on their children's labor than those in more rural areas (Strauss, 1962; Lawrence, Tasker, and Babcock, 1983). These findings imply that as families became increasingly urbanized and as fewer grew up on farms, children were involved less in family tasks. But we do not know how much change is really involved, or which children have participated most in it. And it has now been decades—even generations—since urban life came to dominate American society.

What is happening to the roles of children in homemaking? Under what circumstances, if any, are children more involved in household tasks and in which families are children's tasks becoming more egalitarian? Have *parents'* experiences of nontraditional family forms in childhood and young adulthood influenced the way they share with their own children? And are divorce and remarriage changing the involvement of children in household tasks? To answer these questions, we will examine how much, and under what circumstances, children share in household work, taking into consideration the nature and amount of work needed to be done and the parents' attitudes and values, particularly those resulting from experience with nontraditional families in their own lives.

Measuring Children's Share in the Division of Household Labor

The women included in the National Longitudinal Studies of Young Women and Mature Women answered a series of questions about a variety of household chores, including cooking, cleaning, laundry, child care, dishes, yard work, grocery shopping and paperwork.[6] From the answers to these questions, we created a detailed scale of how much responsibility children took for 7 of these tasks. (Children's share of family paperwork is not included. Appendix B contains a description of the scale and the questions on which it is based.) In brief, the scale takes on a higher value the more tasks children do and the more responsibility they take for them, from a value of 0 if children do no tasks at all to a high of 28 if children do all tasks completely by themselves.

In order to interpret the answers women gave, we translate them into percentage terms. So the range of answers (0–4) given for each task can be interpreted to mean that women who said that children did not share in a given task, share none of that task with children; women who said their children shared "some but less than half," share about 25 percent; women who said they shared "about half" a task with children, share 50 percent of that task with their children; and so on.

In our analysis, we consider only families with at least one child between the ages of 6 and 18, although they could have younger and older children, too. Some families begin to give children regular chores when they are as young as 2 years old (White and Brinkerhoff, 1981b), but this is relatively rare. Further, the way the questions asked in this survey were phrased requires that a child be reported as having at least "some responsibility" for a given chore, which seems unlikely for children aged 5 or less. Hence, we do not examine families whose children are all very young. We also feel that the nature of sharing with children changes fundamentally when the children become adults, so the upper age cutoff was set at 18, eliminating families whose only children at home are adults, although we will show that this is an important group for further study.

How Much Do These Children Share?

Children take relatively little responsibility for most household tasks, although the list of tasks we consider includes some that are often shared with children as well as some that are virtually never shared. Overall (averaging children's sharing across the set of 7 tasks), children contribute a relatively small proportion of total household labor—15 percent; but their share is quite substantial for some tasks (fig. 9.1). Mothers report that their children take a good deal of responsibility for washing dishes and for cleaning the house, taking more than a quarter of the responsibility for these tasks (and more than their fathers do). Equally clearly, most families do not give children any responsibility for paperwork, or much responsibility for grocery shopping or child care. Laundry, cooking, and yard work fall in between, with children doing 12 to 15 percent of these tasks. Thus, children's participation in household tasks depends very much on *which* task.

Which Children Share?

The NLS questions on household labor allow a woman to report that her children share some responsibility for various household tasks, but they do not provide information on which of her children are actually sharing in these tasks. So two women could report identically that children have sole responsibility for the dishes and for the yard, but in one family, one of the children always does the dishes and the other always cuts the grass, and in the other

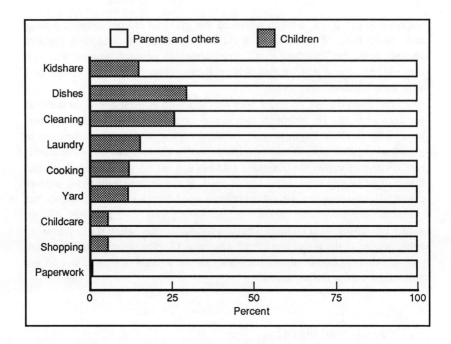

Figure 9.1   Children's Share of Responsibility for Household Tasks

family, the two children share equally in both tasks. The questions do not allow us to distinguish easily between these two women and their children.

But we want to know whether there are differences in the involvement of children, between younger and older children, and particularly between boys and girls. Previous research and common sense suggest that the age and sex composition of the children in the household will affect whether a woman shares with any of her offspring. Many families assign tasks to children along lines segregated by traditional notions of gender (Thrall, 1978; Berk, 1985). Further, children clearly become better able to take on household tasks as they grow, with preteens able to perform fewer tasks than teenagers. So the presence of an "appropriate" child for a given task is likely to lead to greater sharing of that task, since the alternative for the mother is to pay an outsider, take on the task herself, or train a less "appropriate" child (Brody and Steelman, 1985).

These distinctions—male/female, preteen/teen—seem straightforward. However, the role of children who have reached adulthood in household tasks is less obvious. On the one hand, they are adults, and might be expected to take an adult's share of responsibilities. On the other hand, simply by reaching this age, the common justification for sharing—as a mechanism for character development—becomes inappropriate. Further, to the extent that grown children spend more time at work than they did at school, they are less available for household chores. Many parents may continue to feel responsibility for investing their own time (and money) in their child's future as long as he or she remains at home. They may reason that in early adulthood, even more than during high school, a social life is necessary to get married and starting careers is stressful; as a result, they may be unwilling to make demands on their grown children for help. So we need to examine sharing with children in families with children of different ages and sexes, even adult "children."

For each family, there are data on how many children live in the household, and the age and sex of each one. It is our view that if families with teenagers tend to share more with children than do families with younger children only, then we can conclude that families probably share more with teens.[7] Similarly, if women in families with girls share more with their children than women do in families with boys, we can reasonably conclude that they are sharing more with their daughters. This allows us to answer in a general way questions about the characteristics of *children* that increase the extent of their sharing in household tasks.

What we found is that even though we cannot know exactly which children are actually sharing a given task with the mother, the pattern of sharing in families is responsive both to the number and type of children present. The more children in the family, the more the mother reports sharing housework with children as a group (table 9.2, Appendix C). This is sensible, since the more potential workers there are, the more likely some of them will be to pitch in.

The children's age and gender also influence the amount of sharing, sometimes very clearly, sometimes not so clearly. Figure 9.2 presents differences in children's share of household tasks, comparing families with children of different ages, boys, and girls. It shows the total amount of sharing for the seven tasks we consider most intensively (excluding paperwork), distinguishing yard and home maintenance from the others.[8]

Considering the younger children first (under 12), there are few differences among families that have only preteen children. It doesn't matter whether all are age 6 to 11, or whether some are younger. Based on our results that husbands share more tasks when there are toddlers in the household than when there are only older children, we had expected that the presence of very young children might increase sharing with older children. Babies and toddlers require extra work, and harassed mothers might press their older children into service (since each family in our analysis has at least one child between the ages of 6 and 18 in the household).

Since it is families with children ages 4 to 6 who share least of all, we infer that older children are helping a little with the toddlers, help that is not as necessary for somewhat older children. But the differences are small, in

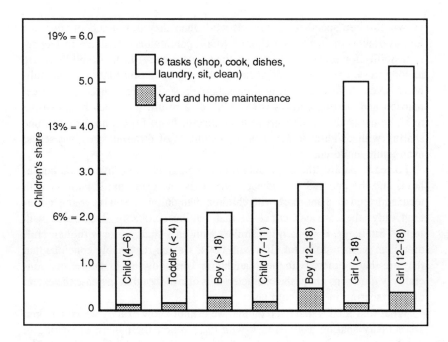

Figure 9.2   Effect of Age and Gender on Children's Share of Yard and Other Household Tasks (Households with Two Children: One 6–11 and One of Given Age/Sex)

part because the level of sharing with children is low across all families that only have children in these ages. (And not surprisingly, such families also get very little help with yard and home maintenance.)

To look at the contribution of older children, we divided families into those with any sons aged 12 to 18 (we call all children of this age "teenagers"), those with any teenage daughters, those with any adult sons (ages 19 and over) and those with any adult daughters. We then compared the amount of housework done by children in these families, to see *which kinds* of children were contributing labor in the family, and how much to "male" as compared to "female" tasks.

As children get older, they clearly become more involved in household chores, in- and outdoors. Families with teenage children share substantially more housework with their children than families with only preteens. Teenage children are most particularly helpful with yard work, with about equal amounts of sharing from teenage boys and girls. But the biggest differences by age and sex are in "female" chores.

Families with teenage girls report sharing *5 times more* of these other tasks with children than do families with boys of the same age. In fact, girls ages

12 to 18 seem to carry the largest share of housework of all children. Mothers with a daughter ages 12 to 18 delegate essentially three-quarters of an entire task (most of the laundry, say, or most of the dishes) compared to mothers with children ages 6 to 11. Although teenage girls do more of all household tasks (except paperwork) than their younger brothers and sisters, they seem to contribute especially large amounts toward doing dishes and cleaning the house, and to share substantially in cooking and laundry. Their teenage brothers, in contrast, share more than younger siblings overall, but only because they do significantly more yard work.

Turning to adult sons and daughters, girls seem to continue their contributions to the household economy as they reach young adulthood, sharing only slightly less after age 18 than before. Older daughters shift their contributions to grocery shopping, child care, and laundry, and away from dishes and cleaning, and drop their share of yard work substantially. However, young adult males contribute no more to housework than do preteen children, and substantially less than their sisters of the same age. In fact, grown sons do significantly less cooking and child care than children 6 to 12 years old. It is not that these young men contribute financially to the family, since most evidence suggests that adult children living at home keep their earnings (Goldscheider and Goldscheider, 1988). Hence, grown sons are being subsidized by their parents both financially and in terms of household services, since although they certainly eat and require clean clothes, they rarely contribute to the performance of these tasks; yet someone has to provide these services to them. Unless grown daughters contribute even less of their earnings to the family than grown sons, staying at home after age 18 seems to provide much less benefit for daughters than for sons. While sons provide virtually no help in housework (even in yard and home maintenance), daughters continue to contribute at a very high level after age 18.

These basic results show that families raising children in the early 1980s share household tasks with them in very traditional ways, giving older children more responsibility than younger ones, girls more than boys, and dividing tasks up so that what are considered female adult tasks are shared with daughters, and what are considered male adult tasks are primarily shared with sons. But what factors influence this division by gender? Are there any that increase young males' sharing in the central tasks involved in making a home?

New Family Experiences and Sharing with Children

Children perform sex-traditional tasks, learning to do—and to like—the tasks usually assigned to adults of their gender. Boys mostly help around the house by cutting the lawn or doing repairs, while watching their sisters cook meals and clean the house. This childhood socialization helps to reproduce the sex segregation of household labor found among husbands and wives. The family is a "gender factory,"[9] serving as a focal point where the importance— especially the symbolic importance—of the division of labor between the sexes is most strongly reinforced.

But for many families, "reproducing" the parental division of labor is not possible, since the traditional parental structure does not exist. The rise in divorce, together with the increase in out-of-wedlock parenthood, means that unmarried women are increasingly heading families with children. How might this influence the children's role in household tasks?

Women who head families alone face enormous pressures with relatively few resources. In many ways, they are the new "farms" in which the labor of children is once again a dire necessity. These families lack two elements generally available in married couple families: the earning capacity and labor power of an adult male. So female-headed families tend to have much lower incomes than do families headed by married couples. Moreover, women who head families show higher rates of labor force participation than do married women, because these unmarried women are almost always responsible for their own support and that of their children (U.S. Bureau of the Census, 1989b). Families headed by unmarried women, then, have both less money and less of the mother's time at home than do families headed by couples; they are in effect squeezed in both directions. Under these circumstances, families may feel more need to turn to the labor power of the children, both in the home and in the market (Tilly and Scott, 1978; Greif, 1985; Sanik and Mauldin, 1986).

The family's need for the children's contribution suggests that women who head families alone will share more with children. In fact, many such mothers say they cannot function without the children's labor (Peters and Haldeman, 1987). But this reasoning does not tell us *which* children will take on extra tasks. Perhaps teenage or young adult males take over only the household duties of the absent male head, increasing sharing in such traditionally male tasks as yard work, leaving girls to take over traditionally female tasks such as cooking, cleaning, and child care. This could lead to more sharing in female-headed families, but no change in the traditional allocation of tasks between boys and girls. However, boys are the obvious candidates for extra responsibilities, even those normally done by females, since the household duties of the absent male head are usually not very onerous (chapter 7), and even in two-parent families, girls do much more work than boys. This situation provides the potential for a less traditional allocation of household tasks among children in mother-only rather than in married couple families.

If mother-only families are more egalitarian, it is also likely that children who spend some time in such a situation may become socialized to greater sharing and to exchanging tasks between the sexes. Even if their mother remarries, the recent experience the mother and children had as a single-parent family may affect their division of household labor in the new, blended family. The effect might extend even further, into the next generation of the children of divorce. Those who spent at least part of their childhood in a female-headed household may have received different training and socialization in the levels and nature of children's participation in household tasks.[10] If female-headed families share more with children than do married-couple families, as we expect, then those raised in such families may transfer this pattern of greater participation by children to their own families. This effect should appear regardless of the structure of the current family.[11]

Mother-Only Families

Children who live in a mother-only family play a key role in the household economy: they share more overall and they share more in every single task. Comparing the children's share of household responsibilities in intact families and in mother-only families (fig. 9.3) shows that children in mother-only families take nearly twice as much responsibility for household tasks as those in standard nuclear (nonblended) families.

Children are drawn into the pool of family labor far more intensively in mother-only families than in any other type of family. This effect takes into account differences in the mother's hours of employment and family income, and so goes beyond the obvious stress these two "shortages" tend to put on mother-only families. Clearly, children are central to the family economy in these households in a way they are not in other families, and as a result, are likely to feel needed and more responsible. Weiss (1979) speculates that single parents develop a very different relationship with their children than do married couples, essentially forming partnerships in which children share responsibility with the parent for decision making and for getting tasks done.

Do all children do much more housework in mother-only than in intact families, or does the burden fall disproportionately on some? We find that both sons and daughters are drawn into more household chores in mother-only as compared to married couple families. Figure 9.4 shows that boys in mother-only families—both teenagers and young adults—take *much* more responsibility for housework than do sons in otherwise comparable families headed by two parents. In fact, sons age 12 and over living with both parents do no more housework than their younger siblings ages 6 to 11. Teenage boys only contribute more than younger children if they live in mother-only families.

We considered the argument that this increased participation results only from the greater involvement of these young men in traditionally male tasks, so that in some sense sons take over the chores that were the province of the absent father. This is the case, but it is not the whole story. Although teenage

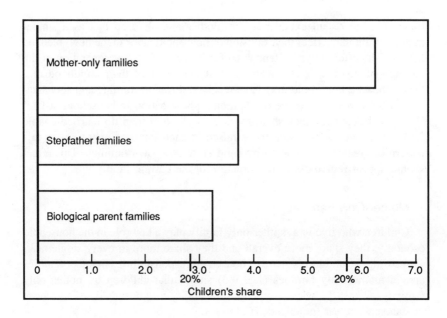

Figure 9.3 Effect of Current Family Structure on Children's Share of Household Tasks

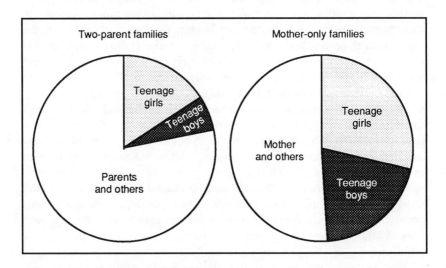

Figure 9.4 Effect of Living in a Mother-Only Family on Sharing Housework with Teenage Sons and Daughters

boys do about twice as much yard work and home maintenance in families headed by their mother only than they do in two-parent families, figure 9.5 shows that they also do more grocery shopping, more cooking and more cleaning if they live with their unmarried mother (and the same result applies to dishes, child care, and paperwork). Similarly, young adult sons share more in every household task except yard work.

What about daughters in mother-only families? We find that teenage girls take more responsibility for housework when they live with a single mother than they do in two-parent families. But the difference between the amount of housework done by children in mother-only and two-parent families is actually larger for teenage boys than for teenage girls, perhaps because girls do so much in all families, whereas boys in two-parent families do very little. As with boys, they share significantly more of nearly every task when they live in a family headed by their mother alone than if they live with two parents. Indeed, teenage boys in mother-only families share considerably more housework than do teenage girls in two-parent families.

We found another surprise in our results: adult daughters are the workhorses in mother-only families. These young women take twice as much responsibility for housework as girls their age in two-parent families, including more of every household task but laundry and yard work (data not presented). Mother-only families with young adult daughters allocate more to children by the equivalent of complete responsibility for two entire tasks—for example dishes and cooking—compared with two-parent families with children ages 6 to 12.

These results show very clearly that mothers heading families do not maintain the traditional segregation of household tasks by sex. Daughters in these families participate much more than girls the same age living with two parents, including greater participation in the two traditionally male tasks in our scale, yard work and paperwork. But these mothers also incorporate teenage boys into virtually all traditionally female household tasks, whereas boys participate very little in families headed by married couples.

Stepparent Families

Children who currently live with their mother and a stepfather take a greater role in household chores than do children who live with both their natural parents, primarily because they wash more dishes and do more child care. However, the differences between stepparent families and other two-parent families are much less than between mother-only and never-disrupted families (fig. 9.5).

Evidently, the increased involvement the children are likely to have experienced before the remarriage does not carry over very much in the new family constellation; perhaps the stepfather takes over many of their chores. It is

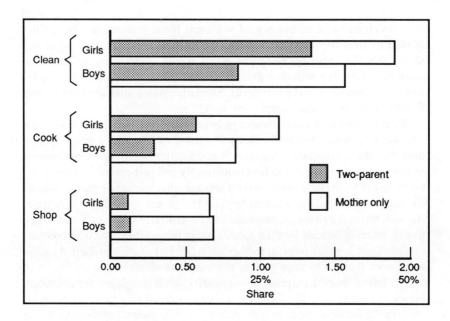

Figure 9.5   Effect of Living in a Mother-Only Family on Sharing "Male" and "Female" Chores with Teenage Sons and Daughters

likely that part of the difference between the effects of mother-only and step-parent families reflects the fact that most children in these stepparent families experienced a shorter period in a mother-only family, and at a much younger age. Data that allow a detailed breakdown of when and how long children were exposed to a mother-only family are needed to see how much of the experience carries over into stepparent families.

We also examined whether the pattern of increased participation in house-hold tasks by boys, established while they were living in a mother-only household, carried over into remarriage. We saw that children in general share more in such households than those living with their natural parents. It turns out this is a general pattern, with few differences by age and sex of children (data not presented). Not only do stepfathers create "Cinderellas," they seem to increase the household contribution of stepsons, as well, so that both are involved in the "extra" work. Stepdaughters are significantly more likely to take responsibility for child care, paralleling the finding in chapter 7 that step-fathers seem less likely to share in the care of small children, even those likely to be theirs. This results in part because their stepdaughters are helping out more. Boys between the ages of 12 and 18 share more in household tasks than younger children in stepfamilies, as they did in mother-only families;

boys with two natural parents do not assume significantly more responsibility when they reach their teens.

The few stepchildren who remain in the household after they become adults, in contrast, do not help out much at all. Unlike adult daughters in mother-only families, otherwise comparable stepdaughters are particularly unlikely to participate in cooking, dishwashing, or shopping for groceries. This pattern also characterizes young adult stepsons, who pitched in when their family was headed only by their mother, but who are very unlikely to share in many tasks—particularly laundry, dishwashing, or household cleaning—when a stepfather is present.

Comparing these three types of families suggests very strongly that the composition of the household has a considerable influence on the exposure of children, and particularly of sons, to household tasks. It may be that women generally try to establish some feeling of teamwork in their approach to housework, but that they generally "team" with a spouse, when one is available. Perhaps women only feel that it is legitimate to divert children from schoolwork to take responsibility for housework when they *feel* they have no one else to turn to.[12] What is clear at this point is that the current period of family disruption, characterized as it is by high proportions of children living at least for some period in mother-only families, is contributing strongly to household competence in men.

Childhood Family Experiences

Does the influence of having lived either in a stepparent or mother-only family as a child persist into the next generation? Does it affect how much mothers and fathers share in household tasks as adults with their own children? Our analysis finds that some small effects linger, but they are not always easy to see, since other factors can obscure them. And our analysis only considers women's experiences, not men's, since only women were asked about sharing household tasks with children.

Women currently heading a family alone share significantly more with their children if they have also had this experience themselves—7 percent on the overall scale (data not shown). Evidently, those women in mother-only families who grew up in nuclear families try to preserve the family dynamics that they knew in childhood and so rely less on their own children for help with housework than do women whose childhood in a mother-only family likely included more responsibility for housework. Further, among married women who are not employed, those whose family experience during their teen years was either of a mother-only or a stepparent family also share more tasks with their children.

These results resemble one that appeared in the analysis of sharing with

husbands (chapter 7), where we found that the wife's childhood family structure only influenced her sharing with her husband when there were no children
present. Evidently, the presence of the respective third party in the three-way
exchange of labor among mothers, fathers, and children serves to blur the
simple intergenerational pattern; children absorb some of the impact on sharing with husbands of their mother's childhood experiences, and husbands absorb the impact on sharing with children. Similarly, women's employment
breaks the intergenerational effect, suggesting that it is important to have time
to supervise the work of young children in order to involve them in useful
ways.

Nonfamily Living
and Sharing with Children

It is also our view that young adults who have had the experience of living
outside a family during young adulthood might change the types of families
they eventually form. We saw that these experiences shift the attitudes, plans,
and expectations of young adults away from traditional family orientations
(chapter 4). Does this experience also affect the incorporation of children into
household tasks? It may be that women with more traditional experiences
of family life share more with daughters as a means of teaching them sex-
traditional skills, while women who have had more independent experiences
may see these skills as less important and require less housework from their
children as a result. Alternatively, such women may simply be more used to
doing things themselves, as we saw occurred in sharing with husbands (chapter 7). Either way, independent living before marriage should reduce sharing
household chores with children.

Consistent with the result for sharing with husbands, we find that women
who did not live independently before marriage share somewhat more with
their children than do those who lived away from home at some point prior
to marriage (fig. 9.6). The women for whom we could observe living arrangements in early adulthood primarily have young children, so their average level
of sharing with children is much less than for the total sample. However, the
mother's experience in living away seems to decrease children's share in
dishwashing (by far the most common task for those with young children),
and to a smaller extent in cooking and housecleaning.

Some effects of family change, then, are leading toward "new families"
in which males and females both learn something about making a home, but
others are leading toward "no families" in which a new generation of children
will grow up even more ignorant of the workings of their own household than
have children in the past. Experiencing childhood family disruption increases
the likelihood that young men will have learned about household tasks by the

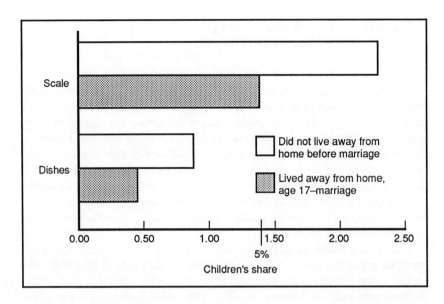

Figure 9.6   Effect of Mothers' Having Lived Away from Home Before Marriage on Children's Share of Household Tasks

time they marry, and our small amount of direct evidence for husbands (chapter 7) indicates that they actually do participate on a more nearly equal basis in running the household. But it is clear that even this experience does not strongly reinforce continuing involvement of children in the workings of the household, since women who remarry and women who experienced family disruption while they were growing up reduce their children's responsibility nearly to the level found in families with no such history. The children's role in the household is peripheral, and, as we will see, is probably becoming increasingly so.

The role of children becomes even more marginal in the families of women who have lived on their own between the time they grew up and marriage. Such women have apparently gained a hard-won independence, and may translate it into a fundamental isolation in the tasks of raising a family. Although we have not yet examined the entire household division of labor, it appears that women who lived in a nonfamily setting are creating a "separate sphere" in their own homes, with less sharing and hence, less interdependence among members of the family. On balance, then, the set of "new family experiences" is having an equivocal effect on the transformation of the home for the next generation of children. This transformation may have to come from other sources, if it is to come at all. In the next sections, we will address whether such changes are likely.

Do Any Factors Augur Change in Children's Household Roles?

A common theme in all the literature on family change is that the home is a central institution in modern society. This would seem to suggest, then, that it is also important to understand whether there are any changes in how each generation is being prepared to manage the home. Yet despite the fact that children take nearly as much responsibility for many household tasks as husbands, we have found little to guide our analyses of how much children share in household tasks. Studies of women's household work only began seriously when the spotlight first fell on them (although never to the extent of the focus on their work in the labor force), but interest in children's work seems to have ended with the passage of child labor laws—*when children's labor vanished into the home*.

For us, this analysis has been an adventure, with so few trails blazed by previous research that it is almost like visiting the dark side of the moon. We looked to see whether there were any differences in how much children share in household tasks by parents' attitudes and values (including sex-role attitudes, and demographic indicators of social contexts such as race, region, community size, and parental education); by the constraints on parents imposed by employment and disability; and by maternal age. We hope that much more research will be done in this area, building on what we and others have done. To this end we offer our results, many of which surprised us when we first saw them, and may surprise others. They suggest that complex forces are operating that are dramatically reducing the extent of children's work in the household, changing what children are doing and which children are getting it done.

Attitudes and Children's Roles in Household Tasks

A wide range of evidence, from studies of school assignments to be done at home to assessments of the number of hours children watch television, shows that children have plenty of *time* to do more chores around the house. How much they actually do, then, depends on how roles and tasks are structured within the family and on what expectations parents set and how willing and able they are to follow through on them. Parental attitudes, then, are important, as well as parental time and energy.

To our knowledge, however, no one has asked parents in any national sample direct questions on their attitudes toward whether and how much children should participate in household tasks. But we expect that those holding more egalitarian attitudes about men's and women's roles generally might share more equally with their sons and daughters and might share more with children altogether. We also thought that group differences in patterns of sharing with children might provide us clues about differences in attitudes, as we discussed in detail in chapter 3. In the analyses that follow, we examine differences in patterns of sharing household tasks with children among those with varying sex-role attitudes, as well as differences by race, region, and city size.

Sex-Role Attitudes.   It was not at all clear to us how measures of sex-role attitudes, which were designed to measure attitudes about *men's and women's* roles in the workplace and in the home (and actually focus much more intensively on women's roles than men's), would relate to sharing household tasks *with children.* Women who are concerned with the importance of the work world would probably rather have anyone else (not themselves) do the housework, and thus might welcome their children's help. However, they may also want their children to be well prepared for that world and so be particularly concerned about taking time away from school responsibilities. They may even feel guilty about denying their children full-time mothering because of their commitment to work outside the home, thus overcompensating by asking little of them (as we saw in chapter 8 was the case in such women's approach to sharing housework with their husbands).

Similarly, traditional women might either involve their children more or less in the tasks of the household. On the one hand, mothers who place a high value on the importance of home-based roles for women might spend more time at home, have higher standards for home maintenance, and so place high demands on their children (and particularly want to train their daughters "appropriately"). On the other hand, what they are saying in their responses to these questions is that they gain tremendous satisfaction from their roles in the home and thus might be less willing to share them. Certainly, as we saw, they were not sharing them with their husbands.

The only clue we can find in the research literature relating sex-role attitudes to children's household tasks is that children do more housework if their mothers are not satisfied with the parental division of labor (White and Brinkerhoff, 1981b). If so, then women with more egalitarian attitudes (and thus less satisfied with their husband's level of sharing) should share more household tasks with their children.

To explore this issue, we examine two general indices of sex-role attitudes (described in detail in Appendix B). One index (FAMILY ROLES) reflects women's views of the importance of their time at home to their children and families. The second (JOB ROLES), measures their feelings about the importance of employment both to their self-esteem and to the economic well-being of their families. A higher score on each of these scales indicates greater acceptance of nonfamilial roles for wives and mothers.

Our results are complex. Women with a modern orientation toward men's and women's roles in the family do involve their children somewhat more, but, as was the case for sharing with husbands, modern attitudes toward women's paid work have an equivocal and often opposite effect. The general picture is that these role indices affect sharing household tasks with children much as they do sharing household tasks with husbands, but a great deal less strongly.

Women who give liberal responses to the FAMILY ROLES questions, who see the home as a less central source of social identity than more traditional women, share more household tasks with their children, as they do with their husbands (fig. 9.7). These women are particularly likely to involve their children in the chores children are usually less involved in—laundry and cooking. Overall, however, differences are not great, since women who are very traditional on the FAMILY ROLES scale share less than three-quarters fewer chores with their children than women who are highly egalitarian—half the effect we found for husband's sharing.[13] Nevertheless, in very modern families, children do 50 percent more cooking and nearly a third more laundry than children in the most traditional families.

Both teenage daughters and teenage sons share more responsibility in families in which mothers hold more egalitarian attitudes on FAMILY ROLES (data not shown). As a result, teenage sons get over a third more responsibility for housework in families with egalitarian mothers than in those with very traditional mothers. This suggests that as such attitudes become more widespread, men will have more competence and confidence with household tasks, based on their experiences as children, and will be that much more able to use their skills to help build a home with their wives.

Nevertheless, the weak or reverse effect of having more liberal attitudes on women's roles in employment (JOB ROLES), which led to *less* sharing with husbands (chapter 8), also appears for sharing household tasks with children, and even more strongly here. Women who value work-related roles for women share less overall, and particularly share less of these same chores— cooking and laundry. This pattern seems to be more intense among younger women, unlike the case for sharing with husbands (data not presented). Since women who hold more modern attitudes on one of these dimensions are also likely to hold modern attitudes on the other (though many do not), the general increase in more egalitarian attitudes may not be having much effect on children.

Indirect Attitude Measures.   As in our other analyses, we wanted to look at all factors that might influence involving children in household tasks. We want to see whether there are other contexts that increase sharing with children, and taking other factors into consideration is also helpful to be sure that

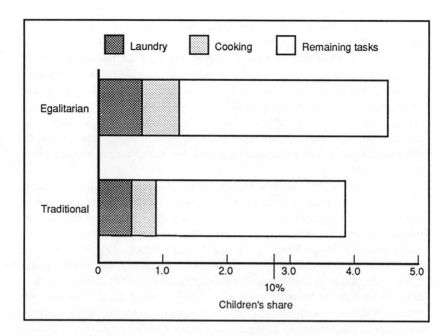

Figure 9.7   Effect of Mothers' Egalitarian Family Role Attitudes on Children's Share of Household Tasks

the results that we see for family structure are not an artifact of leaving out some important influence on household sharing. This could happen if, for example, the differences between those in mother-only families and two-parent families were really a black-white difference (since black families are much more likely to be mother-only). We consider differences by race, region, city size, and educational level, both of mothers and of fathers, where applicable.

First, we find that black families share significantly more responsibility with children for household tasks—21 percent more—than otherwise comparable nonblack families do. Black families involve their children more in common chores, like doing the dishes, but also in more responsible roles, such as grocery shopping and child care. These effects do not arise from the higher prevalence of female-headed families in the black community or from other characteristics of the family that we have held constant; in fact, we found in our analyses that the black-nonblack difference *only* characterizes two-parent families. Black mother-only families are no different from other mother-only families on this dimension: children share more responsibility in all mother-only families.

Hence, we suggest that black families hold different attitudes about children's roles than do comparable white families. We cannot ascertain whether this arises from differences in how families value their children's contribution, how important they feel these specific tasks are for training purposes, or other differences among the many reasons parents give for involving their children. In chapter 8, we also saw that husbands in black families share less in household tasks than comparable white families, at least on traditional "female" chores, so that the mother-child axis is strengthened, in contrast to the husband-wife axis. Understanding these differences in family relationships would seem to be a challenging avenue for further research on the black family.

We also found that families who live in the South share about 15 percent less with children than do families living in other parts of the country, a somewhat smaller difference than that for race. Children in southern families share particularly little in dishwashing and cleaning up, as well as in cooking. The South also had lower levels of sharing with husbands. This suggests that southern women have created a very separate sphere for themselves in the home, with minimal involvement with others in the family. This pattern is likely to have arisen from the lower cost of hiring external labor that has long characterized the South, but southern women may find it difficult to reclaim their family's involvement as the costs of labor rise.[14]

Finally, families share significantly less with their children as the size of the community they live in gets larger (a difference of 18 percent between the smallest and largest places). In part, this reflects a very strong decrease in the amount of yard work shared with children as city size increases, given the smaller size of lots (and greater likelihood of apartment living) in larger places. But more urban children are also significantly less involved in cooking and systematically less responsible for all other tasks, suggesting that larger places may shape a more general orientation that decreases children's participation, rather than being simply a reflection of the difference in the structure of tasks, say, between cities and farms.

Our last indirect measure of attitudes that might relate to sharing with children is education, which we can measure both for mothers and fathers. Husband's education was one of the strongest predictors of *his* involvement in household tasks. However, when we consider its impact on sharing with children we find almost no effect (table 9.2, Appendix C). Children's share in household tasks is almost totally unaffected by differences in the educational levels of their fathers.

Maternal education, in contrast, does influence the participation of children: children's share in household tasks decreases with increases in the number of years of schooling that the mother has completed (table 9.2, Appendix C). Children share about a third of a chore less for every 4 additional years of education she has attained (for example, from high school graduate to college graduate). Children with more educated mothers share less in most chores, particularly yard work and grocery shopping. Highly educated mothers evidently prefer that their children spend time studying algebra or writing their English compositions, rather than on household chores.

Some more highly educated mothers may also want to prepare their sons for domestic independence. There is a general tendency for more educated mothers to share less with their daughters but to share more with their sons (fig. 9.8). Among teenage children, the girls do less cooking if their mothers have a high level of education, but boys do somewhat more, so that teenage girls do only a third more cooking than teenage boys if their mothers have a postgraduate education, compared with nearly twice as much (80 percent) in families with more poorly educated mothers.

The male-female similarity is also marked among young adults living with highly educated mothers. For example, in these families grown daughters do somewhat less dishwashing than those whose mothers have less education, but grown sons do much more, reaching nearly the level of their sisters. Gender parity is less evident in laundry, although again greater at higher levels of maternal education than low. This finding for laundry is particularly interesting, since it is the only chore in which more educated mothers share more with adult children than less educated mothers do. But in no case is the level of sharing very high.

Despite the fact that we have no data on change over time in children's participation in household tasks, it is difficult to escape the interpretation that it must have declined, perhaps substantially. It is generally the case that family patterns that relate strongly to educational level and size of place are responding to the broad social trend loosely called "modernization," which encompasses the network of factors influenced by economic and social development. Increases in urbanization and education have had strong effects on family and demographic processes, leading to declines in fertility and mortality and increases in divorce and migration levels.

Hence, our finding that families with more education and those living in more urban places share less with children makes it unlikely that children have become *more* rather than less involved in household tasks over the twentieth century, which has seen dramatic increases in educational levels and in urban living; quite the contrary. This interpretation is reinforced by considering that most black women in this sample are at least one or even two generations closer to a rural life than nonblack women, given that blacks remained in the South for most of the early period of urbanization. Further, those who moved north during the 1930s and 1940s remained close to kin in the South, frequently sending children back to grandparents for extended periods of time (Cromartie and Stack, 1989). This indicates that the greater sharing of black families can also be expected to be transient.

The South, which has been shown to be rather "traditional" in male-female relationships (chapter 8), seems to be an exception to the simple generaliza-

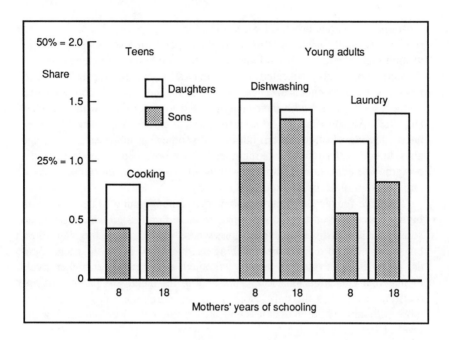

Figure 9.8 Effect of Mothers' Education on Sharing Tasks with Teenagers and Young Adults

tion that "modernization" reduces the role of children in household tasks, since children in the South share less, rather than more in household duties. But whether this has resulted from an ultradomestic definition of women's roles in the South or because the ready availability of cheap labor in this area made them actually move "ahead" in the transformation of the ideal child's role to one of exclusive preparation for the future (and hence, current "uselessness"), it seems more likely that the North will become more like the South on this dimension rather than that the South will become more like the North. Even the "modernization" of family attitudes seems to be having at best an equivocal affect on increasing the involvement of children in household tasks.

There is, however, one major social trend that we have not yet considered, which may be strongly contributing to children's domestic education. The few analyses of children's participation in household tasks have focused on whether the children of working women take up some of the slack as their mothers increase their time away from the household. This factor has so far been controlled in our analysis; we have looked at sharing with children independent of how much mothers (and fathers) are employed outside the home. What do we find? The next section considers this issue in detail.

Parental Time and Resources

Since household tasks take time, we included measures of the availability of parents for household work. For each, we consider the number of hours spent on the job and also the presence of a health disability. For mothers, we consider as well simply being employed, following the same reasoning we tested in the analysis of husband's household participation: that *the fact* of being a working mother (in this case) might shift the roles of children in the household, increasing their participation in order to "help out," whatever the actual number of hours their mother is working.

Women who hold jobs outside the home share with single parents a relative lack of time—both to do housework themselves and to supervise their children while they do it. Much of the research on the impact of mothers' employment on children's role in the family division of labor finds a positive effect; however, it seems to be relatively modest and also to depend on how much the mother works (Roy, 1961; Propper, 1972; Cogle and Tasker, 1982; Timmer, Eccles, and O'Brien, 1985). But since employed mothers reduce their own time in housework, children of employed mothers might nevertheless increase *their share* considerably relative to children whose mothers remain at home, even if they spend little more time on household chores, similar to the dynamic that appears to operate for husbands' labor time at home when the wife works.

In our analysis, however, we find little evidence that mothers' employment has much, if any, effect on the extent to which children share in household tasks. If she decreases her involvement in household tasks when she takes a job outside the home, so, too, do her children. In this analysis, neither the fact of maternal employment nor the number of hours worked has a significant effect either on the overall level children share in household chores, or for any particular chore (table 9.2, Appendix C).

We were concerned with this result, since it varied from effects found in other studies. Although these other studies found weak results, our analysis has tended to be successful at distinguishing even very small differences (for example, the effect of wife's income on how much husbands share, reported in chapter 7). When we examined the issue of mothers' employment more closely, we found that we could generate a significant (but weak) effect of the single variable "employed" if we transformed our dependent variable logarithmically (data not shown). What this means is that in families in which children do *very little* household work, maternal employment does lead to an increase in the children's share, but among families in which children contribute moderately or more, there is much less effect. Hence, mothers' employment, per se, is not having an effect on children's sharing beyond the most minimal level.[15]

We looked more closely to see if other dimensions of the mother's employment affected the children's share in household tasks. We reasoned that greater earnings could allow mothers to buy substitutes for their own and their children's labor, while mothers who earned relatively little would need more assistance from their children. However, table 9.2 in Appendix C shows that children's contributions do not increase—or decrease—with the women's income, suggesting that if women use their earnings to hire help with housework, this help substitutes proportionately for their own time and their children's. (This was also the case with the husband's earnings, which had no effect on the extent to which children share in household tasks.)

As we puzzled over the weak-to-nonexistent effect of maternal employment, we thought about what it might mean. We wondered whether employed mothers' greater need for help with the housework, on the one hand, might be balanced in some fashion by their greater difficulty in supervising children's chores, on the other. If so, this might shift *who* is doing the helping from younger to older children, even while having no overall effect on the extent of children's sharing.

This is the case. Teenage daughters of employed mothers share significantly more than do teenage daughters of mothers at home and teenage sons do more, as well; younger children do considerably less. But there is no shift in the sex composition of tasks, as figure 9.9 shows, since the daughters are doing more cooking, as well as other "female" tasks, while the sons are taking more responsibility for chores related to yard and home maintenance.

Yet the young adult daughters of employed mothers do significantly *less* cleaning and dishes than those whose mothers are at home (data not presented). This may reflect their own greater likelihood of being employed, an issue we do not explore in detail here. Overall, then, employed mothers differ little from other mothers in sharing tasks with their children because while they are sharing more with their teenage children, they are sharing less both with their younger children and with their young adult children.

In contrast to these effects for women's employment, the number of hours their *husbands* work does influence children's participation in housework systematically, both overall and for many tasks. The more hours their father works, the more children take responsibility for dishwashing, cleaning up, and yard work (see table 9.2 in Appendix C). These results suggest that when it comes to the *relative availability* of the two parents, children substitute for their fathers, not their mothers. Fathers help out if they have time. Mothers evidently find the time for housework, even if they work many hours outside the home.[16]

Children do, however, pitch in if their mother is disabled, and to about the same extent as when their father is disabled (see table 9.2, Appendix C). If either parent has a health condition that limits the amount or kind of work they can do, their children share more household responsibility than if there were no limitation. They particularly chip in on the cooking (40 percent more)

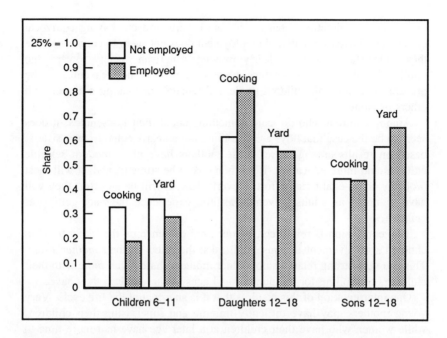

Figure 9.9   Effect of Mothers' Employment on Sharing Tasks with Older and Younger Children

and the laundry (35 percent more) if it is their mother who is disabled. Disabled fathers increase children's sharing primarily in yard work (nearly 60 percent more) and grocery shopping (by 45 percent).

But children whose mothers report some limitation are *less likely* to share in yard work. This result appeared for husbands, as well (in chapter 8). This suggests that for mothers, involving children in yard work requires active supervision, while fathers' tasks are more easily delegated to a child working alone. It may also be that men are more likely to do yard work because it is sex-role appropriate—they have to; if they cannot, others are assigned. But women who work in the yard probably do so because they *enjoy* it, and when they become less able to continue it, find it easier than other household tasks to be contracted out to others outside the household, reducing the involvement of everyone.

How are Families Changing?

On the basis of these indirect indicators of change in children's household participation, it is difficult to escape the conclusion that it must have declined substantially. Trends in education and urbanization would seem to point clearly in this direction, changes in family structure are having equivocal effects, and increased maternal employment does not seem to counterbalance these. One factor that is clearly moving American society toward "no families" as the twentieth century draws to a close is the weakening of the preparation among all children (male and female) for making a home, with others or alone.

Among children who do learn something about their households, it does seem to be the case that boys are becoming more nearly equal to their sisters, based on results among those whose mothers have more modern sex-role attitudes and more education. If the home is to be strengthened, it will most probably be an egalitarian effort. Nevertheless, it will be an effort they will have to begin as adults, given how little experience they are getting as children.

This conclusion is reinforced by our final evidence on the likely trend in children's involvement in household tasks: the effect of their *mother's age*. This is a very strong relationship—older mothers share much more with their children, controlling for the number and ages of the children they have.

One interpretation of this result is that it is an effect of the life cycle. Very young mothers may have difficulty training and supervising their children, while women who have their children at a later age have had more time to develop these skills. The alternative explanation is that there are real declines underway in the extent children share in household chores—meaning that what older mothers are doing reflects patterns of sharing with children that younger mothers are not following, so that there is a strong trend toward reducing children's involvement in making the homes they are growing up in. We very much wanted to distinguish between these two possibilities, since they have important implications for the interpretation of our results.

First, we looked to see whether there were any differences either in which chores are being shared or in the sex patterns of sharing as clues for distinguishing these interpretations. We found much greater differences with mother's age for some chores than others. There are almost no differences in the extent children share in dishwashing and yard work by the age of their mother, but differences are greater for cooking, greater still for laundry, and most for household cleaning. It is not easy to come up with a life-cycle interpretation of these patterns, in which younger mothers find dishwashing easier to supervise than cleaning up. These chores seem instead to suggest that increasingly, children are doing little more around the house than dishwashing and yard work, getting less and less experience in other areas of homemaking.

We also found that differences with mothers' age in the ways they share tasks with sons and daughters are more plausibly related to "real" patterns of change over time than to the mother's greater maturity with age. Younger women are sharing less with their children, but even less with their daughters;

the effect of age is much weaker for sons, as figure 9.10 indicates. The overall decline in sharing chores with teenage children amounted to more than half a chore between mothers of teenage children who were about age 57, who bore these children in their late thirties and early forties, compared with 37-year-old mothers, who had borne their children in their late teens and early twenties. But the comparable drop for teenage girls was nearly three quarters of a chore, while for teenage boys, it was considerably less than half a chore.

This means that the "greater experience" interpretation, in which women become more able to supervise their children with age, is having more effect on their daughters than on their sons. Whereas among the children of older mothers, teenage girls share 41 percent more responsibility for household tasks than teenage boys, among those with young mothers, teenage girls only share 28 percent more responsibility. This result makes the alternative interpretation of change over time even more plausible, particularly since it resembles the effects we saw earlier for maternal education, in which the "trend" is toward less sharing with children, but greater equality.

Conclusions

We began this analysis of children's sharing of household tasks with the expectation that traditional family experiences—growing up in a family headed by the child's own parents and remaining there until marriage—might beget traditional families, while those with some exposure to the world outside the highly sex-segregated two-parent family would take a more creative stance to the problem of equity in the division of family responsibilities. We are also concerned that children's experiences in the home will affect the families they later form. Our analysis in this chapter suggests that few families are reacting in ways that include children. Parents are not preparing them for more egalitarian homes in the future—or even for living alone prior to or between marriages.

This is despite the fact that it is in mother-only families where children—both daughters and sons—play the greatest role in the household, assuming high levels of responsibility on a wide range of tasks. But this effect seems to wear off rapidly, at least in the homes of women who have had this experience, and we must wait for better data to get a fairer evaluation of how these experiences are affecting men. When we focus on the characteristics and attitudes of the mother, we find that "new experiences" and "new attitudes" are leading toward a definition of the child's role in the home that excludes regular responsibilities for more than a very narrow range of tasks.

If we take our age results literally, holding constant the other characteristics of families, our estimates lead us to predict that children have reduced their involvement in household tasks by the equivalent of approximately half

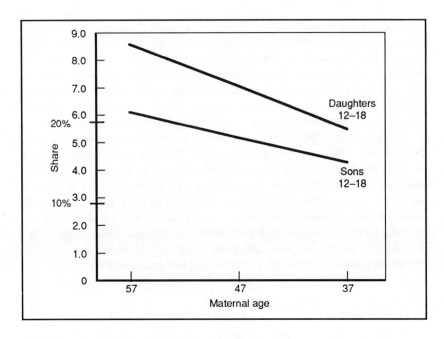

Figure 9.10   Effect of Mothers' Age on Sharing Household Tasks with Teenage Sons and Daughters

a complete chore every 20 years. And if we assume that over time, as the women in our sample who were educated during the Depression and World War II are replaced by younger women who have achieved considerably more education, this level will go down further. And as even fewer families have rural backgrounds, exposed to a strong tradition of children's involvement in the work of the household, even greater changes can be expected.

At present, despite the few signs of change we saw, the home is still very much a "gender factory." Daughters, particularly teenage daughters, take a great deal of responsibility for household tasks, while older daughters mostly continue to help, shifting as they mature (and get their driver's license) to tasks outside the household such as grocery shopping and child care, perhaps chauffeuring their younger siblings around. Boys contribute very little to household chores, participating only in yard work and only as teenagers and are mostly exempt from any contribution whatsoever when they reach adulthood.

Families seem to be recognizing increasingly that imposing heavy domestic responsibilities on daughters will not be appropriate for them when they become women, as women's roles outside the home have become more important, and hence are reducing their effort to prepare them for an adult role of housewife. But there is much less evidence that boys are being prepared even for independent living, much less for helping their wives shape "new families" in the next generation. Parents still seem to want their children to marry and have families (Thornton, 1990). But while they probably want their *daughters* to marry liberated men, who will share in the housework so that these daughters can be successful, they are preparing their *sons* to marry traditional women, who will carry the household burden themselves to further their son's career. They are not yet ready to prepare their sons for someone else's ambitious daughter.

10

The Domestic Economy: Husbands, Wives, and Children

For the last three chapters, we have focused our analysis closely on what is happening in the home, on what might lead to more sharing of household tasks between husbands and wives, and on what increases or decreases the involvement of their children, particularly their sons, in those tasks. We wanted to know whether the home is likely to become more egalitarian, as has happened in the workplace, perhaps making marital and parental roles more attractive to modern working women and their daughters, thus clearing the way for "new families." We looked at children to see whether boys—or any children—are learning the necessary skills for making a home.

The results made it clear that husbands make a significant contribution to household tasks, and that children share in important ways, though primarily daughters, not sons. However, we have not examined the family economy as a whole, including wives, husbands, and children as potential workers. For in addition to focusing on what husbands and children do, it is important to study how they are trading off with each other and with their wives and mothers. Most tasks can be done, at least in part, by children or by either parent. And the amount that needs to be done by any family member depends on how much the others are already doing. The vast majority of studies of husband-wife sharing exclude the role of children and are seriously incomplete; the few studies on children's role in the household may also have missed something important by not including the extent of the husband's share.[1]

Historically, it is not at all clear what sort of patterns have characterized the domestic economy as a whole, or how they have been changing. We know that most families did not *hire* domestic help.[2] And few had access to grannies and maiden aunts to help with chores. In the United States throughout its history, most families have been nuclear (Laslett, 1973; Ruggles, 1987).

It seems likely that until the nineteenth century (as on family farms today), men, women, and children worked hard around the household, doing the tasks defined for them. Our own results on children's share in household labor suggest strongly that children participated in home-based chores much more in the relatively recent past than they do now (chapter 9). We speculate that this decline is the result of relatively recent changes in parental attitudes toward childhood, emphasizing its role in preparation for adult roles *only outside* the household.

In the 1980s husbands have become increasingly involved in housework (chapter 2). This raises the possibility that wives can expect some relief from the double burden of paid and household work they have borne since the rapid increases in married women's employment began during and after World War II. But it is also possible that a quite different restructuring of the family is underway. When *men's* roles expanded in the world outside the home, wives substituted for their contributions, taking on many traditional male tasks around the house (including lawn care, snow shoveling, automobile and appliance maintenance, and child discipline)—without necessarily changing children's share of domestic tasks.

It may now be that fathers are taking their children's share, without necessarily relieving their wives. If this is so, then the increased involvement of husbands is making marriages more egalitarian, as husband and wife share more equally both in earning and homemaking. But the decreased participation of children in housework will make having a family *with children* more burdensome for parents, reducing their willingness to rear them. And it will further weaken the next generation's skills and ability for making homes of their own.

In the results of our prior analyses of husbands' and children's sharing, in which we did not take into account the other's contribution, we noticed evidence of many such trade-offs. Nontraditional family experiences in childhood, such as living in a mother-only family or in a remarried family, increased sharing with children but decreased it with husbands; we saw the same pattern for black families. The wife's education increased sharing with husbands and decreased it with children and we speculated that these results suggested exactly such a trade-off—that more educated families were reincorporating men at the expense of children.

But we also saw instances in which important factors were having similar influences both on husbands' and on children's sharing. Women with more modern attitudes about their role in the family reported greater sharing with both husbands and children, as did women who either were disabled themselves or had a disabled spouse. And we wondered if there were not other situations that led to a greater involvement among all members of the family, a greater sense of mutual participation on the "household team."

It also seems likely that many factors might influence the division between husbands and wives, but not affect children, or that would affect children's involvement, but not husbands'. The *reasons* for involving husbands and children in household tasks differ substantially. Presumably wives attempt to involve their husbands in the domestic economy to have a sense of equity and teamwork, and to get the work done. But few *parents* give this response about children's help around the house, justifying their children's participation more in terms of "character development."[3]

We found that a woman's earnings increased her husbands' sharing, and suggested, consistent with previous research literature, that by increasing her earnings, she had also increased her relative power in the relationship and was thus able to use her earnings to induce her spouse's participation. We found no effect of a mother's earnings on her children's sharing, and were not surprised by that result, since the power gradient in parent-child relationships is not usually attributed to the parties' differential earning capabilities, and we thought that perhaps her earnings might be used to hire help that would relieve them all. In this chapter, we can test these interpretations directly.

Measuring Sharing
Household Labor in the Family

Our analyses use data from the National Longitudinal Surveys of Young Women and Mature Women (see chapter 3).[4] Since the focus here is on tradeoffs *among* men, women, and children, we restrict the sample to those families eligible to share across all three categories. Thus, the sample for the analyses reported consists of married women with at least one child in the household who is over the age of 5 and under the age of 19.[5] As before, the families may include children older than 18 or younger than 6, but must have at least one child old enough to share housework and not yet be an adult.

We use the same information on how families share household tasks in the early 1980s as in the previous chapters. Women were asked about 8 household tasks ranging from grocery shopping to family paperwork. For each, they reported whether they shared the task with anyone else and how much responsibility that person took for the task. Appendix B describes the questions on division of household labor and the measures that we created from them.[6] We will focus primarily on a summary measure of 5 of these tasks shared among husbands, wives, and children. These chores are the predominately "female" jobs of dishwashing, laundry, housecleaning, cooking, and grocery shopping, the same set that was used for the analysis of husbands' sharing. Where appropriate, we will consider factors influencing sharing on these specific chores, as well as on the others included in the interview.

Our scales were created from these items by summing the extent of responsibility for each chore. We followed the same procedure to create scales of sharing with husbands and with children. The resulting scales each had a possible range from 0, if the wife reported no sharing on any of the 5 tasks, to 20, if she reported either that her children or her husband takes complete responsibility for all 5 tasks. In most families, the wife reports only modest amounts of sharing with both husband and children, but some families distribute chores more equally than others.

How Do Families Divide Household Tasks?

Wives report that they have the largest share of responsibility for most of the chores we examined. Their estimate is that their share is around 80 percent for laundry, shopping, and cooking; and around two-thirds for housecleaning, dishwashing, child care, and family paperwork. Only for tasks associated with yard work and household maintenance do women claim less than half of the responsibility (40 percent) (fig. 10.1).[7] Overall, the husband's share is larger than the children's, which is the case for 5 of the 8 tasks, except for dishwashing, housecleaning, and laundry, in which the children's share is reported to be larger.[8]

Very few women report much involvement of other kin or hired help in household tasks; in almost all cases, they report either always performing a task alone or sharing it with their husband or children. Women are no more likely to report that other kin help with child care than they are to report such help with cooking or dishwashing, suggesting that few working mothers in this sample turn to their extended family for day care. And paid help with yard work is rarely reported.

The only chore that is more commonly shared with paid outsiders is housecleaning. (Four percent of the women report some sharing with paid help, but since women also do a lot of cleaning, the paid total only reaches 2 percent.) These patterns reassured us that it was reasonable to focus on the triangle of spouses and their children as the basic team for our analysis, confident that our results really reflect variation in children versus fathers, and not the effects of hiring outside workers.[9]

Children Versus Husbands

Do families substitute the household labor of husbands for children? Or do households with more contribution from husbands also involve their chil-

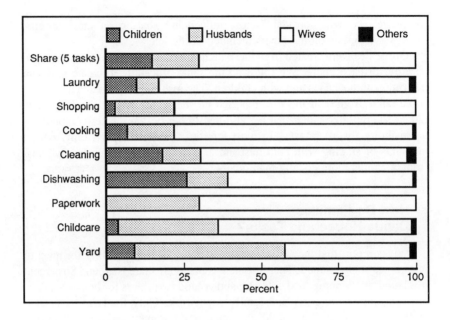

Figure 10.1   Sharing Responsibility for Household Tasks

dren more, thus reducing the wife's share? Given the fact that children and husbands participate in housework at relatively low levels (chapters 7 and 9), families have much more leeway to reduce the amount of housework done by the wife/mother than they do to reduce the already low amount done by husbands or children.

Our results show that families appear to treat husbands as substitutes for children, but to treat children as substitutes for the wife (fig. 10.2).[10] Each additional task performed by the husband reduces the children's contribution by nearly one task (87 percent). Apparently the wife gets very modest relief from her mate's efforts on housework. He reduces the tasks that need to be done, and so children are not called on to do them; but the wife still does the rest. The factors that lead to high levels of husbands' sharing are likely to lead, therefore, to lower levels of children's sharing.

This is much less the case for factors influencing children's sharing. Each task done by children decreases the husband's participation in domestic chores by only about a sixth of 1 task; for every 6 additional tasks children do, husbands do only 1 fewer. These results suggest that when children take over housework they take over chores that would otherwise be done by their mother, or not get done at all.[11] But the work done by fathers appears to lighten the children's load almost on a one-for-one basis, and to reduce the wife's responsibility only very modestly.

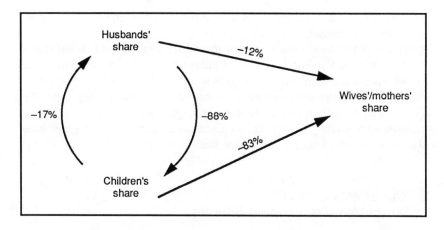

Figure 10.2   The Effects of Sharing by Husbands and Children on the Household Division of Labor

This result could have important implications for our understanding of the factors influencing the extent to which children share. It opens the possibility that the results that we have interpreted in terms of mother-child relationships could simply reflect variation in husband-wife relationships, since the influence of variation in men's sharing is felt so strongly on their children's share. This is much less likely for our results on husbands' sharing, since they are relatively unaffected by variation in the overall involvement of their children. In both cases, however, we will carefully consider how stable our previous results are when viewed in this new format.[12]

This substitution of fathers for children also complicates our understanding of the results we present here. When we examine the effects of, say, a woman's remarriage on the extent to which her children share in household tasks, we will see that the effect can operate through two pathways: its direct effect on how much children share, *independent of how much their new husbands share*; and its indirect effect on the husband's share, which in turn affects the children's share as a result.

The only substantive change in our understanding of the ways fathers and children trade off their shares of household tasks appears for teenage daughters (table 10.1, Appendix C). This result also nicely illustrates the complexities of this more complete view of the household. We saw earlier that married men living with older (young adult) daughters shared less in household tasks (chapter 8, fig. 8.6). In the present analysis, this is also the case, but only because of the effect of the presence of older daughters on the average amount that children in general share and the effect of the children's share on the husband's share. Therefore young adult daughters have an indirect effect on the husband's share. When we take this effect into account, the presence of an older daughter has little direct effect on the involvement of their fathers in household tasks.

This result is most clearly seen in the analysis of separate chores (table 10.2, Appendix C). For no chore do husbands significantly decrease their contribution when there are teenage girls in the family, once the overall effect of children's contributions to these chores is taken into account (with the single exception of child care). In fact, men significantly *increase* their share of household cleaning when living with a teenage daughter, even though these daughters are also taking a substantial share.

The Effects of Family Structure on Household Sharing

The focus on the family as a unit is particularly helpful for understanding how young people's experiences outside a stable two-parent family might influence the balance of sharing household tasks. These experiences—whether in mother-only or stepparent families, in living independently prior to marriage, or in divorce and remarriage as adults—affect all family roles. The absence of a father or the presence of a stepfather shapes children's experiences of family roles, while parents who remarry experience shifts in both marital and parental roles. And nonfamily living takes young people out of the role of child, leaving them in their own homes with no family roles at all. But to see what these effects are requires that we study them together.

Stepfather Families

The analysis of the effects of family structure on household sharing is particularly challenging because these effects have been changing, generally leading to more, rather than less, household sharing. This is certainly the case for stepfamilies. On average, and particularly in families with older wives, children generally share more and husbands less in stepfamilies, in housecleaning, dishwashing, and child care. This finding is consistent with the conclusions of chapter 9, in which children in mother-only families assume higher levels of household responsibilities than children in two-parent families, so that patterns established during the period of single-parenthood might well carry over when the mother remarried. Stepfathers have responded by withdrawing from the domestic scene more than otherwise comparable fathers, with a level of sharing only 88 percent of that of biological fathers,[13] thereby increasing children's responsibility by 5 percent. The net effect for women is that the wife shares fewer of the household tasks with her family when she has remarried.

However, this pattern does not characterize the youngest wives. For them, remarriage appears to increase the extent of sharing with husbands, although not significantly so (table 10.3, Appendix C). This suggests to us that as remarriage has become more common, the difficulties that remarried couples have faced on this issue have been eliminated.

Childhood Family Structure

In chapter 7 we observed a similar pattern, in which a new family experience was leading to more, rather than less, sharing among the youngest wives. In that case, it was the effect of experiencing a mother-only household growing up that was changing, and it led to sharing more with husbands among young wives, while older women shared less. In chapter 9, we found that the mother's experiences growing up in a nontraditional family consistently increased the children's role in housework. Putting these two results together suggests that a woman with some experience outside a stable two-parent family shares somewhat more with both her husband (about 4 percent) and particularly her children (10 percent). Differences are particularly marked for clothes washing, housecleaning, and grocery shopping (predicted from table 10.1, Appendix C).

Nonfamily Living

We examined the impact of having lived independently during young adulthood on the family allocation of labor, using the subset of the NLS Young Women for whom we can construct complete histories of living arrangements from age 17 onward, as described in Appendix B. For these young women, we looked at the proportion of the years since age 17 that they lived away from the parental home in college dormitories, apartments, by themselves, or with roommates. Such independent living has a dramatic impact on young women's attitudes and plans about future families (chapter 4), on their likelihood of marriage (chapter 5), and on the timing of parenthood within marriage (chapter 6). We wanted to see if it also affects the division of labor in the families they themselves form.

Our results show relatively weak effects of independent living, but the effect is the opposite of what we found in the separate analyses: living outside a family setting before marriage *increases* sharing with both children and husbands (table 10.3, Appendix C). This effect emerges because any factor that increases the husband's share decreases the children's share, and vice versa. Once both effects are controlled, the underlying positive effect of nonfamily living on increasing sharing shows clearly. In terms of separate chores, nonfamily living significantly increased children's sharing in cleaning and laundry, although it reduces the extent to which children share in shopping (table 10.4, Appendix C).[14]

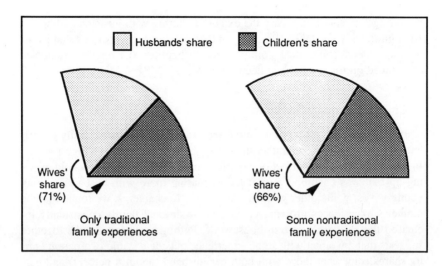

Figure 10.3 Effect of Young Wives' Nontraditional Family Experiences on the Household Divison of Labor

Young People's New Family Experiences

Reviewing the effects of family structure and living arrangements on sharing household tasks with husbands and children over the last several chapters shows a mixed picture. Some of these experiences appear to lead to more sharing and some to less, depending in part on whether all family members are included in the analysis, or whether the focus is solely on husbands or on children. In this analysis, however, in which we consider husbands, wives, and children simultaneously, all the results point in the same direction. At least for young women in their late twenties and early thirties, the new experiences of mother-only or stepfamilies in childhood, of nonfamily living in young adulthood, and of remarriage as an adult increase sharing both with husbands and children, although in each case the differences were small.

Because of the consistency in the patterns, we decided to combine our analyses of these separate experiences, in order to show how much of a difference family change is making. Taken together, more than half the young women whom we could follow for 15 years into adulthood starting at ages 14–17 in 1968 had had one or more of these new experiences. In figure 10.4 we show that these experiences make an important difference in household sharing, increasing husbands' sharing by 22 percent and children's sharing by 13 percent.[15]

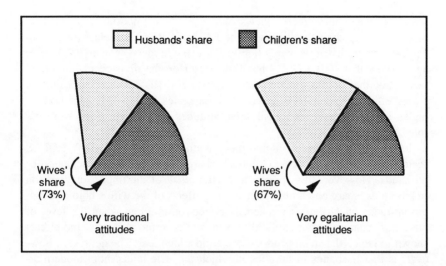

Figure 10.4   Effect of Attitudes About Women's Family Roles on the Household Division of Labor

Hence, it appears that new family experiences were having a mixed or negative effect on household sharing among the women who pioneered them, particularly among those who experienced parental divorce (when few of their peers had known that experience) or who themselves were divorcing and remarrying (when this was still rare). But as these experiences have become more common, they are leading to greater family cohesion, at least in terms of increasing sharing in the household division of labor.

It seems unlikely that the experiences themselves have changed. Rather, the very different contexts in which they are taking place are likely to be affecting young people's *attitudes* toward these experiences. At the time when most were experiencing traditional families, those with new family experiences may have felt strange and isolated, forming attitudes toward family roles that emphasized independence. But as such experiences have become more common, shared by peers and marriage partners, they no longer impede communication and interdependence, and instead can lead to increased sharing.

Attitudes and the Household Division of Labor

Overall, many of the patterns we saw in previous chapters repeat themselves in this one. Our two measures of sex-role attitudes, the JOB ROLES scale (focusing on women's views of the practical importance of work to themselves and their families) and the FAMILY ROLES scale, which indicates the centrality of women's family roles (the home as women's "place"), again show that JOB ROLES has little effect on the division of household labor, but that holding modern attitudes on FAMILY ROLES has quite a strong effect. (Appendix B describes these scales in detail, but for both, a higher score indicates more egalitarian attitudes toward men's and women's roles.)

In our earlier analyses, holding modern attitudes on the FAMILY ROLES scale had a weaker effect on children's sharing than for the participation of husbands. However, this appears to be the result of the impact of variation in husbands' share on children. The strong effects of the wife's holding modern attitudes *on husbands* weaken its effects on children when the level of husbands' sharing is not explicitly taken into account. Actually, the effects shown in table 10.1 in Appendix C are almost identical. The net result, however, is that husbands in families in which the wife holds more modern attitudes[16] share 44 percent more than husbands in families with traditional wives; children only increase their level of sharing by 5 percent. These increases by both husbands and children relieve women of some of the household burden, but not dramatically—even wives with very modern attitudes carry 86 percent of the share of very traditional wives (see fig. 10.5). Nevertheless, the effects on the involvement in housework of both husbands and children are substantial. The chores that are most likely to be shared are laundry, dishwashing, and housecleaning (table 10.2, Appendix C). On the other chores—cooking, child care, and yard work—it is primarily husbands who are drawn in by wives with relatively modern attitudes. Only sharing grocery shopping and paperwork remains unaffected by family-related sex-role attitudes.

Holding more modern attitudes about women's role in paid employment, in contrast, has much less effect, influencing the participation of husbands (but not children) in a limited and somewhat equivocal way. In families in which wives hold more liberal attitudes on JOB ROLES, husbands increase their responsibility for cooking, but *reduce* their responsibility for yard work (table 10.2, Appendix C). Perhaps, a wife with a strong job commitment needs to relieve her husband's domestic responsibilities to some extent, and "make it up to him" by taking on one of "his" responsibilities.

Turning to our three less direct measures of tastes—race, region, and community size—we again see many of our previous findings reinforced. In figure 10.5, we see that children in black two-parent families share significantly more (30 percent) than children in white families, while southern children share significantly less, only 85 percent of the level of children living elsewhere. There are fewer differences among husbands by race or region.

Black children also take much more responsibility than comparable white

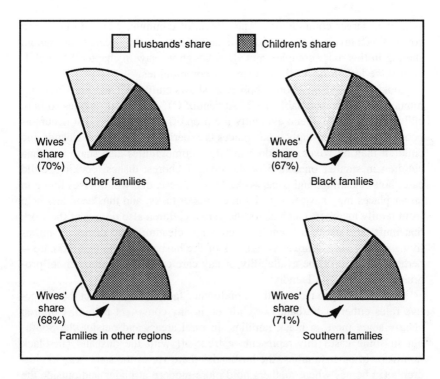

Figure 10.5   Racial and Regional Differences in the Household Division of Labor

children for every single task except grocery shopping (table 10.2, Appendix C). Black families may differ from white families in their division of household labor because of their long experience with mother-only families and poverty. We have seen that mother-only families incorporate children more into the division of household labor than do others (chapter 9). And although neither mothers' nor fathers' earnings appeared in that analysis to influence children's share in household labor, it seems unlikely that this was the case in the past. So black experiences might increase sharing with children, regardless of the situation the family faces itself, by establishing norms and ideals that affect behavior.

In contrast, families who live in the South assign substantially less responsibility to children for housework than those in other regions of the country (table 10.1, Appendix C). Southern husbands' comparatively lower share of housework may account for the lowered fertility expectations of southern women (chapter 4). Although their mothers have had more access to outside cleaning help (see footnote 8), young southern women evidently expect not to have such help and to carry a greater burden themselves.

The household responsibilities of husbands and children are consistently smaller in larger communities. The effects of community size do not reach conventional levels of statistical significance for the overall scale of household sharing in this more complex model, although we saw in chapter 9 that children share less in larger than in smaller communities.[17]

Looking at separate chores, however, shows children sharing less as community size increases (table 10.2, Appendix C). One result applies to both children and their fathers: evidently the drop off in yard work that occurs as people live in increasingly urban places is experienced more by husbands and children than by wives. Children in larger communities also share less than children in smaller ones in 5 of the other 7 chores: dishes, cooking, child care, housecleaning, and paperwork. This suggests that while wives living in larger places may have fewer of some sorts of tasks, and thus need less help from family members (such as for the yard), children also do less of the work that must be done in all families—cooking, cleaning, and dishes. Families living in large urban areas assign less of the husband's time to child care— perhaps because of the availability of day care centers and after-school programs—and more to laundry.

We have seen, so far, that these preference factors do not affect the respective roles either of husbands or children in any consistent pattern. Children clearly share more in black families, in rural areas, and outside the South, but in some cases this represents a trade-off with the husband (in black families). In other families, the husbands' share varies the same way as children's (in homes where mothers hold more modern attitudes and outside the South). Community size, however, seems to have little effect on how much husbands share in household tasks.

The black pattern is clearly distinctive. However, our results for region of the country and sex-role attitudes suggest a trend toward greater household sharing: as the traditional patterns associated with the South and with attitudes reinforcing sex-segregated roles in the home weaken, women can expect greater sharing of their domestic tasks with their husbands and children. But the other result, for community size, suggests that the trend toward urbanization has deprived women of their children's help, at least, if not their husbands'. How do the effects of parental education fit into this picture?

Recall that we found in chapters 8 and 9 that more highly educated spouses seemed to share more between themselves and less with children than did families in which the husband and wife had less schooling. Our results here reinforce this finding. Husbands share more in families in which either the husband or the wife has more education, although the husband's education has a considerably greater effect than the wife's, increasing his participation substantially in all chores. The wife's education further increases her spouse's contribution to washing dishes and child care.

The primary effect of increased male education on the children's share is indirect, since a greater husbands' share reduces the children's share. Highly educated husbands appear particularly to replace their children in cooking and child care (although their children take more responsibility for yard work and home maintenance than others). Maternal education has a stronger effect on reducing the children's participation: the more schooling the mother has received, the less she shares grocery shopping, child care, housecleaning, yard work, and paperwork with children (and the less she shares yard work and paperwork with her *husband*).

In figure 10.6, we show the power of higher education in trading off the shares of fathers and children. In families in which both parents are highly educated,[18] the husbands' share of household tasks is 80 percent greater than in families in which the parents have only completed grammar school. In contrast, children in highly educated families share only 68 percent of the level of children in poorly educated families. Thus it is clear that most of the effect of increasing education has been to shift *who* is helping the wife/mother; *her* share decreases, but only slightly (from 71 percent to 67 percent of all housework). To the extent that the growth in household sharing exhibited by husbands in recent years is the result of increases in education, then, it is not at all clear that women have gained much relief from their double burden; their husbands have basically substituted for the share previously taken by children.

We also tested to see whether children's own participation became less sex segregated in families with higher parental education, and found this to be the case, although some of the patterns differed, depending on whether we were considering fathers' or mothers' education. There was a general tendency for more of the benefit to be felt by teenage girls than by teenage boys, primarily because their level of sharing is so much higher. There is even some indication that in families in which it is the mother with high education, teenage boys actually participate more in dishwashing, cooking, and cleaning (data not presented).

Thus, children in more educated families *observe* greater sharing in household tasks between men and women. But they *participate* much less in these tasks than children in families in which parents have less education. The increase in egalitarianism in more educated families, then, provides children with more positive role models for egalitarian families of their own, but this may also mean that neither gender will come of age with any feeling of competence or pleasure in homemaking.

Parental Employment: Time Constraints and Parental Power

One of the most critical questions facing modern families is how to get the housework done when the housewife—whose "job" it is—also has a full-time job outside the home.[19] We found in chapter 8 that husbands of working

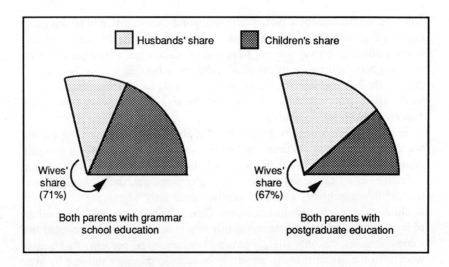

Figure 10.6   Effects of Parental Education on the Household Division of Labor

wives do take over some housework, but the effect is a limited one. We went to extremes and compared traditional families with a workaholic husband and a housewife to "role reversal" families (a workaholic wife and a househusband) and still found that we could not predict a great deal of difference. Wives in the latter situation were responsible for almost as many chores as wives in the first situation (a difference of about 1 chore out of 5). And one of the most startling results of chapter 9 was the almost total lack of effect of mothers' employment on children's sharing in household tasks. Our weak results linking wives' employment with husbands' participation have been mirrored by the results of others,[20] and one of their most common conclusions has been that while "everyone thinks" that husbands participate more in household tasks, *their* scientific study shows little or no effect of the wife's employment.

It turns out that the effects of women's employment on their family's participation were being masked almost entirely by the reciprocal relationship between how much fathers and children share. By looking separately at each member, we were seeing part of the pressure on, say, the husband (posed by the employment of his wife), *offset* by the response of the children to the employment of their mother, and vice versa. As a result, the small substitution of children for fathers weakened the observed impact on husbands, and the strong substitution of fathers for children totally wiped out the evidence of any effect on children. In fact, there is a strong and very similar pure effect of female employment on both children and husbands, although children continue to benefit more from their fathers' participation than fathers from their children's (table 10.1, Appendix C).

When we look at each household task separately, we find that both husbands and children share more grocery shopping, cooking, and laundry the more hours their wife or mother works;[21] husbands (but not children) of women who work more hours in paid jobs are more likely to share household cleaning and dishwashing (table 10.2, Appendix C). It also turns out that it is necessary to consider the contributions of both husbands and children to find any of the "pure" effect of employment that social psychologists have posited.[22] Net of the number of hours women work, simply being employed leads both their children and husbands to share more in dishwashing as well as in child care, even if wives work very few hours. Thus, between the effects of employment, per se, and the effects of the number of hours worked, the only chores for which husbands and children do not increase their responsibility commensurate with increases in women's employment outside the home are yard and household maintenance and paperwork, tasks that are not stereotypically "female."

The child care result is particularly interesting. Other research points to shift work as a strategy used by some families to allow parents to take care of children themselves.[23] The focus of this research tradition has been on the coordination of the schedules of both parents. However, it appears from our results that families also draw children into this arrangement, so that older children may babysit for younger siblings for an hour or two after school until a parent returns from work.

It seems, then, that women's employment is having a much greater impact on household sharing than earlier analyses had shown. But is this all? Are there other effects of employment that this more precise analytical technique reveals? We saw in chapter 8 that a wife's *earnings* also had some (but weak) effect on their sharing domestic tasks, while no effects were seen on children (chapter 9)—and we did not expect any.

In fact, we find that sharing with *both* husbands and children increases significantly as the wife's earnings rise (table 10.1, Appendix C). The higher the wife's earnings, the more husbands and children assume responsibility for housecleaning, laundry, and paperwork. Husbands also replace wives in yard work, grocery shopping, dishwashing, and cooking as her income rises (table 10.2, Appendix C).

These findings suggest that even though families hire help, at least with household cleaning, as their income rises,[24] they also often substitute the labor of husbands and children for that of the wife as her earnings rise, increasing the value of her time outside the home. This implies that a woman's resources are not necessarily used to free the rest of the family from the burden of housework, but rather to shift it from her to others.[25] Evidently, a wife's power in the family increases with her earnings, providing her with the leverage to shift some responsibility for housework not only onto her husband but also onto her children. We had not expected this result, since most feel that parents, regardless of their earnings, should stand in an authority relationship to children. However, it seems that the importance of money as a yardstick of worth has entered the family in the most direct way, so that children respect their mother and cooperate more with her when she too has earnings in the outside world.

To grasp the extent of the combined effects our model predicts for women *with careers*, we estimated husbands' and childrens' shares in families in which the woman works 50 hours a week and earns $25,000. Figure 10.7 shows that in such families, the wife's share of housework drops from 75 percent to 56 percent of the total, with substantial increases from both husbands and children, compared to nonworking wives. This is an important group of families, since by 1987, about 1 out of 8 (12.7 percent) working women earned this much or more.[26] And if she earns $50,000 a year, our model predicts that husbands who are working normal hours and earning average salaries join with their children to take over more than half the household tasks measured here, leaving the wife with only about 45 percent.

Although the resources brought into the family by the wife reduce her share of housework, the husband's earnings have no impact on either the share that he does overall or the amount done by children (table 10.1, Appendix C). For the tasks considered separately, higher-earning husbands are slightly less likely to share grocery shopping and housecleaning,[27] and much more likely to take responsibility for the family paperwork, perhaps because this function includes managing investments and savings more frequently for higher-income families—tasks husbands may prefer to retain for themselves.

As we did for parental education, we also examined whether our various indicators of mothers' employment shifted responsibilities *among* children in a more egalitarian direction. Recall that in chapter 9, where employment effects were generally weaker, there was no sign of such shifting, with mothers who worked more hours sharing slightly more with both teenage boys and teenage girls, relative to younger children. The greatest increases in boys' sharing occurred for less stereotypically "female" chores while the girls increased their share of washing, cleaning, and cooking. The same pattern appears in this analysis.

Given the importance in the current analysis not only of maternal employment but mothers' earnings, we looked to see whether children's response to their mothers' employment differed, depending on which dimension of employment was being considered—employment, number of employment hours, or earnings. An interesting result emerged. Although both teenage girls and boys increase their participation when their mothers work, as we indicated above, girls are much more responsive to maternal employment than boys,

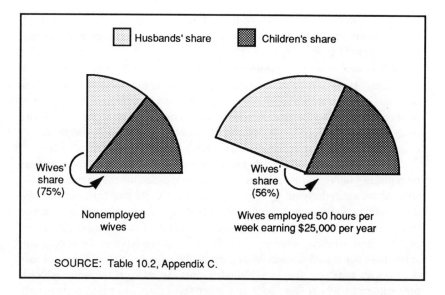

Figure 10.7   Effects of Women's Careers on the Household Division of Labor

whereas boys are more responsive to maternal earnings (table 10.5, Appendix C). Children's sharing in shopping, cleaning, and yard work increases as maternal earnings rise when there are teenage boys in the family; this effect does not appear either for employment or work hours. In contrast, children's sharing in laundry, cooking, and child care increases as mothers work more hours and there are teenage girls in the family, but only laundry increases in response to greater maternal earnings. To the extent, then, that earnings increase mothers' clout in their negotiation with their children, it is primarily felt by sons. Daughters are substituting directly for mothers in their absence.

Prospects for Change in the Household

What are the prospects for bringing men back into the household? Or for bringing children back in? Can they both be brought in together, or do the factors that increase the involvement of men decrease children's sharing and vice versa? What are the implications of the patterns we have seen for prospects of change in the household?

It is clear that *substitution* is an important dynamic in American households, in which husbands and children alternate in the role of chief helper for their wives and mothers. In both black families and older stepparent families, children take the dominant role. In black families mothers gain from the high, absolute participation of their children, while in older stepfamilies, the child-centered pattern is in part the result of the stepfather's withdrawal from household tasks.

Such substitution is most dramatic when we consider the effects of parental education. At each rung of the educational ladder, the father's participation increases and the children's decreases, with only a very small net gain to mothers in highly educated families. Male education is a powerful factor in increasing husbands' participation in the household, but it comes almost entirely at the expense of decreased children's participation.

But not all factors influencing the household division of labor operate only by replacing fathers with children, and vice versa, despite the strength of substitution as an underlying dynamic in the process. At one extreme, we saw that southern families are characterized both by low male participation and by extremely low children's involvement, a pattern that focuses the domestic realm around women, with greater help in wealthier families from paid outsiders than among families in other parts of the country. But this route clearly does not lead to "new families." What it most resembles is the twentieth century pattern in which fast foods and other substitutes are being increasingly used by families who rarely sit down to a meal together but whose children spend many hours watching television. Yet for housework to be valued as the contributor that it is to family well-being, it should be shared by men and children, and not relegated to women. Moreover, young people need the experience of and training in housework that will give them the option of a rich home life when they reach adulthood.

Three processes are operating that increase the chances that married couples will move toward the more equal sharing of "new families." The most powerful is the growth not only in women's employment but in the share women are contributing *financially* to the family. Women's earnings are inducing more participation from both husbands and children—particularly from sons. But participation that results primarily from the high value of women's work outside the home may not do much to increase anyone's appreciation for the home and its tasks.

Families in which wives hold more "modern" attitudes that deny the centrality of the home as a "woman's place" also involve both husbands and children more in its tasks. But the primary effect of these attitudes is on husbands' sharing, with much less influence on children. This is likely to be the case with husbands' attitudes as well, if we could only measure them. As such, the growth of these attitudes will help in providing children with more egalitarian role models, but will do little to halt the erosion in their own involvement and experience.

In some ways, the results we presented for very young families with some sort of nontraditional family experiences form a paradigm for what is needed for the development of "new families"—greater participation of children without the withdrawal of fathers. These young women, who experienced a mother-only family, perhaps followed by a stepfather, in childhood, who lived independently in young adulthood, or who have already been unmarried mothers, involve not only their husbands more, but particularly increase the participation of their children. It seems that the basic—fundamental—nitty-gritty experience of children's being needed to help in the household has effects on parents and, later, on the next generation of children.

The effects of childhood family structure appear strongly in mother-only families. In families with children and two parents, however, the roles of all parties must be considered in order for many effects to appear clearly. This pattern also characterizes the effects of nonfamily living. These effects might even appear more clearly if we were able to take into account *men's* nontraditional family experiences. We have seen that such experiences greatly increase boys' participation in the household *as children*, and, at least in terms of marriage, seem to lead more directly to egalitarian families as adults.

The study of the domestic economy in the late twentieth century is in its infancy. Clearly, we need to look at the roles of all family members, particularly taking into account how husbands and children substitute for each other, instead of reducing the burden on wives and mothers. But it has been reassuring to learn that as more families include a working—and properly paid—mother, and as more families come to accept the modern definition of a woman's place extending beyond the home, the prospects are improving for "new families" rather than "no families."

11

The Future
of the Home in the
Twenty-First Century

For the last generation, the United States and other modern countries have watched the march of women out of the home and into the workplace, a movement so dramatic and complete that it often appears that only the most traditional women will remain to fill classical domestic roles.[1] Throughout this period, although there have been occasional studies revealing that even very egalitarian couples still leave most family-related tasks to women,[2] most observers, both among the public and in the scholarly community, have focused their attention primarily on how the sex-role revolution was affecting the workplace, as women increasingly took traditionally male positions. Thus observers seem to have noted and commented on change *outside* but not inside the home.

Our study has taken the home itself, the primary site of family interaction, as its focus, and tied it to the broader social and demographic trends affecting the family. We asked how a changing home life, in which some young people have experienced their parents' divorce and remarriage and others have left early to live independently, has influenced their later lives; and we have examined how men and women manage their tasks *within* the home as their work roles become more equal. This focus has given us a new view of the changes in marriage, fertility, and divorce associated with the sex-role revolution. We can see more clearly the pressures placed on families as women who want both to be wives and mothers and yet contribute financially to their families and have the security of economic independence struggle to carry "the double burden" of work and family roles. And we have seen the changes in their children as they have reacted to their parents' divorces and as they have left to live independently. These analyses show that the real threats to the family have been almost totally ignored in the inordinate concentration on women in the workplace; the real challenges are in the home.

The growth of independent living among the unmarried during the last generation has provided for the first time an *adult* option to marriage—a "home of one's own." Thus marriage is not only being challenged from the inside by the sex-role revolution but is being threatened from the outside, since it is no longer the only game in town. And we learned something we had not at all anticipated: children—particularly sons but increasingly daughters—are not being taught the fundamental skills that underlie making a home. If men and women in the last generation have had difficulty sharing home tasks because of *men's* lack of training and experience, it may be that the young men and women of the future will have even less confidence about their ability to take them on.

Our results on these issues presented to us a mixed picture of what the future might hold, as we examined factors that influence young men's and women's work and family plans, whether they marry, have children or divorce, and how they allocate responsibility for family tasks. Some results suggest to us "worst case" scenarios about family cohesion—particularly what appears to be the dramatic decline in children's involvement in household tasks—while others provided more hope for the home in the twenty-first century. Here we will tie these results together, both in order to clarify what they imply about the future and to provide a new view of the home as it is today, at the end of the twentieth century. We think it is important to study what goes on in the home in detail for its own sake; it is time to stop taking the home for granted. Like the environment, it is a precious resource, one that can be lost simply because too few are looking at it in a scientific way when it first shows real signs of strain.

Families Planned and Formed;
Dissolved or Functioning

We have examined a wide range of phenomena. We started with very young adults, and looked at the work and family plans first formulated by young women and at various aspects of young men's and women's attitudes toward women's work and family roles. We then followed these young men and women further into adulthood, to see what influenced their chances of marriage, their patterns of family building (and dissolving), and their participation in household tasks, focusing closely on husband's and children's roles and how they form a family economy.

In each case we looked for any effects that might result from exposure to different family structures in childhood and from independent living in young adulthood, and we considered as well how much differences in "tastes," (whether measured directly in terms of sex-role attitudes or indirectly by parental educational level) led to differences along the early adult life course. And as the young adults grew older, we increasingly took into account the possible effects of their adult work and family experiences, as well as the characteristics of their spouse and children, in order to assess the range of forces affecting the family economy.

Although we focus primarily on the natural history of a single group of young adults who began their entry into adulthood in the late 1960s and early 1970s and who reached their thirties during the early 1980s, we also sought wherever possible to study broader patterns of change more directly. Thus we look at how our young adults were influenced by their parents' experiences and how, in turn, they influenced their own children; and we examine differences by age and time directly. In this chapter, we attempt to meet the challenge of tying together our findings on the factors that shape attitudes, marriage, fertility, divorce, and sharing among husbands, wives, and children. We then use our results to speculate about the future of the home and family.

The Effects of Family Change

Our greatest concern has been with the effects of family change itself. How are the new family experiences of current generations—in childhood, in young adulthood, and as adults—echoing in the lives of later generations? When considering only the effects on young women, it is difficult to see beyond the powerful ways these new family experiences lead women to reject traditional family roles, with little sign that they might lead to "new families" rather than "no families." Both those young women who experienced parental marital disruption and those who lived outside a family setting prior to marriage show the same essential response: increased plans for lifetime employment, greater approval of mothers' working, delayed marriage, and, for those who married, delayed childbearing.

The only exceptions in some sense "prove the rule." While most of those who experienced family disruption in childhood delay both marriage and childbearing within marriage, others with this experience are particularly likely to marry very young, and to begin their marriages pregnant. It may be that these characteristics are contributing to the frequently shown finding that young people from broken homes face heightened risks of divorce.

Even in the area of sharing household responsibilities with spouse and children, most of our results suggested that these new family experiences weakened household interdependence, increasing the burden on women by reducing their sharing with husbands and children. Women from nonintact childhood homes appeared to share less with their husbands; those who lived independently in early adulthood shared less both with husbands and children;

and currently remarried women seemed also to share less with their new husbands than once-married women did with theirs.

When we focused on the youngest women, however, *and considered the entire household jointly*, it began to appear that new family experiences might be leading to "new families." Among younger women, the experience of a mother-only household in childhood increased rather than decreased sharing with husbands, and their own remarriage showed no negative effect on sharing with husbands. The strong antisharing responses of those who first experienced the rise in divorce, either as children or adults, are less common among those who have grown up with high levels of divorce in their families and communities. Our final test (chapter 10, fig. 10.4) even found that the youngest women were using their new family experiences to find ways to include both husbands and children more in household tasks.

Our results were most dramatic for boys. Although boys of any age generally participate little in the domestic work of the household, teenage boys in mother-only families actually share more in household tasks than do teenage girls in two-parent families, building a foundation of knowledge and experience for making "new families" when they grow up. And the few direct tests we could make on young men also produced some basis for hoping that the twenty-first century will build "new families" via the greater participation of husbands and fathers. Although the experience of family disruption in childhood slowed young men's progress to marriage (but not as much as for young women), it appeared to make their attitudes toward women's roles more egalitarian and to increase their actual sharing of "women's work" in the household. The experience of independent living in young adulthood also led to more egalitarian attitudes and behavior, and actually increased young men's success in the marriage market. Taken together, it seems that new family experiences in childhood and young adulthood may be making young men more open to participating in "new families."

The pattern of results for young men made the lack of detail available for them one of the most frustrating aspects of our analysis, since it seems increasingly clear that the road to "new families" will lead through men, who must decide whether they want homes, families, and children enough to share responsibility for them. But we could not look at how remarriage affected males' sharing with their wives, or at how any of these experiences might affect their likelihood of divorce, their plans for fatherhood, or their relationships with their children, because so much less information is collected on the family lives of men than of women.

Nevertheless, it is clear that new family experiences, whether of parental divorce or of independent living early in adulthood, are not necessarily destructive to familism in later life. Such experiences may not be supportive of traditional families, since approval of women's combining work with parenthood was increased both among young men and young women who had had these experiences, but "new families" seem to have been reinforced. Particularly among younger women, such experiences are leading to the greater integration of husbands and children in the household economy, and men who lived independently in young adulthood are both more modern in their attitudes and more likely to marry.

Sex-Role Attitudes and Families

Those holding modern sex-role attitudes, like those with new family experiences, are often considered to be "antifamily." But again, our results suggest instead that although such attitudes may be anti "traditional families," they are much less clearly anti "new families." Women with more "modern" attitudes about family roles are more successful in involving not only their husbands, but also their children—including their sons—in domestic tasks. As these modern attitudes become more common, the next generation of men should feel more comfortable doing these tasks, based on their own experience and their awareness of their importance. And although we were unable to test the effect of men's sex-role attitudes on their family-related attitudes and behavior, recent results suggest that men with modern attitudes toward the traditional gender-based division of labor between men and women may also be marrying at a slightly younger age than other men, paralleling the result found in this study for independent living among young men (Goldscheider and Goldscheider, 1990).

Yet even with the evidence we have, it is clear that many of the changes under way in family patterns are not necessarily "antifamily" but simply anti "traditional" family. Changes in *women's* sex-role orientations may make them less willing to assume exclusive responsibility for family roles; and changes in *women's* employment patterns that leave them little time for such an exclusive responsibility may lead women to reject their traditionally defined family responsibilities. But the implications of the sex-role revolution look very different when we turn them around, and consider their effects on men. If modern sex-role attitudes among men lead them to become more interested and involved in being responsible for their homes, children, and possibly aging parents, can we call this an "antifamily" trend? Particularly if this results in their assuming an essentially equal responsibility in these matters? This dimension of the sex-role revolution could be profoundly *profamily*. Traditionally, men are socialized to sacrifice almost none of their career goals, or any of the other items on their agenda, for their families. They have been taught to feel that in developing their own careers, increasing their earning ability, and achieving occupational success, they are best serving their families. But this is no longer the case.

A recent economic analysis of women's difficulties in the labor market concluded that women's "problem" is that they have a greater "demand for children—both in terms of wanting to be a parent and of caring about children after they are born [than men]" (Fuchs, 1988, p.154). But it is unclear that men have a low "demand for children." Traditional family attitudes put great pressure on men to put work roles ahead of family roles. If the development of modern sex-role attitudes means that these pressures are reduced, men could more easily increase their involvement with their families. This would reduce the pressure on working women not to become mothers. If the burdens were shared, many more women might be willing not only to have one child but to have a second or even a third child.

Family Differences by Race, Region, and Community Size

In the course of our analysis, we considered differences by race, region, and community size. We were using these groupings as indirect indicators of differences in "family values." Our results suggest that some communities may not take the same paths to "new families."

Black Families.   Black families seemed focused particularly closely around the mother-child axis. Black women are more likely than other women to expect to work as adults, to approve of mothers' working, to expect and have more children, and to involve them more in household tasks. But they are no more likely to involve their husbands in the household, and less likely to marry. Hence, black men have the experience of involvement in the household as children, but this does not carry over into more egalitarian marriages, or to increased familism.

It may be that black men's childhood experiences in the family are not leading them to "new families" with greater family involvement in adulthood because they associate their childhood experiences with father—absence, racism, and discrimination. Black women, who have worked outside the home for generations, often did not share the view of middle-class white women that employment was a "liberation," since for them it meant that they often could not care adequately for their own home and children. In the same way, black men moving into adulthood may feel an increased need to "make it" as white men always have, to have intense professional work lives, and to be taken care of by women at home.

Southern Families.   Southern families also do not present a simple picture. Young southern adults appear to be quite familistic in a traditional way, given their earlier age at marriage and low probability of divorce. But this greater familism does not extend to southern children, who appear to be particularly uninvolved in their home and its tasks. Their mothers appear to respond to this by expecting fewer children, and by postponing childbearing within marriage.

This suggests that previous studies that showed an early transition to motherhood in the South (Michael and Tuma, 1985; Rindfuss et al., 1988) were simply reflecting the South's early marriage pattern. A more comprehensive analysis, such as this one, is needed to separate the various components of familism, and to show that the southern pattern is quite complex.

Families in Rural Areas and Big Cities.   The larger the community, the less traditional families in them appear to be. In larger places, women are more approving of mothers' working and more modern in their views of women's family roles in general; they also marry later. But they are not moving clearly toward more egalitarian families. Husbands are no more likely to participate in domestic tasks and children are particularly unlikely to share in the domestic economy.

The effects of community size, however, were neither very strong nor particularly systematic. In the late twentieth century, rural Americans are no longer very rural, sharing many of the experiences and attitudes evolving across the society as they develop. It is likely that only a small remnant of family distinctiveness remains in the small towns and rural areas of the United States.

Education and Family Patterns

It may be that the relevant axes of American communities are defined more by educational differences than by residence in smaller or larger places. Certainly this is the case for family patterns. Differences by educational level are pervasive in our results, and since men and women tend to marry those with similar levels of education, differences among families are reinforced.

Focusing first on the effects of female education, it is clear that increased education reduces adherence to traditional family roles, with more educated young women making firmer plans for working during adulthood, delaying marriage, and delaying childbearing within marriage, but also generally expressing greater approval of mothers' working. The effects of male education, however, appear to support marriage, increase its stability, and make it relatively egalitarian, with higher levels of participation by men in household tasks.

Yet it is also in the most educated families that the children's role in the family appears most minimal. Educated families not only delay childbearing and expect fewer children, they also are least willing or able to incorporate their children in the everyday activities of the household. Demographic theory often posits that modern families have few children in order to maximize their investment in schooling for each one, but it may also be that the reduced fertility in modern families is a response to the parent-child relationships they have observed among their family and friends, in which the children's "work" at school is seen as more important than their mothers' (and fathers') work in the home, and "independence" often appears as noncooperation. In any event, however, this pattern results in fewer children being exposed to more egalitarian marriages and gaining little practical experience in the domestic skills needed to make such a marriage.

Further, the forces that our results point to as leading to a reduced role for children in the household seem to be strengthening in society as a whole, affecting not only educated families, but also younger families, suggesting to us that the more educated are, as is often the case, simply leading a trend that is becoming pervasive throughout American society (Schultz, 1975). However, it is also the case that the more educated can lead trends *back*. The more educated have led trends in fertility, so that when fertility has been declining, the educated have had the lowest fertility. But when fertility is rising, as it did during the baby boom, the more educated have fertility rates that are relatively high compared to those of the less educated. The same phenomenon has occurred with trends in smoking and breastfeeding. Rates of breastfeeding rose first and fastest among college-educated women during the dramatic resurgence in these rates that began during the 1970s (Haaga, 1988).

Dual Worker—and
Dual Career—Families

It is our results regarding maternal employment, however, that present the strongest evidence that the home is finally responding to the sex-role revolution in the workplace, and responding in such a way that both husbands and children are beginning to assume some of the double burden borne by their wives and mothers. Employment has one of the strongest effects in reducing women's orientation toward traditional female roles, leading young women to plan to continue to work, to approve of mothers' working, and to plan smaller families. But it does not delay marriage; quite the contrary. As is the case for men, a woman's being able to earn appears to facilitate marriage.

And once married, female commitment to employment at least as measured by female earnings does not appear to deter childbearing and also leads to greater involvement of both men and children in the tasks of the household. The effects on the division of labor, however, only appeared when we took into consideration all family members. The substitution between fathers and children means that the studies that have only looked at the trade-offs between men and women (and the few that have looked at mothers and children) are often misled into seeing little effect.

But our result must be strongly qualified, since it is clear that these effects are not coming from female employment, per se, or even so much from the number of hours women are spending on the job. To get important amounts of sharing from others in the household, a woman's job has to pay considerably more than average for women in today's job market. Only career-level jobs command the resources—or the respect—to involve other family members, and particularly sons, in "women's work" in the home.

Alternative Family Futures

Taken together, these results sharply pose our general concerns about the future of the family. There are many factors at work that could lead to a "no families" future, in which few marry and have children, and many live alone outside of families altogether. The most ominous of these forces may be the withdrawal of children from the family and its tasks. But we also see significant signs that "new families" might be on the horizon, as men and children seem to join increasingly with their wives and mothers in the home and its tasks as women's work outside the home becomes more regular—full time and financially rewarding.

Until now, we have paid little attention to other possible family arrangements. Why are we confident that our results do not imply an eventual return to "old families" in which women focus their identities on the roles of wife and mother and spend most of their lives preparing for and carrying out those roles? And what of mother-only families, the fastest growing family form of the last several decades? Might this be the family of the future?

We should make clear that in discussing the future of the family we are focusing not on individual families, and the varieties of people in them, but on overall family systems—the institutions that provide the framework around which people make plans and within which they work out their own lives. When we criticize both mother-only and traditional families below, it is as total systems; many of these families are wonderful both for the adults and children in them. But we will make the distinction clear between individual families and family systems by using another example—the voluntary childless couple.

Childless Couples

Such couples, which have grown in numbers and proportions in the recent past, may be very happy together with the choices they have made, and they may also be making many important contributions to society. They usually feel very comfortable with their choice, and increasingly their friends and families are accepting it. These marriages tend to be the most egalitarian, since all studies show that the arrival of children puts pressures on couples to follow more conventional parental roles, as we discussed in chapter 8.

As a *family system*, however, rejection of parenthood has obvious difficulties. It is no longer the case that almost all adults' energies must go into raising the next generation. We now have both the resources and the knowledge to realize that the simple reproduction of the species is not a sufficient goal for a "good life" or a "good society." Nevertheless, the fact remains that at some point we will need a system that ensures replacement, and this means that most adults will still have a lot of child care to do. Each generation of young adults feels that the world is theirs for the indefinite future, but they learn in a very few decades that the children they raised or did not raise, whether raised well or not, are beginning to take over—as trendsetters, stars, heroes, and workers with their own skills and experiences. Any society needs to commit substantial resources to developing each new generation, providing them of course with schools and health care, but also with families. So most adults must be prepared to parent.

Mother-Only Families

But which adults should parent? The growth of mother-only families has a clear message—that the increase in women's responsibility for parenting relative to men's that began in the nineteenth century (chapter 7) is nearing its maximum, as women take total responsibility for direct care, with fathers providing funds either through child support payments or through the taxes they pay that provide "Aid to Families with Dependent Children" (AFDC), the primary welfare system in the United States. As with voluntarily childless couples, we again do not think this is a good *system*—without deprecating in any way individual mother-only (or father-only) families, most of whom are doing a good job under difficult circumstances.

As a system, making women responsible for most of the child raising presents important problems—problems that focus primarily on *men*. Boys in mother-only families face a number of difficulties. Although the early discussions in the psychological literature emphasized the lack of "role models" to teach boys how to be "men," it eventually became clear that boys in mother-only families do not lack *models* of "ideal" men; such models are amply provided by other relatives, by friends of their families, and by the media. What they lack is experience with "real" men with whom they can be close enough to see that men can deviate in healthy ways from sex-role stereotypes, fail and recover, mourn a parent and not lose face, help a tired spouse and still have a loving relationship (or even have a better one). "Role models" do not provide boys these insights, since they serve only to reinforce stereotypes; only having a close relationship with a normal man has this effect (Pruett, 1987).

The mother-only family presents even more difficulties for men as adults and fathers. There is considerable evidence that marriage provides major benefits for adults, and that being unmarried is particularly problematic for men. Research demonstrating this is clearest for mortality—married people are less likely to die than unmarried people—but comparable findings have emerged for measures of physical and mental health. Women have been shown to be much less dependent on the marital tie for social support than men (Berkman and Syme, 1979; Umberson, 1987), so the mother-only family form is less problematic for them in this respect. And the unmarried men who are at greatest risk of premature death are those living alone (Kobrin and Hendershot, 1976).

The mother-only family form also bars men from the experience of dealing again with the pleasures and problems of growing up, which parents do as they relive their own childhoods in new ways with their children, reading them their favorite books, playing games that brought them joy as children, teaching skills that they had enjoyed mastering. There has been far too little research on what has happened to the *fathers* of the children in mother-only families, who appear at best to move on to parent, at least a little, their next mate's children (Furstenberg, 1988). But it is hard to believe that these experiences will contribute to a healthy sense of accomplishment as men move into their retirement years—and seek whatever support they can from the family ties they have woven as adults.

And women need help. Despite the numbers of superwomen who take on both parental and economic roles, not all women can do so; few can parent totally alone. If the burden is to fall entirely on women, it seems unlikely that they will be willing to have the numbers of children needed for population replacement. Women who have experienced family disruption as children expect and have fewer, not more children (chapters 4 and 6), as do women on welfare (Rank, 1989). They need time to work for their own support, since the current social expectation is that noncustodial parents should provide only for their children's financial needs, no child care, and often minimal "quality time." For men, the knowledge that marital breakup will in most cases lead to diminished and frustrating contact with their children has undoubtedly led to some resistance to having children at all, and thus risking this loss. Not all men have a low "demand for children," but they will have little chance to realize their preferences in the event of divorce. This is another cost of the mother-only family.

Old Families

Why can we not return to the old balance of men's and women's work and family roles, which were "fair" to each in terms of hours, and which provided children with mothers who cared for them intensively and fathers who supported them adequately? It is clearly better in many ways than our current emphasis on mother-only families, since it provides for children's needs and reinforces family roles for men as children, adults, and in old age. What is wrong with "old families" as a family system? The answer to this question takes us back to the origins of the sex-role revolution, since the problems "old families" create are disproportionately for women.

The major problem for women posed by "old families" is demographic. With the increase in life expectancy and the decline in fertility, homemaking is no longer a lifetime career for women as a group. Either there has to be a division within their adult lives, with about half their time devoted to raising two or so children to adulthood[3] and half spent in other occupations, or women have to be divided into mothers and workers, or "real" workers and "mommy track" workers (Schwartz, 1989).

Perhaps we should remember, in the context of the recent outpouring of women's anger against men for being unhelpful and insensitive (Townsend and O'Neil, 1990), that it was only recently that men were writing in extraordinarily angry ways about traditional women, *for being too involved with their children*. In the 1940s, women who did not work outside the home but had achieved small families were walking a very narrow line. They were called unfeminine if they worked outside the home, and overinvolved and overcontrolling if they focused too much attention on their children. They were accused of "momism" not only in popular contemporary nonfiction (Wylie, 1942) and in scholarly writings (Strecker, 1946) but also in novels reflecting growing up during that period (Roth, 1969).[4]

The rise in divorce has also raised the cost of "old family" roles for women. When few families ended voluntarily, women could invest all their energies in the family, and expect that the responsibility for their maintenance in old age would be borne by their husbands—or if necessary, their sons. But even moderate levels of divorce changed the wisdom of this course. Women who decide to interrupt their careers to raise children are taking a calculated risk, and it is likely that only those who are the most publicized for doing so (the "new executives") can afford to take "time out," since they already have the skills that will make them desirable in the reentry job market, even if they never reach chief executive officer as a result. But women who have scrambled beyond the pink-collar ghetto, but only just beyond, are much less likely to risk what they have gained. They return to work quickly (often too quickly) after childbirth in an industrial climate that often offers at most short maternity leaves, paid or unpaid.[5] So most women will work, and "old families" simply means that they have the double burden of work and home.

It is also the case that increasingly, men are rejecting "old families" for themselves. Being relieved of at least some part of the economic burden has obvious advantages and many men have also found rewards from intensifying their family lives by developing closer relationships with their wives and children. "Old families" preclude much of that for men, and for the children growing up in these families. Sons, in particular, experience limited options as well, since they are not being prepared for the possibility of "new families" in the sex-segregated world such families create.

No Families

This leaves us with the choice of "no families" or "new families." "No families" means that too many adults make the decision not to have children to provide population replacement, as we discussed above under "childless couples," and it also means that most will forgo developing close, intimate, long-term relationships, choosing instead to live alone. Again, we want to make clear that such people may have rich lives of satisfying employment and contribution to society; they may as well experience and provide others with strong friendship and support that those bound up in family obligations often cannot.

But even going beyond the problem of population replacement, nonfamily living as a system, in which many adults expect to spend much of their lives living alone, is untested. Although people may be able to maintain close and giving relationships, it not clear that their circumstances will teach them how to do so; *they will have to go out of their way* to make and maintain such relationships across the distances created by residential separation. It seems likely that commitment and intimacy will be more difficult to achieve and maintain.[6]

New Families

What then, of "new families"? We have reached them at this point in the argument by process of elimination. We have also suggested that such families have the potential to solve critical problems facing families today. But what do we really know about them? What effects does this pioneer family form have on marriages and families and on the men, women, and children who live in them? Are more egalitarian and sharing families possible? This is largely uncharted territory. In this study we have looked at factors that might *lead* to more egalitarian families, but we have not attempted to consider their consequences.

In fact, as we suggested in our introduction (chapter 1), most students of the family have resisted considering that men might take a greater role in family matters, usually raising the possibility only to dismiss it. One of the most systematic and sympathetically feminist discussions of family problems considers the prospect of increased male involvement in household tasks only to dismiss it as bizarre or pathological.[7]

But will "new families" be so bad for men and for children that they will offset their benefits for women who want both family and economic lives? Certainly there will be some costs. The most obvious consequence is that, as for women, the hours men spend in housework are likely to decrease the time available for paid employment or for related activities such as training, travel for work, or overtime. One study found that time spent in domestic activities reduced the wages of both men and women, and affected the sexes about equally (Coverman, 1983).[8]

However, the job-related pressures placed on men by an egalitarian division of labor at home are on the wane. Fewer and fewer of their competitors in the workplace are men married to full-time housewives, and more and more of them are not only other men with relatively egalitarian marriages, but also women carrying a double burden themselves, as single parents or working wives in traditional marriages. The growth of on-site day care, and fathers' involvement with their children there, could also reinforce family orientations among men at work.

Further, marriages that are more egalitarian in sharing domestic labor appear to have positive consequences for *both* spouses outside the workplace. Wives whose husbands "help" with the housework report lower levels of depression than those whose husbands do not help (Ross, Mirowsky, and Huber, 1983). And their husbands do not suffer—at least in terms of *their* mental health—as a result of helping around the house. And the more housework the husband does, the lower the chances that the wife has considered divorce.[9]

And what of the children? How does participation in the domestic sphere affect them? One study argues that children become more independent when they have more responsibility and greater demands placed upon them (Weiss, 1979). The study focused only on children living in single-parent families, who are given substantially more decision-making power and responsibility for household tasks than are children living with two parents, becoming almost equal partners in the business of running a single-parent family. But it seems likely that even in two-parent families, working regularly together on the tasks that enrich their lives would not only increase children's skill levels, when they leave to form homes of their own, but would reinforce ties and respect between parents and children in the home.

Research Needed

Much research is needed on the factors leading to "new families" and to "no families" and to provide us with information to shape public policy wisely in the years ahead. In many ways, our analysis has raised even more questions than it has answered, since it has revealed rather starkly how much we do not know about the home. Nevertheless, we hope it will also serve as a stimulus to study this important sphere much more systematically. In that spirit, the section that follows specifies some of the gaps we see as particularly problematic.

New Research on Men

The most critical omission in the study of the family in recent years is information, theorizing, even attention—to men. What have *their* parenthood trends really been? A substantial amount of creative and painstaking research has been done on women's fertility and marital histories, relating them to their children's ages to portray how these histories become the contexts for children's experiences of divorce and remarriage as they are growing up. And we have begun to learn a little about children's relationships with their absent fathers after divorce and remarriage, but we know almost nothing from the perspective of these fathers. Men have almost never been the focus of analysis in family research, so that we know very little about what is happening to them, much less how they feel about it. There have been no national studies of men's relationships with the children they fathered but no longer live with (or the stepchildren they no longer live with), and none that focus on their relationships with those they did not father but currently live with.

Further, the questions asked men about changing family roles have been almost entirely focused on women, as if men's roles would not be affected at all by women's changing lives. The sex-roles scales that have been developed ask about how mothers' working affects children, but not about how different forms of fathering might affect them. There are some studies of men in detail (Komarovsky, 1976) but no one has taken the results of these in-depth studies and developed general instruments for inclusion in multipurpose surveys. As a result, there is no way to look at the effects of these experiences and attitudes toward marriage, willingness to parent, or the likelihood of divorce *among men*.

New Research on the Home

Another major area that needs more research is the home. We know relatively little about how families function together—what they do and how they feel about it. We do not know how the quantity of time people spend together affects their relationships nor do we know what "quality time" really means— whether between parents and children or between spouses. These issues will have to be unraveled before we understand enough to know what processes build solid families, based on interdependence, interaction, and sharing.

The greatest omission is research on children's role in the home. Family scholars are adults, who do research and teach children who are nearly grown up (and are thus used to learning via lectures and readings). When they think about younger children, they normally focus on what must be done *for them*. But teachers of younger children have known for generations that children learn best by doing, by being given the opportunity to experience and feel mastery directly. Thus it is not surprising that boys rarely turn into men with domestic skills, even those who developed egalitarian ideals in young adulthood.

Recent Trends Toward New Families

Our study, by focusing in detail on the lives of young adults between the late 1960s and early 1980s, is also limited as a basis for assessing change and predicting the future. A similar study of young adults who grew up in the late 1920s and 1930s, who had the smallest family sizes on record to date, or of those growing up in the 1940s and 1950s, who created the baby boom, would be equally problematic, as the demographers who made predictions based on the experience of those cohorts learned to their dismay. But is there other evidence about broader trends which might justify optimism or pessimism? Are the "no families" trends we outlined earlier (chapter 2) continuing in force, or are changes underway that portend either a return to "old families" or the advent of "new families"?

It is much too soon to give a definitive answer. But there are clues that justify our optimism about the growth of "new families." Some recent evidence suggests that we are experiencing a "return to the family" and that these families are "new families." Among young people, the trend toward support for remaining single plateaued in the 1970s, remaining stable or declining in the 1980s.[10] Similarly, approval for divorce "when there are children in the family, and the parents don't get along" peaked in 1977 and approval of childlessness peaked in 1980. But the increases continue unabated in employment among mothers of young children, in egalitarian sex-role attitudes, and particularly in husband's helping around the house—which in the latter case may even be accelerating.

By the 1980s, married men were increasing not only their share of household responsibilities (a trend that developed earlier as employed women began to cut corners) but were actually increasing their total number of hours.[11] This means that many more children are observing at least some participation in household tasks by their fathers, which is probably a more fundamental recognition than their awareness that the sharing is not precisely equal.

Recent trends in Sweden provide another straw in the wind. Sweden, far more than any other country, has taken an actively egalitarian approach to family policy, pioneering in the provision of a wide variety of family-based services during the 1940s, institutionalizing "maternity leave," and then, in the 1970s, redefining it as "parental" leave. Although Sweden is portrayed as a country in "family decline" and still very sexist, it is only sexist in contrast to total equality. For example, the participation of men in parenting is rather summarily dismissed with a mention that "only" 25 percent of fathers take advantage of paternity leave (Popenoe, 1988). But in fact, fertility trends over the past 4 years have brought Sweden to one of the highest, not lowest, fertility levels in Western Europe, close to population replacement with a total fertility rate of 2.0 (Population Reference Bureau, 1989). Swedes have struggled longest with the sex-role revolution, and may well be furthest ahead in reaching a solution.

It is also the case that pressures have recently been building on men to become more involved in the family and its tasks whether they want to or not. Men who still hold traditional definitions of their appropriate adult role are increasingly having difficulty finding wives willing to take the full burden of family obligations left by a husband whose only responsibilities are to work. Some of these men have given up on "modern" women, and have turned to importing wives from the less-developed countries of Asia. Such women are often slavishly grateful for the opportunity to live a better life and to have children with far greater opportunities than would be possible for them in the Philippines or Korea. But as immigration is not a long-term solution for the fertility problem (chapter 2), so neither is it a long-term solution for the marriage problem. And most men will prefer a wife with more shared ideas and experiences, even if she insists on their sharing at least a little in household tasks.

It may become even more difficult for the next generation of men to find any wife, much less a traditional one, thereby increasing the pressure on males of the 1990s and beyond to be desirable as husbands. Their experience is likely to be very different from that of their fathers. Their fathers felt very little pressure to increase their involvement in family tasks with the result that the youngest generation of men has become quite used to women who both work full time and carry total responsibility for the home, since that is what their mothers did. What is changing? Their fathers' experiences in the 1960s and 1970s may have resulted from women's unwillingness to be "too demanding," given conventional definitions of femininity; but it might also have resulted from some rarely thought about consequences of the demographic imbalances of that period often called "the marriage squeeze" (chapter 5).

The baby boom dramatically increased the numbers of younger women relative to older men. This affected not only the first marriage chances of women, but also the *remarriage* chances of older men. As divorce rates rose, married men may well have become increasingly tempted to look more closely at the "new models" of younger women that the baby boom, together with the sexual revolution, seemed to be offering them.

But the new opposing marriage squeeze will change this, putting increased competitive pressure on men. A shortage is developing of younger women relative to men a few years older, since the baby boom began to ease in the late 1950s and was followed by a full-fledged "baby bust" in the early 1970s. Men born in the mid– and late–1960s, entering the marriage market in the late–1980s and early–1990s, are finding many fewer women in the age group just below them. And these young women are not at all traditional. They may still expect to do more than half the housework, but they expect more sharing than their young suitors are planning to offer.

This will increase the competitive advantage of men whose views of marriage and family life include an interest in sharing parenting and home life.[12] Older women have known for a generation that younger men are often more flexible—more giving—in their relationships with women than most older men, although market conditions meant that few such men were available to women willing to risk social taboos about age differences. But these numbers are changing, too, as young men find few women their own age or younger, and look elsewhere for warmth and companionship. So older men of the 1990s and 2000s may feel the same kind of pressure to accommodate in order to retain their spouses that older women of the 1960s and 1970s felt.

It is possible that we may have to go into the twenty-first century with several generations of very small cohorts—as the children of chaotic families have few and unstable marriages producing few and insecure children—until a new balance of egalitarian norms is in place. But our research makes us hopeful that this will happen eventually, so that more children will be raised in "new families," learning how to handle egalitarian marital relationships and share in parenting pleasures and responsibilities. For it is such young men and women who will increasingly become the adults and parents of the future.

Appendix A
The National
Longitudinal Surveys

This appendix provides detailed information on the National Longitudinal Surveys of Labor Market Experience, the data sets used in this volume. These surveys began in the late 1960s, when the Department of Labor began funding a series of studies of the American population, in an attempt to gather information that would aid policymakers in developing legislation on issues from Social Security to job-training programs. The National Longitudinal Surveys were designed by the Ohio State University Center for Human Resource Research and conducted by the U.S. Bureau of the Census.

Each of the 4 original National Longitudinal Surveys (or NLS, as they are commonly called) focused on an age group of particular interest. There was a sample of "young men," ages 14 to 24; a sample of comparable "young women"; a sample of "mature women," ages 30 to 44; and a sample of "older men," ages 45 to 59. Each of these groups included approximately 5,000 individuals of the appropriate age and sex and began with an initial interview at some point between 1966 and 1968; they have been continued for at least 15 years.[1]

We rely entirely on the two cohorts of women—the NLS Young Women and the NLS Mature Women—and on the young male cohort, the NLS Young Men.[2] Each of these groups has been interviewed in most of the succeeding years through the mid–1980s. The respondents constituted national probability samples of the noninstitutionalized population of females 14 to 24 in 1968, males 14 to 24 in 1966, and women 30 to 44 in 1967. Each was interviewed annually over the next several years, and then either annually or every other year for a total of at least 15 years.[3] Attrition from the sample over the panel period has been relatively low; three-quarters of the original Young Women's sample was reinterviewed in 1978 and seventy percent of the Young Men's sample was reinterviewed in 1976, the last years used for the analysis of attitudes and plans in chapter 4. The NLS cohorts lost relatively few respondents through the early 1980s (the last years used in the analysis of division of household labor) so that from 65 to 70 percent of the initial sample was reinterviewed in those years.

The interview lasted in most cases for about an hour, and consisted of detailed questions on the family background of the individual, as well as current work-, school-, and family-related activities and opinions on a wide range of issues. These interviews were done in person, either face-to-face (particularly in the early years) or over the telephone. As a result, answers were obtained to nearly all the questions asked, unlike other surveys of young adults that relied on mailed questionnaires, in which many questions are unanswered by those who return interviews.

In the initial interview, the NLS respondents provided extensive details on themselves and on the families in which they grew up. They were asked about their parents' education, occupation, and income; whether their mother worked; the number of brothers and sisters they had; the size of the city (or rural area) in which they grew up; and a number of characteristics of their home. They were also asked about the structure of the family in which they grew up, with their answers coded in great detail. This information allows us to create a number of measures of childhood family structures that we discuss in Appendix B.

In each year the NLS also obtained a complete listing of everyone in the household, their relationship to the respondent, age, sex, and in some cases a number of other characteristics such as education and employment. This listing only includes relatives of the young women in early survey years but includes all household members (relatives and nonrelatives) for the young men in all years and for the young women in later years. These listings formed the basis for our constructions of living arrangements in young adulthood, allowing us to count years of nonfamily living.

The NLS respondents also provided annual information on their activities over the preceding year. The key activities of interest to us here are schooling, employment, and military service. At each survey respondents were asked about their current marital status, and in later years complete marital and fertility histories were obtained, allowing us to date first marriage, any divorce or separation, and the births of all children. They also answered questions about their husbands and wives, including their educational attainment, employment, income, and work hours. Respondents answered questions about their health and that of their spouse. And, of course, the surveys covered many topics not of particular interest to us here, for example political participation or volunteer work.

The NLS data sets have important strengths for the type of study that we present in this volume. First, they represent the entire population of people of a particular age in the United States, allowing us to generalize our results to the nation as a whole. Second, the NLS cohorts include large numbers of respondents, so that we can observe even fairly small differences between groups, or focus intensively on certain particular subgroups, say mother-only families. Third, the NLS follow people over extended periods, allowing us to map changes in the outcomes of interest to us, and to witness the unfolding of the lives of our respondents.

Appendix B
The Creation of
Key Measures

This appendix provides the interested reader with technical details on the measures used in our analysis. Three sets of variables required complex constructions. One set measures the extent of sharing of responsibility for household tasks among family members, which we use as a dependent variable in chapters 7–10. Another set scales attitudes toward appropriate roles of men and women at work and in the family, which we use as a dependent variable in chapter 4, and to explain differences between individuals in all our outcomes in the subsequent chapters. The third set includes the two key predictor variables in our analyses: childhood family structure and nonfamily living. We present our methods for constructing our complex variables and then provide a table outlining the logic used for the rest of our measures.

Measuring Division of Household Labor

The men and women included in the National Longitudinal Surveys of Young Men, Young Women, and Mature Women answered a series of questions about a variety of household chores, including cooking, cleaning, laundry, child care, dishes, yard work, grocery shopping, and paperwork. Most of our analyses are based on answers the women gave, since the questions were asked in much more detail than those asked of young men. The series for women allow us to determine *who* shared a given task, and how much the task was shared. The young men, in contrast, were asked about a comparable list of tasks (actually longer, with separate questions on yard and home maintenance, which were combined for the women, and including as well whether they ran errands) but without any information on with whom the task was shared.

The NLS Mature and Young Women data contain identical sets of items on household tasks. The questions, which are reproduced at the end of this appendix, ask: "Now I would like to ask you a few questions about work around the home (even though you live alone). Would you say that—week in and week out—you have the sole responsibility, someone else has sole responsibility, or that you share responsibility with someone else for—grocery shopping? Child care, including helping with children? Cooking? Cleaning the dishes after meals? Cleaning the house? Washing the clothes? Yard and home maintenance? Family paperwork, like paying bills and balancing the checkbook?" For each task, the woman could report that she has sole responsibility, others have sole responsibility, or she shares responsibility with others. For all tasks, the majority of women reported that they had sole responsibility; husbands most often share in grocery shopping and least often in laundry. (The respondent could also indicate that the particular task is not applicable, for example if she had no children and thus did not have or share responsibility for child care.)

We also learn who (besides the wife) did the task, since, for each task that was shared or for which others had responsibility, the woman was asked: "Who usually performs this task or shares it with you?" The response categories included husband, children, hired help, and other. Women report very little sharing with either hired help or others (fewer than 10 percent of those who share with someone share with hired help or others on any task). These categories allow us to distinguish between categories of others but not, except for husbands, the *particular individual* with whom the woman shares. Thus, we do not know which child is doing the dishes, or whether her mother-in-law is the "other" sharing the responsibility for child care.

If the woman reported that she shared responsibility for a task, she was asked: "Would you say that you are responsible for this task—less than half of the time, about half of the time, or more than half of the time?" We treat these answers as indicating the wife's share to be about 50 percent of a task if she replied "about half the time," about 25 percent of a task if she reported "less than half of the time," and about 75 percent if she replied "more than half of the time."

This measure provides information on *responsibility* for various commonly done household tasks. It ignores the number of hours spent on the tasks or how efficient each person is. It also does not allow for sharing with more than one other category of others. For example, a woman might share grocery shopping with both her husband and one of her children, but cannot name both since she is allowed to name only one class of individuals with whom she shares. And those who occasionally (or often) perform tasks but take no responsibility for them might not be mentioned at all, if the respondent focused only on the word "responsibility." However, given that in these questions "responsibility" is necessarily shareable, we feel that the responses reflect in most cases actual sharing of the *doing* of the task, and are thus closer to a time measurement than they appear to be. The consistency of our results with those of others reinforces our feeling that respondents generally understood the questions in this way.

The reader will note that the list of household tasks above includes a sizable number usually considered "female" and two—yard and home maintenance and family paperwork—that are either stereotypically male (like yard) or neutral (like paperwork). Together, these tasks account for about 90 percent of all household time inputs, according to a Walker and Woods (1976) landmark study.[1] But the 6 traditionally female tasks clearly predominate in the list, as they do in the time they require in the average household.

Creating Measures of Sharing

We created a number of different indicators reflecting different dimensions of sharing. Most are based on the series of questions, described above, asked of the young women in 1983 and of the mature women in 1982.[2] One measures the amount of responsibility for household tasks for a given task assumed by children. For each separate task, such as cooking, we created a measure of sharing that ranged from 0, if the woman did not share at all with children, to 4, if children had sole responsibility for the task (a rare occurrence). The complete coding of this measure is presented below:

0 if mother does not share with children[3]
1 if children do less than half
2 if children do about half
3 if children do more than half
4 if children have sole responsibility

In order to interpret these answers quantitatively, we translated them into percentage terms. So the women who said that children did not share in a given task (and who were scored 0) are sharing 0 percent of that task with children; women who said their children shared "some but less than half" (and were scored 1) are interpreted as sharing 25 percent; women who said they shared "about half" a task with children (scored 2) are treated as if they shared 50 percent of the task with their children. If children were reported as taking "most" of the responsibility (scored 3) we treated them as sharing 75 percent of the task, and if women said that children took "all or almost all" responsibility for a task (scored 4), we interpret this response as meaning that children

took 100 percent of the responsibility for that task. We created parallel measures of sharing each task with husbands, based on the same questions and
with the same scoring.

Measuring Overall Sharing

We also wanted to be able to discuss the extent to which children and
husbands share responsibility for household tasks *in general*. To consider
household tasks as a group, we needed measures of overall sharing, which
we construct for sharing with children and for sharing with husbands. To combine the individual tasks into a single measure of overall sharing, we first
examined the relationship among tasks on sharing. This exercise informed us
that the pattern of sharing with children on all the tasks was essentially similar
and appeared to provide a measure of the same phenomenon, with the single
exception of family paperwork. Families virtually never share this task with
children, although husbands and wives often divide responsibility between
them, as we will see later. So we omitted paperwork from our measure of
sharing with children.[4]

Our analysis of inter-item homogeneity for sharing with *husbands* showed
that 3 of the tasks did not fit well into a unidimensional scale. These were
yard work, child care, and, as in sharing with children, family paperwork.
Yard and paperwork are traditionally male tasks, and patterns of sharing differ
for these than for the other, traditionally female, tasks. Child care may be
unique because it tends to be concentrated in the years when the family has
small children, a relatively short period in the life cycle of the typical family.

For the analysis of the children's share (chapter 9), we summed sharing
scores for the 7 remaining tasks to yield a single scale that ranges from 0, if
children do not share at all in any of the tasks, to 28, if children are solely
responsible for all 7 tasks. Table B.1 gives the distribution of the resulting
scale. This scale indicates that a sizable minority of families with children
do not involve them in responsibility for any household tasks, but that most
do share. However, the average extent of sharing is relatively modest, with
children typically assuming some responsibility for only a few tasks.

For the analysis of husbands' sharing, we summed the 5 chores, with a
range from 0, if the husband takes no responsibility for any of the tasks, to
20 if he has sole responsibility for all 5. The mean on this scale is quite low,
indicating that husbands share in only a few tasks and for these take relatively
little responsibility.

These scales rest on different chores, 7 for children and 5 for husbands.
In order to analyze sharing with husbands and children jointly, we created
an additional scale for children that matched the husbands' chores—and
examined only shopping, dishwashing, laundry, cooking, and cleaning.

Measuring Sex-Role Attitudes

Given the growth in women's roles in the labor market and the pressure this puts on working wives and mothers who are seeking to continue to maintain their traditional roles in the home, we were interested in examining as much information on sex-role related attitudes and behaviors as we could. The NLS is a relatively rich source of information on this subject, much more so than most national, longitudinal data sets, although much more detail was provided for women than men. There were general questions on sex-role attitudes and a set of more specific questions on when mothers should work.

We constructed two general indices of sex-role attitudes from questions asked in the National Longitudinal Surveys of Young Women and Mature Women. The questions, which are reproduced at the end of Appendix B, deal primarily with the impact of women's employment on their families, and ask respondents for value judgments about the appropriate roles for men and women. These were Likert-type questions coded as 5-point scales from strongly agree to strongly disagree. These questions were asked, with some modest variations, in a number of survey years, 1972, 1978, and 1983 for the young women and for the mature women in 1972, 1977, and 1982.

The variables used in our analyses are the composite indices (or factor scores) derived from the coefficient matrix of a factor analysis done with oblique rotation. Our factor analysis of each of the series produced two distinct dimensions. One, which we call FAMILY ROLES, reflects the importance of women's time at home to their children and families. The second dimension, JOB ROLES, measures views of the importance of women's employment to their self-esteem and to the economic well-being of their families. A higher score indicates greater acceptance of nonfamilial roles for wives and mothers. These two dimensions had a correlation of .3 with each other.

Finding two distinct dimensions of sex-role attitudes in this series of questions replicates results from a number of other studies. Mason and Bumpass (1975) and Mason, Czajka, and Arber (1976) found, using questions overlapping to some extent with those that we use, that respondents answered relatively consistently to all questions on the appropriateness of the traditional division of labor within the family, and to those on women's roles in the labor market, but apparently saw little need to connect their views across these two dimensions.

Measuring Childhood
Family Structure

Respondents to the NLS were asked in the first year of the panel about the structure of their family when they were children. They were asked with whom they lived when they were 14 years old. The NLS coded the answers in great detail, allowing us to identify those who lived with both natural parents, who we refer to as living in INTACT families; those who lived with their mother only as head of the family, called MOTHER-ONLY families; and those who either lived with one parent (usually the mother) and a step-parent or those who lived with other relatives, not their mother or father, which we call STEPFAMILIES.

This measure is limited, as we discuss in chapter 3, by its focus on a single age. The detail available, however, allows us to separate those living with a married couple into those living with two parents and those living with a re-married parent. An ideal measure of family structure during childhood would include the child's age at which his parents divorced or separated, how long he or she spent in a mother-only family and at what ages. It would also allow the researcher to separate children who lived in mother-only families because their parents divorced, from those born to single mothers, a distinction we cannot make.

Measuring Nonfamily Living

One of the key tenets of this book is that young adults are changed in some important ways through the experience of living independently during the transition to adulthood. We operationalize this experience by examining the amount of time that young adults spend living away from their parents' home before they form their own families.

The National Longitudinal Surveys provide detailed information on living arrangements, more than any of the other major longitudinal studies on young adults.[5] A household listing is obtained at each interview, and information is collected there on all members of the household, including their relationship to the respondent. Thus, we can easily identify those respondents living with their parents, those living with other relatives, and those living alone.

For the NLS Young Men, these listings reflect actual living arrangements at the survey date. But for the young women, those away at college who returned home for the summer were allocated by the Census Bureau back to their parents' home. Since a substantial minority of all college students live at home while going to school, we could not assume that all young women enrolled in college lived away.

We were able to resolve this ambiguity in living arrangements for female college students by using the year-to-year migration records in the NLS. These reflect actual residence of the respondent, not the residence of the parental family. Thus, those young women who moved in the same year that they entered college are almost certainly living away in group quarters in that year, given the very low migration rates of adults with college-age children.[6] The information in the household listing allows us to code unmarried female respondents as living with parents (the reference category), in college dormitories, or in more independent living arrangements, that is, with nonrelatives, alone, or with her own children.

To the extent that our measure of female respondents' living arrangements contains error, we will tend to miss those actually living away and underestimate the extent of independent living. This will bias our results against finding an effect of nonfamily living and make our tests of these effects conservative. For males we do not need to make these assumptions about the living arrangements of college students, since their actual living arrangements were recorded. Although different information is initially available on the NLS for the sexes, we have designed our coding of the living arrangements variables to produce measures nearly identical for males and females.

These measures of nonfamily living for each follow-up survey have been aggregated to produce a continuous measure indicating the number of years that the respondent has experienced such living arrangements. We track living arrangements beginning at age 18. We compiled a complete and detailed history of living arrangements from the yearly interviews by beginning with respondents 14 to 17 years old at the first interview. Some young adults live with their parents until they marry; they have no experience in independent living. Some live in dormitories while attending college, some live in apartments with or without roommates, some live in military barracks. All of these experiences constitute independent living.[7]

For some analyses, such as those in chapter 5 on marriage, we separate independent living into its components. For other analyses in chapter 5, we look only at whether the person was living away at the beginning of the interval during which they are at risk of marrying for the first time. And in other analyses we look at the *proportion* of years the young persons were eligible to live away that they actually did so. We assume for purposes of calculating this proportion of time spent living away that the clock started at age 17 for girls and 18 for boys and stopped with first marriage. Using this strategy, some young adults—those who married by age 17 (girls) or 18 (boys)—had no opportunity to live away. Others who married in their late twenties could have lived independently for more than a decade.

Sex-Role Attitude Questions, 1972

a. Modern conveniences permit a wife to work without neglecting her family.
b. A woman's place is in the home, not in the office or shop.
c. A job provides a wife with interesting outside contacts.
d. A wife who carries out her full family responsibilities doesn't have time for outside employment.
e. A working wife feels more useful than one who doesn't hold a job.

f. The employment of wives leads to more juvenile delinquency.
g. Working wives help to raise the general standard of living.
h. Working wives lose interest in their home and families.
i. Employment of both parents is necessary to keep up with the high cost of living.

Sex-Role Attitudes
Questions, 1977 and 1978

The 1978 series includes items a, b, d, e, f, and i. It also includes the questions listed below.

j. It is much better for everyone concerned if the man is the achiever outside the home and the woman takes care of the home and family.
k. Men should share the work around the house with women, such as doing dishes, cleaning, and so forth.
l. A working mother can establish just as warm and secure a relationship with her child as a woman who doesn't work.
m. Women are much happier if they stay at home and take care of their children.
n. A woman should not let bearing and rearing children stand in the way of a career if she wants it.

The 1982 and 1983 questions included all those asked in 1978 except item n.

Items a and c had no relationship with either dimension in the 1972 scales and were dropped, and items a and k were deleted from the 1978 scores for the same reason. Items e, g and i loaded highly on score #2 (jobs), and the remaining items loaded highly on score #1 (family).

Attitudes Toward Mothers' Working

"Now I'd like you to think about a family where there is a mother, a father who works full time, and several children under school age. A trusted relative who can care for the children lives nearby. In this family situation, how do you feel about the mother taking a full-time job outside the home: a. If it is absolutely necessary to make ends meet? b. If she wants to and her husband agrees? c. If she prefers to work, but her husband doesn't particularly like it?"

Table B.1. Children's Share of Household Tasks (share scale: 0 = none of any task; 28 = all of every task)

Scale	Frequency	Percent
0	1621	46.2
1	74	2.1
2	102	2.9
3	196	5.6
4	345	9.8
5	69	2.0
6	151	4.3
7	71	2.0
8	241	6.9
9	86	2.5
10	51	1.5
11	31	0.9
12	184	5.2
13	40	1.1
14	13	0.4
15	12	0.3
16	99	2.8
17	7	0.2
18	10	0.3
19	2	0.1
20	66	1.9
21	1	0.0
22	2	0.1
23	1	0.0
24	21	0.6
28	12	0.3

Appendix C
Tables

Table 4.1. *Description of Independent Variables Used in the Analysis of Family Plans*

Explanatory Variables	*Description*
Nonfamily living	Proportion of years spent in nonfamily living between age 17 and first marriage or age in question
Work 35 at 17	Plans to work when age 35 as measured at age 17
Black	1 = yes, 0 = no
Nonintact	Did not live with 2 natural parents at age 14
Parents' education	Average years of school completed by parents
Employed	Current full-time or part-time employment
Enrolled	Enrolled in school full time
Size	Scale ranging from 1 (rural) to 8 (urbanized areas of 3 million or more)
South	Census region
Year	Year became age in question
Married	Currently married for the first time (1 = yes, 0 = no)
Divorced/separated	Currently divorced, separated, or widowed (1 = yes, 0 = no)
Remarried	Currently remarried (1 = yes, 0 = no)
Husband's total income	In 1967 constant dollars (thousands)
Kids	Living with own children (1 = yes, 0 = no)
Education	Years of schooling completed

Table 4.2.   *Factors Predicting Young Women's Plans to Work at Age 35*

Explanatory Variables	Age		
	20	22	24
Nonfamily living	0.110*	0.120*	0.068
Black	0.195**	0.179**	0.063
Nonintact	0.095*	−0.044	0.120**
Parents' education	−0.004	0.005	−0.005
Employed	0.044	−0.024	0.148**
Enrolled	0.286**	0.184**	0.114
Size	0.004	0.009	−0.003
South	0.060*	0.043	0.053
Year	0.010	0.021	0.038*
Married	−0.023	0.029	−0.080
Divorced/separated	0.024	0.038	−0.059
Remarried	0.033	0.167	0.059
Husband's total income	−0.010	−0.010	0.002
Kids	0.067	0.051	0.142**
Employed * Kid	0.092	0.079	−0.062
Educational attainment	0.037**	0.059**	0.042**
N =	1227	740	928
2* log-likelihood ratio (df=18)	240.43	113.93	103.01

One-tailed test of significance:
** = p ≤.025
* = .025 < p ≤.05

Table 4.3. Unstandardized Coefficients for Models of Young Women's and Men's Family Plans and Attitudes

| | Approval of Mothers' Working | | Girls Only | | | |
| | | | Expected Family Size | Ideal Family Size | Sex-Role Attitudes | |
Explanatory Variables	Girls 1972	Boys 1976	1973	1973	Family 1978	Jobs 1978
Nonfamily living	1.000**	0.261	-0.211**	-0.084	0.181**	0.108*
Black	0.453***	0.517**	0.077	0.290**	0.019	0.182**
Nonintact	0.246*	0.271	-0.197***	-0.153*	-0.033	0.061
Parents' education	0.026	0.052**	-0.021*	-0.017	0.003	-0.012*
Employed	0.269***	-0.126	-0.122	-0.058	0.380**	0.285**
Enrolled	-0.013	-0.163	-0.256***	-0.217**	0.523**	0.131
Size	0.042*	0.037	-0.012	0.009	0.024*	0.010
South	0.465***	0.045	-0.265***	-0.173***	0.037	0.027
Age at first survey	0.076	0.063	-0.140***	-0.058*	-0.007	0.027*
Married	0.074	-0.153	-0.092	-0.062	0.124	0.260**
Divorced/separated	0.451	0.333	-0.517***	-0.431*	0.208**	0.021
Remarried	-0.877	0.246	0.056	-0.273	0.060	0.140**

Table 4.3. (continued)

	Approval of Mothers' Working		Girls Only			
			Expected Family Size	Ideal Family Size	Sex-Role Attitudes	
	Girls	Boys			Family	Jobs
Explanatory Variables	1972	1976	1973	1973	1978	1978
Husband's total income	0.003	—	-0.004	-0.010	0.006	-0.007**
Kids	0.401*	—	0.396**	0.002	-0.172*	-0.266**
Employed * Kid	-0.341	—	-0.228*	-0.054	0.010	0.221**
Education	0.055	0.116**	0.037*	0.013	0.059**	-0.012
N	1472	1153	1344	1365	1223	1223
R-squared	0.064	0.091	0.230	0.229	0.233	0.182

One-tailed test of significance:
** = p ≤ .05
* = .05 < p ≤ .10

Table 4.4. *Transformed Logit Coefficients for Models of Young Women's Plans, Attitudes and Expectations (controlling for all variables in table 4.2)*

	Plans for Work at Age 35		
	20	22	24
Model 1			
College * Away	0.171**	0.204**	0.147**
College * Home	0.118***	0.107**	0.046**
Noncollege away	0.000	0.007	-0.014

Girls Only

	Attitude Toward Mothers' Working		Expected Family Size	Ideal Family Size	Sex-Role Attitudes	
	Girls 1972	Boys 1976	1973	1973	Family 1978	Jobs 1978
Model 1						
College * Away	0.235*	0.378*	-0.017	0.000	0.259**	0.036
College * Home	-0.145	0.016	0.038	0.076	0.115*	-0.061
Noncollege away	0.551**	-0.077	-0.199**	-0.083	0.055	0.043

One-tailed test of significance:
** = $p \leq .05$
* = $.05 < p \leq .10$

Table 5.1. Description of Independent Variables Used in the Analysis of the Transition to Marriage

Explanatory Variables	Description
I. Market:	
Black	1 = yes, 0 = no
Size	Scale from 1 = rural to 8 = urbanized areas of ≥ 3 million
South	1 = yes, 0 = no
Year	Year from which observation comes (1968–77, girls; 1966–78, boys)
II. Concurrent roles at beginning of interval:	
Enrollment	Enrolled in school full time (1 = yes, 0 = no)
Away	Living outside the parental home (1 = yes, 0 = no)
Employed	Current full- or part-time employment (1 = yes, 0 = no)
Military	Active military duty (1 = yes, 0 = no)
Kids	Presence of own (1 = yes, 0 = no)
Pregnant	Had live birth within seven months (1 = yes, 0 = no)
Work at 35	Plans to hold job at age 35
III. Desirability:	
Intact	Living with two natural parents when respondent age 14
Education	Years of schooling completed
Parents' education	Average years of schooling completed by parents
Household head's occupation	Score on the Duncan SEI when respondent age 14
Family income	Parental family income when respondent about age 17 (constant US$ thousands)

Table 5.2. Transformed Logit Coefficients for Model of First Marriage for Males (age at end of interval)

Age	Males				Females			
	18–21	22–25	26–29	All	18–21	22–25	26–29	All
Intercept	−0.729	0.290	0.203	−0.198	−0.907	1.412	−0.994	0.209
Experiences outside traditional families								
Intact	0.005	0.039*	−0.013	0.011	−0.017	0.040*	0.160**	0.011
Away	0.020*	0.003	0.006	0.014*	−0.007	−0.024	−0.029	−0.011
Family background								
Parents' education	−0.002*	−0.002	0.005	−0.002*	−0.009**	−0.002	−0.006	−0.007**
Head's occupation	−0.001**	−0.001*	−0.001*	−0.001**	0.000	0.000	0.000	0.000
Family income	0.000	0.001	−0.001	0.000	−0.001	−0.002	−0.003	−0.001*
Plans for work at age 35	−0.029**	0.004	−0.058**	−0.017**				
Black	−0.041**	−0.046**	−0.004	−0.038**	−0.146**	−0.111**	−0.080*	−0.132**
City size	−0.003*	−0.005*	−0.010**	−0.005**	−0.008**	−0.006*	−0.001*	−0.006**
South	0.027**	0.015	−0.046**	0.016**	0.050**	0.010	−0.020	0.036**
Education	0.008**	0.008**	−0.001	0.010**	0.018**	0.018**	−0.001	0.019**
Enrollment	−0.076**	−0.005	−0.062*	−0.068**	−0.081**	−0.065	0.003	−0.080**
Employed	0.039**	0.088**	0.097**	0.051**	0.024**	0.029	0.097**	0.025**

Table 5.2. (continued)

Age	Males				Females			
	18–21	22–25	26–29	All	18–21	22–25	26–29	All
Year	0.007**	−0.009**	−0.006	−0.001	0.010**	−0.026**	0.009	0.007**
Military	−0.045**	−0.069	−0.125	−0.044**				
Kids					0.036	−0.029	−0.009	0.003
Pregnant					0.206**	0.171**	0.144**	0.200**
2 log likelihood ratio	277.06	60.34	23.86	337.36	519.20	142.85	34.49	599.70
N =	7400	3190	1137	11727	5630	2703	556	8889
Annual proportion marrying	0.083	0.156	0.113	0.105	0.120	0.167	0.110	0.134

One-tailed test of significance:
** = $p \leq .05$;
* = $.05 < p \leq .10$
Distributed as χ^2 with 13 degrees of freedom.

Table 6.1.   Description of Independent Variables Used in the Analysis of Fertility and Divorce Variables

Explanatory Variables	Description
Intact	Living with two natural parents when respondent age 14
Black	1 = yes, 0 = no
Parents' education	Average years of schooling completed by parents
Age at first marriage	In years
Size	Urbanization scale ranging from 1 = rural to 8 = urbanized areas of ≥3 million
South	Southern residence indicator (1 = yes, 0 = no)
Hiatus	Proportion of time that respondent lived in a nonfamily setting prior to first marriage
Plans for work at age 35	Plans to be working at a job when age 35 (question asked when respondent was age 17)
Respondent total income	Respondent total income from all sources (point in time varies with the analysis)
Family roles	See Appendix B
Job roles	See Appendix B
Husband's education	Years of schooling completed
Husband's total income	Husband's total income from all sources (point in time varies based on analysis framework)
Education	Years of schooling completed
Number of siblings	Number of respondent siblings in 1968

Table 6.2. *Transformed Logit Coefficients for Model of First Birth for Married Women*

	Months since Marriage				
	1–6	7–18	19–30	31–48	Total
Intercept	1.709	3.311	1.963	-0.694	2.033
Experiences outside traditional families:					
Intact	-0.530**	0.222	0.552*	0.478	0.400**
Hiatus	-0.872*	0.130	-0.397	-0.155	-0.117
Parents' education	-0.007	-0.023	0.012	-0.064	-0.018
Number of siblings	-0.017	0.069+	0.093+	-0.036	0.037
Plans for work at age 35	-0.035	-0.192	-0.017	0.039	-0.071
Black	0.882**	0.110	0.513+	0.487	0.466**
Size	-0.025	-0.034	0.026	-0.036	-0.013
South	-0.495*	-0.037	-0.516*	0.071	-0.198+
Education	0.008	-0.089+	0.026	0.040	-0.017
Age at first marriage	-0.131**	-0.151**	-0.122**	-0.069	-0.123**
Family roles	-0.305*	-0.296*	-0.099	0.057	-0.183**
Job roles	0.286	-0.044	-0.013	-0.390+	-0.034
Husband's:					
Schooling	-0.047	-0.020	-0.170**	0.028	-0.050**
Total income	-0.000	-0.000	0.000	0.000**	0.000**

Two-tailed tests of significance:
** = p ≤ .01
* = .01 < p ≤ .05
+ = .05 < p ≤ .10

Table 6.3. *Transformed Logit Coefficients for Model of Marital Disruption, Women*

	Months since Marriage					
	1–12	13–24	25–36	37–48	49–60	Total
Intercept	-0.171	-0.582	-0.997	2.159	-3.056	-1.235
Experiences outside traditional families:						
Intact	-0.551	-0.194	-0.185	-0.103	0.500	-0.013
Hiatus	-0.259	-0.406	-0.028	0.763	0.496	0.134
Parents' education	0.048	0.033	0.032	0.095	0.073	0.555+
Plans for work at age 35	0.343	-0.049	-0.038	0.240	0.144	0.113
Black	0.066	1.105**	0.590	0.220	0.339	0.525**
Size	-0.065	-0.059	0.059	0.032	0.735+	0.034
South	-0.211	0.028	-0.332	-0.741+	0.164+	-0.118
Education	-0.214	0.128	-0.166	-0.115	0.037	-0.053
Age at first marriage	-0.028	-0.155*	-0.026	-0.148*	-0.038	-0.074**
Family roles	-0.014	0.414	-0.186	0.431	-0.033	0.118
Job roles	-0.229	-0.347	0.503	-0.016	0.232	0.053
Husband's:						
Schooling	-0.043	-0.123*	0.007	-0.133*	-0.103	-0.083**
Total income	0.000	-0.000	-0.000	-0.000	-0.000*	-0.000**
Respondent's total income	-0.000	0.000	0.000	-0.000	0.000	0.000

Two-tailed tests of significance:
** = $p \leq .01$
* = $.01 < p \leq .05$
+ = $.05 < p \leq .10$

Table 7.1.   Description of Independent Variables Used in the Analysis of Husband's Share of Household Tasks

Explanatory Variables	Description
Age	The age in years of the respondent minus 27
Educational attainment	Years of schooling completed
Employed	Current full-time or part-time employment (1 = yes, 0 = no)
Stepfamily	Indicator that there was a stepparent in the household when the respondent was age 14 (1 = yes, 0 = no)
Stepparent	Indicator for the presence of a stepparent in the current household (1 = yes, 0 = no)
Mother-only family I	Respondent lived in a female-headed household when she was age 14 (1 = yes, 0 = no)
Hiatus	Proportion of time that respondent lived in a nonfamily setting prior to first marriage
Girl 12–18	Number of female children ages 12–18 in the household
Girl > 18	Number of female children older than 18 in the household
Boy 12–18	Number of male children ages 12–18 in the household
Boy > 18	Number of male children older than 18 in the household
Total kids	Total number of children in the household
Kid < 4	Presence of at least one child less than 4 years old in the household (1 = yes, 0 = no)
Kid 4–6	Presence of at least one child between the ages of 4 and 6 in the household (1 = yes, 0 = no)
Prekid	Indicator that the couple has never had children (1 = yes, 0 = no)
Empty nest couple	Indicator showing that the couple had children in their household and now have none (1 = yes, 0 = no)
Husband's share	Sum of the 8 independent measures on the husband's role in sharing household tasks
Groceries	Measure of husband's role in grocery shopping (the scale ranges from 0 for the husband who has no responsibility for grocery shopping to 4 for the husband who has total responsibility for the grocery shopping)
Dishes	Measure of husband's role in washing dishes (the scale ranges from 0 to 4 and is similar in concept to Groceries)

Table 7.1.   (continued)

Explanatory Variables	Description
Cooking	Measure of husband's role in cooking meals (the scale ranges from 0 to 4 and is similar in concept to Groceries)
Child care	Measure of husband's role in child care (the scale ranges from 0 to 4 and is similar in concept to Groceries)
Cleaning	Measure of husband's role in cleaning the house (the scale ranges from 0 to 4 and is similar in concept to Groceries)
Laundry	Measure of husband's role in washing the clothes (the scale ranges from 0 to 4 and is similar in concept to Groceries)
Yard work	Measure of husband's role in performing yard work (the scale ranges from 0 to 4 and is similar in concept to Groceries)
Paperwork	Measure of husband's role in doing household paperwork (the scale ranges from 0 to 4 and is similar in concept to Groceries)
Black	1 = yes, 0 = no
Size	Urbanization scale ranging from 1 = rural to 8 = urbanized areas of ≥ 3 million
South	Southern residence indicator (1 = yes, 0 = no)
Wife's current work hours	Number of hours that wife normally works during a workweek
Wife's disability	Indicator for a health limitation on the amount of work that the wife can do (1 = yes, 0 = no)
Wife's income	Wife's total income from all sources
Family roles	See Appendix B
Job roles	See Appendix B
Husband's educational attainment	Years of schooling completed by husband
Husband's current hours of work	Number of hours that husband normally works during a workweek
Husband's total income	Husband's total income from all sources
Husband's disability	Indicator for a health limitation on the amount of work that the husband can do (1 = yes, 0 = no)

Table 7.2. Ordinary Least-Squares Models of Husbands' Share of Household Tasks: Total Population

Dependent Variables	Share Scale	Grocery Shopping	Dishes	Cooking	Child Care	Cleaning	Laundry	Yard Work	Paperwork
Dep mean	3.835	1.067	0.826	0.808	1.678	0.730	0.401	1.650	1.043
R-squared	0.138	0.062	0.102	0.061	0.104	0.089	0.063	0.074	0.022
N =	4789	4800	4798	4799	2711	4797	4800	4622	4794
Model DF	27	27	27	27	27	27	27	27	27
Intercept	2.089**	0.816**	−0.028	0.557**	0.225	0.495**	0.233*	2.118**	0.569**
Childhood family:									
Stepfamily I	−0.310	−0.069	−0.076	−0.077	0.172	−0.047	−0.050	0.098	0.022
Mother-only family I	0.107	0.022	0.017	0.062	0.052	−0.021	0.023	−0.024	−0.089
Stepparent	−0.372*	0.009	−0.147*	−0.084	−0.220**	−0.090	−0.054	0.180*	0.129+
Hiatus	0.707***	0.373***	0.048	0.174*	−0.563***	0.080	0.032	0.148	−0.018
Prekid	0.844***	0.245*	0.285***	0.092	−1.331***	0.104	0.096	−0.053	0.182
Children in family:									
Child under 4	0.414+	0.104	0.187*	−0.016	0.099	0.153*	−0.013	0.134	0.226**
Child 4–6	0.210	−0.007	0.142*	0.051	−0.041	0.024	−0.001	0.001	0.190*
Girl 12–18	−0.620**	0.003	−0.298***	−0.078	−0.076	−0.144*	−0.105*	−0.131+	−0.093
Girl > 18	−0.918***	−0.069	−0.298***	−0.190*	−0.187	−0.221***	−0.149*	−0.211*	−0.029
Boy 12–18	−0.080	0.020	−0.044	0.031	0.076	−0.034	−0.061	−0.195*	0.003
Boy > 18	0.550*	0.201*	0.105	0.089	−0.152	0.103	0.046	−0.193*	0.026
Total number	−0.109	−0.021	−0.020	−0.025	−0.001	−0.032	−0.010	−0.042	0.039

Black	-0.307+	0.030	-0.223**	-0.075	-0.223**	-0.060	0.016	-0.063	0.248**
Size	0.019	-0.015	0.005	0.009	-0.019	0.010	0.011	0.012	0.000
South	-0.213	-0.127*	0.032	-0.058	-0.208**	-0.033	-0.026	-0.147*	-0.004
Education	0.012	-0.008	0.020*	-0.008	0.066**	-0.002	0.011	0.010	-0.014
Employed	0.083	-0.139+	0.161*	0.092	0.215*	0.027	-0.052	-0.147+	-0.003
Wife's:									
Current hours	0.032**	0.007**	0.004*	0.008**	0.003	0.007**	0.006**	0.003	0.002
Disability	1.122**	0.285**	0.197**	0.158*	-0.053	0.297**	0.182**	-0.190*	0.056
Income	0.000**	0.000*	0.000**	0.000*	-0.000	0.000**	0.000**	0.000	0.000
Age	0.039**	0.016**	0.021**	0.002	0.019**	0.003	-0.003	-0.034**	0.001
Sex-role attitudes:									
Family roles	0.487**	0.065*	0.104**	0.118**	0.115**	0.134**	0.067**	0.014	0.027
Job roles	-0.230*	-0.021	-0.073*	-0.051+	-0.098*	-0.084**	-0.003	0.067+	-0.045
Husband's:									
Education	0.108**	0.025**	0.030**	0.017**	0.046**	0.022**	0.014**	0.008	0.027**
Earnings	-0.000**	-0.000**	-0.000	-0.000	-0.000	-0.000*	-0.000***	0.000	0.000*
Current hours	-0.020**	-0.005***	-0.006**	-0.002	0.001	-0.005***	-0.003***	0.001	-0.001
Disability	0.062	-0.097	-0.060	0.106+	0.197*	0.042	0.077+	-0.110	0.062

Two-tailed tests of significance:

** = $p \leq .01$

* = $.01 < p \leq .05$

+ = $.05 < p \leq .10$

Table 7.3. Ordinary Least-Squares Models of Husbands' Share of Household Tasks: Hiatus Sample, Hiatus Population

Dependent Variables	Share Scale	Grocery Shopping	Dishes	Cooking	Child Care	Cleaning	Laundry	Yard Work	Paperwork
Dep mean	3.877	0.903	0.792	0.806	1.715	0.848	0.528	2.156	1.187
R-squared	0.144	0.044	0.111	0.093	0.093	0.097	0.099	0.053	0.056
N =	900	900	900	900	766	899	899	860	900
Model DF	28	28	28	28	27	28	28	28	28
Intercept	1.555	0.385	0.294	0.370	0.794+	0.404	0.102	1.772**	0.535
Childhood family:									
Stepfamily I	−0.174	0.001	−0.022	−0.035	−0.030	0.002	−0.121	0.326	0.225
Mother-only family I	1.077**	0.074	0.202	0.338*	0.177	0.207	0.256*	−0.123	−0.161
Stepparent	0.565	0.214+	0.004	0.367**	0.172	−0.030	0.010	0.116	0.188
Hiatus	−1.297+	−0.493*	−0.018	−0.504*	0.214	−0.253	−0.032	−0.654*	−0.345
Empty-nest couple	−0.009	−0.104	0.540	−0.400	—	0.123	−0.167	−0.208	−0.400
Prekid	0.353	0.388*	0.085	0.170	−1.706*	−0.092	−0.202	0.297	0.299
Children in family:									
Child under 4	0.657*	0.162	0.128	0.099	0.198+	0.232*	0.035	0.153	0.184
Child 4–6	0.123	−0.078	0.087	0.144	0.011	0.009	−0.039	−0.176	0.191
Girl 12–18	−0.750+	0.037	−0.332*	−0.042	−0.246	−0.195	−0.218+	−0.279	−0.051
Girl > 18	−0.816	−0.242	−0.041	0.671	0.400	−0.267	−0.937	0.490	−1.327

Boy 12–18	-0.444	0.040	-0.235	-0.163	-0.379*	0.020	-0.107	-0.234	0.205
Boy > 18	-5.228	-1.139	-1.204	-1.386	-0.441	-0.955	-0.542	-0.375	-1.663
Total number	-0.344*	-0.013	-0.023	-0.099+	0.041	-0.121*	-0.088+	-0.004	-0.062
Black	-0.302	0.172	-0.285**	-0.126	-0.213+	-0.057	-0.006	0.251+	0.187
Size	0.022	-0.027	0.018	-0.002	-0.011	-0.009	0.042*	0.019	0.060*
South	0.029	-0.122	0.038	0.065	-0.116	-0.008	0.056	-0.116	0.087
Education	0.121	0.018	0.014	0.039	0.022	0.027	0.023	0.028	-0.024
Employed	0.730	0.268+	0.286*	0.052	0.290+	0.089	0.034	-0.122	0.006
Wife's:									
Current hours	0.008	0.001	-0.005	0.006	0.007	0.003	0.003	0.005	0.001
Disability	0.569	0.063	0.103	-0.031	-0.135	0.310	0.124	-0.420	-0.075
Income	0.000**	-0.000	0.000*	0.000	-0.000+	0.000*	0.000**	0.000	-0.000
Age	-0.094	0.005	-0.030	-0.069+	-0.036	-0.011	0.012	-0.077	-0.040
Sex-role attitudes:									
Family roles	0.182	-0.066	0.079	-0.062	-0.035	0.117+	0.113*	-0.164+	0.020
Job roles	0.376	0.107	0.065	0.220**	-0.035	0.053	-0.067	0.119	-0.088
Husband's:									
Education	0.090**	0.013	0.028*	0.015	0.036**	0.021+	0.014	0.033*	0.051**
Earnings	-0.000	0.000	0.000	0.000	0.000	-0.000	-0.000*	-0.000	0.000*
Current hours	-0.017+	-0.002	-0.005+	-0.006*	-0.001	-0.002	-0.001	-0.000	-0.002
Disability	-0.424	-0.053	-0.163	-0.070	0.246	-0.045	-0.092	-0.384+	0.154

Two-tailed tests of significance:

** = p ≤ .01
* = .01 < p ≤ .05
+ = .05 < p ≤ .10

Table 7.4.   Ordinary Least-Squares Models of Men's Sharing Household Tasks with Their Wives

Explanatory Variables	All Married Men	Married Fathers
Intercept	−11.78**	−11.68**
Intact family growing up	−.67*	−.78**
Black	.91**	.90*
Education	.34**	.33**
Enrolled in school	1.21	1.16
Wife employed full time	1.34**	1.04**
Wife employed part time	.54	.36
Log of wife's income	.08*	.10**
Unemployed	2.75**	3.80**
Employment hours	.02**	.02**
Occupational prestige	.00	.00
Log of own income	.05	.04
Parents' education	.06	.06
Size	.08	.09
South	−.33	−.39
N	2246	1939
Mean[a]	−5.32	−5.61
R-squared	.10	.08

Two-tailed tests of significance:
** = $p \leq .01$
* = $.01 < p \leq .05$

[a]Based on summing responses to questions on 9 chores with the responses scored −2=wife does all; −1=husband does some; 0=they share equally; +1=husband does most; +2=husband does all.

Table 7.5.   Husbands' Sharing of Household Tasks: Interaction Coefficients[a] with Household Structure (full sample)

Model and Variables	Coefficient	Probability
I. Interaction of childhood family structure and childlessness		
Stepfamily I	.078	.842
No kids	.814	.041
Stepfamily I * No kids	−1.486	.051
Mother-only family I	.363	.125
No kids	.862	.035
Mother-only family I * No kids	−.917	.038
II. Interaction of stepfather with teenage children[b]		
Stepparent	−.008	.871
Boy 12–18	.047	.376
Stepparent * Boy 12–18	−.126	.090
Stepparent	−.024	.618
Girl 12–18	−.098	.066
Stepparent * Girl 12–18	−.092	.218

[a]Based on regressions otherwise identical to those presented in table 7.2.
[b]Based on logged version of the dependent variable.

Table 7.6.   Teenage Children's Sharing of Household Tasks: Interaction Coefficients[a] Mother-Only Families and Age (full sample)

Dependent Variables	Share Scale	Cooking	Cleaning	Grocery Shopping
I. Interaction of family structure and teenage children[b]				
Mother-only family	2.503**	.270*	.521**	.285**
Girl 12–18	2.626**	.369**	.798**	.015
Mother-only family * Girl 12–18	.990**	.286**	.030	.264**
Mother-only family	2.347**	.317*	.395**	.356**
Boy 12–18	−.115	−.123*	−.077	−.070
Mother-only family * Boy 12–18	1.494**	.222**	.320**	.142*

Table 7.6.   (continued)

	Cooking	Dishes	Laundry
II. Interaction of maternal education and teenage children			
Mother's education	−.004	−.016	−.006
Girl 12–18	.591**	.549**	.465**
Mother's education * Girl 12–18	−.012	.017	.004
Mother's education	−.019*	−.019	−.010
Boy 12–18	−.328*	−.216	−.092
Mother's education * Boy 12–18	.022	.023	.011

	Cooking	Yard Work
III. Interaction of maternal employment and teenage children		
Employed	−.076	.004
Girl 12–18	.290**	.193**
Employed * Girl 12–18	.264**	−.020
Employed	.062	−.072
Boy 12–18	−.018	.176**
Employed * Boy 12–18	−.064	.154*

	Share Scale Kid's Share
IV. Interaction of maternal age and teenage children	
Mother's age	.087**
Girl 12–18	2.074**
Mother's age * Girl 12–18	.069*
Mother's age	.141**
Boy 12–18	.952*
Mother's age * Boy 12–18	−.050*

Two-tailed tests of significance:
** = p ≤ .01
* = .01 < p ≤ .05

[a]Based on regressions otherwise identical to those presented in table 7.2.

[b]Families with two children, one between 6 and 11 (the reference category), one the relevant teenage child.

Table 8.1.   Husbands' Sharing of Household Tasks: Interaction Coefficients[a] with Wife's Education and Age (full sample)

Model and Variables	Coefficient	Probability
I. Interaction of wife's education and childlessness[b]		
Education	.017	.031
Education * No kid	−.033	.009
II. Interaction of wife's age and sex -role attitudes[b]		
Age	.040	.001
Family roles	.286	.003
Job roles	.448	.038
Age * Job roles	−.044	.001

Two-tailed tests of significance:
** = $p \leq .01$
* = $.01 < p \leq .05$
[a]Based on regressions otherwise identical to those presented in table 7.2.
[b]Based on logged version of the dependent variable.

Table 9.1.   Description of Independent Variables Used in the Analysis of Children's Share of Household Tasks

Explanatory Variables	Description
Age	The age in years of the respondent minus 27
Educational attainment	Years of schooling completed
Employed	Current full-time or part-time employment(1 = yes, 0 = no)
Stepfamily	Indicator that there was a stepparent in the household when the respondent was age 14 (1 = yes, 0 = no)
Stepparent	Indicator for the presence of a stepparent in the current household (1 = yes, 0 = no)
Mother-only family I	Respondent lived in a female-headed household when she was age 14 (1 = yes, 0 = no)
Mother-only family II	Respondent lives in a female-headed household (1 = yes, 0 = no)
Hiatus	Proportion of time that respondent lived in a nonfamily setting prior to first marriage
Girl 12–18	Number of female children age 12–18 in the household
Girl > 18	Number of female children older than 18 in the household
Boy 12–18	Number of male children ages 12–18 in the household
Boy > 18	Number of male children older than 18 in the household
Total kids	Total number of children in the household
Kid < 4	Presence of at least one child less than 4 years old in the household (1 = yes, 0 = no)
Kid 4–6	Presence of at least one child between the ages of 4 and 6 in the household (1 = yes, 0 = no)
Intact	Living with two natural parents when respondent age 14
Kids' share	Sum of the 8 independent measures on the children's role in sharing household tasks
Groceries	Measure of children's role in grocery shopping. The scale ranges from 0 for children who have no responsibility for grocery shopping to 4 for children who have total responsibility for the grocery shopping

Table 9.1.   *(continued)*

Dishes	Measure of children's role in washing dishes (the scale ranges from 0 to 4 and is similar in concept to Groceries)
Cooking	Measure of children's role in cooking meals (the scale ranges from 0 to 4 and is similar in concept to Groceries)
Child care	Measure of children's role in child care (the scale ranges from 0 to 4 and is similar in concept to Groceries)
Cleaning	Measure of children's role in cleaning the house (the scale ranges from 0 to 4 and is similar in concept to Groceries)
Laundry	Measure of children's role in washing the clothes (the scale ranges from 0 to 4 and is similar in concept to Groceries)
Yard work	Measure of children's role in performing yard work (the scale ranges from 0 to 4 and is similar in concept to Groceries)
Paperwork	Measure of children's role in doing household paperwork (the scale ranges from 0 to 4 and is similar in concept to Groceries)
Black	1 = yes, 0 = no
Size	Urbanization scale ranging from 1 = rural to 8 = urbanized areas of $\geq$ 3 million
South	Southern residence indicator (1 = yes, 0 = no)
Wife's current work hours	Number of hours that wife normally works during a work week
Wife's disability	Indicator for a health limitation on the amount of work that the wife can do (1 = yes, 0 = no)
Wife's income	Wife's total income from all sources
Family roles	See Appendix B
Job roles	Factor score based on respondent's answer to attitude question related to respondent's attitude toward work and family
Husband's educational attainment	Years of schooling completed by husband
Husband's current hours of work	Number of hours that husband normally works during a work week
Husband's total income	Husband's total income from all sources
Husband's disability	Indicator for a health limitation on the amount of work that the children can do (1 = yes, 0 = no)

Table 9.2. Ordinary Least-Squares Models of Children Sharing Household Tasks: Complete Sample, Total Population

Dependent Variables	Share Scale	Grocery Shopping	Dishes	Cooking	Child Care	Cleaning	Laundry	Yard Work	Paperwork
Dep mean	4.234	0.224	1.181	0.479	0.225	1.040	0.613	0.472	0.042
R-squared	0.341	0.111	0.160	0.169	0.135	0.212	0.204	0.116	0.029
N =	3467	3467	3467	3467	3467	3467	3467	3467	3467
Model DF	25	25	25	25	25	25	25	25	25
Intercept	-1.112	-0.095	0.148	-0.232	0.005	-0.113	-0.580**	-0.246	0.025
Childhood family:									
Intact	-0.283	-0.052	-0.059	-0.009	-0.017	-0.054	-0.072	-0.019	-0.016
Stepparent	0.465*	0.054	0.210**	0.048	0.061+	0.069	0.025	-0.002	0.003
Mother-only	3.003**	0.419**	0.353*	0.414**	0.144*	0.536**	0.430**	0.707**	0.118**
Children in family:									
Child under 4	-0.383	-0.029	-0.113	-0.064	-0.005	-0.016	-0.095	-0.061	-0.022
Child 4–6	-0.557**	-0.011	-0.269**	-0.052	0.003	-0.096	-0.060	-0.072	-0.004
Girl 12–18	2.916**	0.092**	0.760**	0.453**	0.106**	0.807**	0.516**	0.181**	0.002
Girl > 18	2.638**	0.312**	0.397**	0.368**	0.295**	0.603**	0.702**	-0.040	0.007
Boy 12–18	0.328+	-0.028	0.063	-0.057	0.016	0.017	0.046	0.270**	-0.025
Boy > 18	-0.276	-0.037	-0.107	-0.136*	-0.123*	0.015	0.038	0.074	-0.023
Total number	0.925**	0.038*	0.206**	0.122**	0.134**	0.147**	0.152**	0.127**	0.012
Black	0.826**	0.082*	0.309**	0.017	0.170**	0.084	0.067	0.098+	0.014
Size	-0.097**	-0.003	-0.011	-0.020*	-0.020**	-0.017	-0.003	-0.024*	0.000

South	–0.513**	–0.040	–0.233**	–0.083+	0.042	–0.159**	–0.051	0.010	0.014
Education	–0.087*	–0.014*	–0.008	–0.009	–0.022**	–0.014	–0.004	–0.016+	–0.008*
Employed	0.071	–0.061	–0.005	0.034	0.043	0.040	0.025	–0.005	–0.027
Wife's:									
Current hours	0.009	0.001	0.003	0.003	–0.001	0.001	0.002	0.000	–0.000
Disability	0.530*	0.057	–0.037	0.181**	0.137**	0.110	0.203**	–0.120+	0.022
Income	0.000	–0.000	0.000	0.000	–0.000	0.000	0.000**	0.000	0.000
Age	0.118**	0.017**	0.008+	0.023**	0.005*	0.030**	0.024**	0.011**	0.005**
Sex-role attitudes:									
Family roles	0.189*	0.035*	0.019	0.055*	0.014	0.023	0.046+	–0.004	0.013
Job roles	–0.262*	–0.026	–0.023	–0.079**	–0.018	–0.049	–0.055+	–0.013	–0.018+
Husband's:									
Education	–0.030	0.003	–0.012	–0.012+	–0.003	–0.012	0.007	0.000	0.003
Earnings	–0.000	0.000	0.000	–0.000	0.000	–0.000	0.000	–0.000	–0.000
Current hours	0.021**	0.001	0.006**	0.002	–0.001	0.007**	0.001	0.005**	0.000
Disability	0.615*	0.095+	0.082	0.063	0.035	0.097	–0.010	0.253**	–0.004

Note: The scale measure of sharing KIDSHARE, which ranges from 0 to 32, was logged for this analysis to reduce the impact of the long right tail on the results. Measures of individual tasks are not logged, since they range only from 0 to 4.

Two-tailed tests of significance:
** = $p \leq .01$
* = $.01 < p \leq .05$
+ = $.05 < p \leq .10$

Table 9.3. Ordinary Least-Squares Models of Children Sharing Household Tasks: Complete Sample, Hiatus Population

Dependent Variables	Share Scale	Grocery Shopping	Dishes	Cooking	Child Care	Cleaning	Laundry	Yard Work	Paperwork
Dep mean	2.212	0.044	0.844	0.181	0.121	0.567	0.199	0.256	0.011
R-squared	0.275	0.064	0.187	0.156	0.100	0.157	0.130	0.119	0.040
N =	758	758	758	758	758	758	758	758	758
Model DF	25	25	25	25	25	25	25	25	25
Intercept	-2.908**	-0.094	-0.545	-0.526*	-0.489*	-0.628+	-0.466*	-0.160	-0.151*
Childhood family:									
Intact	0.707	-0.013	0.048	0.206*	0.106	0.288+	-0.031	0.103	-0.013
Stepparent	0.399	0.033	0.005	0.008	0.010	0.120	0.068	0.154+	-0.019
Mother-only	-0.910+	-0.059	-0.431*	-0.182	-0.177+	-0.188	0.073	0.055	0.053
Children in family:									
Child under 4	0.336	-0.004	0.203	0.037	0.058	0.164	-0.071	-0.052	-0.016
Child 4–6	2.130**	0.103	0.156	0.323*	0.321**	0.690**	0.250+	0.287	-0.001
Girl 12–18	-0.385	0.007	-0.122	-0.050	-0.015	-0.129	-0.054	-0.022	-0.038+
Girl > 18	-0.756***	-0.016	-0.348**	-0.068	-0.023	-0.228*	-0.104+	0.031	-0.008
Boy 12–18	2.228***	0.053	0.644***	0.454***	0.061	0.535***	0.386***	0.094	-0.026
Boy > 18	0.867***	-0.003	0.230+	0.134+	0.107+	0.052	0.071	0.276**	0.016
Total number	0.897***	-0.010	0.297***	0.072*	0.094**	0.222**	0.113***	0.109**	0.015
Black	0.641*	0.051	0.306***	-0.035	0.076	0.145	0.106+	-0.009	-0.002
Size	-0.007	0.002	0.003	-0.016	-0.014	0.016	0.018	-0.015	0.005

	(1)	(2)	(3)	(4)	(5)	(6)	(7)	(8)	(9)
South	-0.572*	-0.013	-0.294**	-0.130*	0.025	-0.187*	-0.061	0.088	0.021
Education	0.024	-0.002	0.013	0.029*	-0.002	-0.005	0.011	-0.021	0.007+
Employed	0.580	-0.007	0.058	0.086	0.054	0.298*	0.065	0.026	-0.019
Wife's:									
Current hours	0.008	0.001	0.006	0.002	0.001	-0.006	0.001	0.002	0.000
Disability	1.112*	0.215**	0.100	0.279*	0.154	-0.206	0.289*	0.282*	0.091**
Income	0.000	-0.000+	0.000	-0.000	-0.000	0.000+	-0.000	-0.000	-0.000
Age	0.122	0.026*	0.056	-0.012	0.031	0.000	-0.027	0.048	0.011
Sex-role attitudes:									
Family roles	-0.026	0.020	-0.030	-0.050	-0.043	-0.038	0.039	0.074+	0.008
Job roles	-0.601**	-0.024	-0.218*	-0.017	-0.027	-0.128	-0.056	-0.130*	-0.023
Husband's:									
Education	0.018	-0.002	-0.017	0.005	0.003	0.014	0.005	0.009	0.001
Earnings	0.000	0.000	-0.000	0.000	0.000	0.000	0.000	-0.000	-0.000
Current hours	0.015	0.001	0.008+	-0.001	0.002	0.005	0.001	-0.001	-0.000
Disability	0.569	-0.017	0.141	0.002	-0.043	0.388*	0.138	-0.040	-0.016

Two-tailed tests of significance:
** = $p \leq .01$
* = $.01 < p \leq .05$
+ = $.05 < p \leq .10$

Table 9.4.   Teenage Children's Sharing of Household Tasks: Interaction Coefficients [a] for Mother-Only Families (full sample)

Dependent Variables	Kid's Share	Cooking	Cleaning	Grocery Shopping
I. Interaction of family structure and teenage children[b]				
Mother-only family	2.503**	.270*	.521**	.285**
Girl 12–18	2.626**	.369**	.798**	.015
Mother-only family * Girl 12–18	.990**	.286**	.030	.264**
Mother-only family	2.347**	.317*	.395**	.356**
Boy 12–18	–.115	–.123*	–.077	–.070
Mother-only family * Boy 12–18	1.494**	.222**	.320**	.142*

		Cooking	Dishes	Laundry
II. Interaction of maternal education and older children				
Mother's education		–.004	–.007	–.009
Girl >18[c]		.591**	.48	.34
Mother's education * Girl >18[c]		–.012	–.008	.032
Mother's education		–.019	–.016	–.010
Boy >18[c]		–.216	–.71	–.37
Mother's education * Boy >18[c]		.023	.053	.036

			Cooking	Yard and Home Maintenance
III. Interaction of maternal employment and teenage children				
Employed			–.076	.004
Girl 12–18			.290**	.193**
Employed * Girl 12–18			.264**	–.020
Employed			.062	–.072
Boy 12–18			–.018	.176**
Employed * Boy 12–18			–.064	.154*

				Share Scale Kid's Share
IV. Interaction of maternal age and teenage children				
Mother's age				.087**
Girl 12–18				2.074**
Mother's age * Girl 12–18				.069*
Mother's age				.141**
Boy 12–18				.952*
Mother's age * Boy 12–18				–.050*

[a]Based on regressions otherwise identical to those presented in table 9.3.

[b]Families with two children, one between 6 and 11 (the reference category), and one the relevant teenage child.

[c]Results for cooking are for sons and daughters aged 12–18.

Table 10.1.   Description of Independent Variables Used in the Analysis of Husband's and Children's Share of Household Tasks

Explanatory Variables	Description
Age	The age in years of the respondent minus 27
Stepfamily	Indicator that there was a stepparent in the household when the respondent was age 14 (1 = yes, 0 = no)
Stepfather	Indicator for the presence of a stepparent in the current household (1 = yes, 0 = no)
Mother-only family I	Respondent lived in a female-headed household when she was age 14 (1 = yes, 0 = no)
Hiatus	Proportion of time that respondent lived in a nonfamily setting prior to first marriage
Girl 12–18	Number of female children age 12–18 in the household
Boy 12–18	Number of male children ages 12–18 in the household
Total kids	Total number of children in the household
Kid < 4	Presence of at least one child less than 4 years old in the household (1 = yes, 0 = no)
Kid 4–6	Presence of at least one child between the ages of 4 and 6 in the household (1 = yes, 0 = no)
Groceries	Measure of person's role in grocery shopping (the scale ranges from 0 for the person who has no responsibility for grocery shopping to 4 for the person who has total responsibility for grocery shopping)
Dishes	Measure of the person's role in washing dishes (the scale ranges from 0 to 4 and is similar in concept to Groceries)
Cooking	Measure of the person's role in cooking meals (the scale ranges from 0 to 4 and is similar in concept to Groceries)
Child care	Measure of husband's or children's role in child care (the scale ranges from 0 to 4 and is similar in concept to Groceries)
Cleaning	Measure of children's role in cleaning the house (the scale ranges from 0 to 4 and is similar in concept to Groceries)
Laundry	Measure of children's role in washing the clothes (the scale ranges from 0 to 4 and is similar in concept to Groceries)

Table 10.1.   (continued)

Yard work	Measure of children's role in performing yard work (the scale ranges from 0 to 4 and is similar in concept to Groceries)
Paperwork	Measure of children's role in doing household paperwork (the scale ranges from 0 to 4 and is similar in concept to Groceries)
Black	1 = yes, 0 = no
Size	Urbanization scale ranging from 1 = rural to 8 = urbanized areas of ≥3 million
South	Southern residence indicator (1 = yes, 0 = no)
Wife's current work hours	Number of hours that wife normally works during a work week
Wife's disability	Indicator for a health limitation on the amount of work that the wife can do (1 = yes, 0 = no)
Wife employed	Current full-time or part-time employment (1 = yes, 0 = no)
Wife's income	Wife's total income from all sources
Wife's schooling	Years of schooling completed
Family roles	Factor score based on respondent's answer to attitude questions related to respondent's role in the household
Job roles	Factor score based on respondent's answer to attitude question related to respondent's attitude toward work and family
Husband's educational attainment	Years of schooling completed by husband
Husband's current hours of work	Number of hours that husband normally works during a work week
Husband's total income	Husband's total income from all sources (thousands)
Husband's disability	Indicator for a health limitation on the amount of work that the husband can do (1 = yes, 0 = no)

Table 10.2.   Two-Stage Least-Squares Models of Sharing with Husbands and Children, Total Population

	Children's Share	Husband's Share
Intercept	0.613	0.750
Husband's share	−0.875+	—
Children's share	—	−0.172*
Childhood family:		
Stepfamily I	0.446	0.221
Mother-only family I	0.420	0.160
Stepfather	−0.171	−0.339+
Children in family:		
Child < 4	−0.211	0.250
Child 4–6	−0.449+	0.093
Girl 12–18	2.103**	—
Girl > 18	1.736**	−0.108
Boy 12–18	−0.070	0.080
Boy > 18	−0.177	0.402
Total number	0.700**	0.014
Black	0.666*	−0.092
Size	−0.052	0.017
South	−0.555**	−0.172
Wife's:		
Schooling	−0.024	0.054
Employed	0.018	−0.110
Work hours	0.033*	0.031**
Disabled	0.638	0.567*
Income	0.070*	0.060**
Age	0.085**	0.035*
Sex-role attitudes:		
Family roles	0.314+	0.310**
Job roles	−0.006	0.065
Husband's:		
Schooling	0.072	0.111**
Work hours	—	−0.011*
Income	−0.004	−0.010
Disability	0.817*	0.502*
N = 2572		
R-squared	0.227	0.116
Mean of dependent variable	2.96	3.01

Two-tailed tests of significance:
** = $p \leq .01$
* = $.01 < p \leq .05$
+ = $.05 < p \leq .10$

Table 10.3. *Polytomous Logit Models of Sharing with Husband and Children for Separate Chores, Total Population*

Dependent Variables	Grocery Shopping		Washing Dishes		Cooking		Child Care	
	Husband	Child	Husband	Child	Husband	Child	Husband	Child
Dep Mean	0.321	0.040	0.218	0.393	0.247	0.111	0.507	0.058
R-squared	0.069	0.098	0.240	0.353	0.114	0.173	0.212	0.177
N =	2573	2573	2573	2573	2573	2573	2573	2573
Intercept	−1.074**	−4.719	−2.871	−2.203**	−1.658**	−3.378	−0.876**	−3.893*
Childhood family:								
Stepfamily I	0.418+	2.086**	0.270	0.052	0.011	−0.184	0.299	0.296
Mother-only family I	−0.071	0.053	0.140	0.230	0.216	0.274	−0.116	−0.082
Stepfather	0.175+	0.151	0.037	0.427**	−0.029	0.092	0.013	0.508*
Children in family:								
Child < 4	0.274+	−0.124	0.129	−0.396*	−0.086	−0.305	0.106	−0.306
Child 4–6	−0.083	−0.162	0.119	−0.466**	0.035	−0.266	−0.133	0.042
Girl 12–18	0.047	0.652*	−0.065	1.524**	0.081	1.629**	−0.298**	0.611**
Girl >18	0.106	2.366**	−0.057	0.484*	−0.227	1.070**	−0.286+	1.224**
Boy 12–18	0.036	−0.054	−0.180	−0.039	0.108	−0.123	−0.229*	−0.208
Boy >18	0.147	−0.305	0.148	−0.474*	−0.082	−0.686**	−0.756**	−1.481**
Total number	−0.014	0.355**	0.117+	0.550**	0.020	0.521**	0.220**	0.966**
Black	0.265*	0.463	−0.094	1.085**	−0.044	0.345+	−0.253*	1.484**
Size	−0.010	−0.019	−0.005	−0.056*	0.031	−0.095**	−0.043+	−0.077+

South	–0.204*	–0.141	–0.125	–0.457**	–0.159	–0.405*	–0.257*	0.312
Wife's:								
Schooling	–0.014	–0.098+	0.063*	–0.026	–0.012	–0.057	0.072**	–0.148**
Employed	–0.258+	–0.811*	0.315+	0.361*	0.092	0.276	0.369*	0.627*
Work hours	0.015**	0.021*	0.010+	0.004	0.019**	0.015*	0.002	–0.007
Disabled	0.540**	0.396	0.450*	0.009	0.057	0.562*	–0.027	0.557
Income	0.020**	0.020	0.030**	0.010	0.030**	–0.010	0.010	0.010
Age	0.001	0.062**	0.006	–0.007	–0.022*	0.014	–0.065**	–0.004
Sex-role attitudes:								
Family roles	0.036	0.209	0.283**	0.224**	0.105+	0.056	0.141**	0.101
Job roles	0.070	–0.050	0.030	–0.100	0.178*	–0.032	0.095	–0.204
Husband's:								
Schooling	0.058**	–0.021	0.060**	–0.000	0.044**	–0.045*	0.046**	–0.053*
Work hours	–0.007*	0.002	–0.006	0.004	–0.005	–0.001	0.000	–0.011
Income	–0.010**	0.000	0.010	0.010	–0.000	0.000	0.000	0.010
Disability	0.074	1.143**	0.099	0.284+	0.386*	0.445*	0.564**	0.393

Two-tailed tests of significance:
** = $p \leq .01$
* = $.01 < p \leq .05$
+ = $.05 < p \leq .10$

Table 10.3. (continued)

Dependent Variables	Housecleaning		Laundry		Yard, Home Maintenance		Paperwork	
	Husband	Child	Husband	Child	Husband	Child	Husband	Child
Dep Mean	0.209	0.306	0.116	0.168	0.705	0.133	0.425	0.007
R-squared	0.202	0.303	0.101	0.220	0.396	0.416	0.049	0.036
N =	2573	2573	2573	2573	2573	2573	2573	2573
Intercept	-2.538+	-2.554+	-3.449	-4.384	0.106**	-2.200**	-1.409*	-2.379**
Childhood family:								
Stepfamily I	0.317	0.321	0.000	0.188	0.117	-0.334	0.077	1.362
Mother-only family I	0.032	0.312+	0.159	0.323+	0.019	-0.006	-0.237+	0.525
Stepfather	0.010	0.280*	-0.106	0.066	0.167	-0.039	0.113	-0.939+
Children in family:								
Child < 4	0.099	-0.112	-0.301	-0.430*	0.321+	0.148	0.401**	-0.410
Child 4–6	-0.046	-0.299*	-0.123	-0.348*	0.030	-0.125	0.252*	0.313
Girl 12–18	0.280*	1.689**	-0.118	1.534**	-0.119	0.361+	-0.088	0.519
Girl > 18	-0.145	0.797**	-0.053	1.707**	-0.286	0.016	0.125	1.620+
Boy 12–18	-0.053	-0.067	-0.193	0.097	-0.130	0.928**	0.015	-0.751
Boy > 18	0.039	-0.294	-0.102	-0.371+	0.055	0.410	-0.001	-2.444**
Total number	0.100	0.445**	0.094	0.502**	0.184**	0.425**	0.035	-0.019
Black	0.130	0.685**	0.137	0.511**	-0.149	0.429+	0.459**	1.181+
Size	0.031	-0.062*	0.057+	-0.046	-0.059*	-0.110**	-0.019	-0.258*

South	−0.080	−0.282*	−0.058	−0.074	−0.080	0.216	−0.158+	0.019
Wife's:								
Schooling	0.027	−0.054*	0.054	−0.042	−0.056*	−0.133**	−0.039+	−0.403**
Employed	−0.234	0.055	−0.272	0.155	−0.076	−0.178	0.041	−0.711
Work hours	0.025**	0.008	0.025**	0.010+	0.007	−0.002	−0.002	−0.022
Disabled	0.552**	0.344+	0.378	0.669**	0.203	0.281	−0.172	0.536
Income	0.050**	0.030**	0.060**	0.040**	0.020*	0.020	0.010+	0.100*
Age	−0.019+	0.016	−0.026*	0.028*	0.018+	0.039**	0.023**	0.117**
Sex-role attitudes:								
Family roles	0.239**	0.119+	0.185*	0.133+	0.141*	0.133	0.008	0.272
Job roles	0.076	−0.060	0.111	−0.087	−0.272**	−0.172	−0.005	−0.401
Husband's:								
Schooling	0.045**	−0.007	0.038*	0.003	0.087**	0.040+	0.068**	0.056
Work hours	0.001	0.010**	−0.003	−0.002	0.009*	0.017**	−0.000	−0.010
Income	−0.010+	−0.000	−0.010	0.010	0.010	0.010	0.010**	0.010
Disability	0.383*	0.334*	0.366+	0.120	−0.171	0.589*	0.109	1.426+

Two-tailed tests of significance:
** = $p \leq .01$
* = $.01 < p \leq .05$
+ = $.05 < p \leq .10$

Table 10.4.   Two-Stage Least-Squares Models of Sharing with Husbands and Children, Model with Measure of Nonfamily Living

	Children's Share	Husband's Share
Intercept	–0.281	0.131
Husband's share	–0.938	—
Children's share	—	–0.365
Childhood family:		
Stepfamily I	0.224	0.204
Mother-only family I	0.656	0.458
Hiatus	0.239	0.123
Stepfather	0.622	0.543
Children in family:		
Child < 4	0.128	0.459
Child 4–6	–0.764*	–0.329
Girl 12–18	1.156	—
Girl > 18	0.000	0.000
Boy 12–18	0.319	0.028
Boy > 18	0.000	0.000
Total number	0.639*	0.074
Black	0.311	–0.294
Size	0.004	0.030
South	–0.070	0.269
Wife's:		
Schooling	0.074	0.130
Employed	–0.023	–0.283
Work hours	0.034	0.032+
Disabled	1.598+	0.841
Income	0.100	0.100**
Age	–0.266	–0.237
Sex-role attitudes:		
Family roles	0.084	0.181
Job roles	–0.190	0.057
Husband's:		
Schooling	0.140	0.145**
Work hours	—	–0.008
Earnings	0.010	0.000
Disability	–0.078	–0.528
N = 527		
R-squared	0.135	0.157
Mean of dependent variable	1.55	3.30

Two-tailed tests of significance:
** = $p \le .01$
* = $.01 < p \le .05$
+ = $.05 < p \le .10$

Table 10.5. Polytomous Logit Models of Sharing with Husband and Children for Separate Chores, Hiatus Population

Dependent Variables	Grocery Shopping		Washing Dishes		Cooking		Child Care	
	Husband	Child	Husband	Child	Husband	Child	Husband	Child
Dep mean	0.360	0.006	0.263	0.301	0.297	0.045	0.650	0.032
R-squared	0.068	0.052	0.260	0.360	0.136	0.195	0.160	0.166
N =	528	528	528	528	528	528	528	528
Intercept	−1.646	−13.175	−3.413	−2.929	−2.814	−5.818	−0.912+	−8.017
Childhood family:								
Stepfamily I	0.185	5.664*	0.054	−0.489	0.235	1.483	0.122	3.536**
Mother-only family I	−0.016	1.379	0.659+	0.447	0.449	0.211	0.161	0.593
Hiatus	−0.026	−3.250	−0.068	−0.395	−0.539	−0.490	0.397	−3.029
Stepfather	0.350	0.429	0.202	0.513+	0.643*	0.222	0.320	0.373
Children in family:								
Child < 4	0.196	−0.282	0.166	−0.669*	0.004	−0.510	0.391	−0.611
Child 4–6	−0.453*	−0.831	−0.216	−0.846**	−0.044	−0.181	−0.275	0.071
Girl 12–18	−0.206	2.091	−0.242	1.629**	0.003	3.087**	−0.426	0.857
Boy 12–18	0.102	−0.127	−0.152	0.181	−0.126	1.127	−0.539+	0.945
Total number	0.098	1.116	0.179	1.017**	0.085	1.034**	0.216	1.427**
Black	0.314	−0.066	−0.119	1.216***	−0.289	0.068	−0.239	1.534*
Size	−0.055	0.521	0.021	−0.106	0.026	−0.222	−0.009	−0.035

Table 10.5. (continued)

Dependent Variables	Grocery Shopping		Washing Dishes		Cooking		Child Care	
	Husband	Child	Husband	Child	Husband	Child	Husband	Child
South	0.077	-0.274	0.117	-0.580*	0.158	-0.681	-0.150	0.269
Wife's:								
Schooling	-0.011	-0.102	0.069	-0.106	0.115+	-0.112	-0.002	-0.137
Employed	-0.062	-1.245	0.098	0.226	-0.261	0.081	0.186	0.057
Work hours	0.011	0.070	0.004	0.015	0.030**	0.041	0.023*	0.024
Disabled	-0.142	7.132*	-0.025	0.161	0.460	6.471**	-0.338	1.432
Income	0.020	-0.190	0.090**	0.050	0.030	0.000	0.010	0.030
Age	0.044	-0.102	-0.146	-0.047	-0.217*	-0.443+	-0.122	-0.085
Sex-role attitudes:								
Family roles	-0.048	0.321	0.363+	0.149	-0.199	-0.784*	0.047	0.163
Job roles	-0.034	-0.120	-0.136	-0.496+	0.338	0.457	-0.166	-1.432*
Husband's:								
Schooling	0.077**	-0.098	0.122**	0.047	0.055+	0.066	0.085**	0.004
Work hours	-0.004	0.064	-0.008	0.006	-0.008	-0.023	0.001	0.004
Income	-0.010	0.010	0.010	0.010	-0.010	0.040	0.010	0.030
Disability	-0.354	-0.832	-0.163	0.382	-0.286	0.086	0.619+	-0.399

Two-tailed tests of significance:

** = p ≤ .01

* = .01 < p ≤ .05

+ = .05 ≤ p ≤ .10

Table 10.5. (continued)

Dependent Variables	Housecleaning		Laundry		Yard, Home Maintenance		Paperwork	
	Husband	Child	Husband	Child	Husband	Child	Husband	Child
Dep mean	0.280	0.193	0.165	0.057	0.746	0.066	0.419	0.002
R-squared	0.212	0.271	0.121	0.168	0.298	0.324	0.057	0.037
N =	528	528	528	528	528	528	528	528
Intercept	-3.436	-4.915	-3.224	-5.426	1.181**	-3.674*	-0.713+	-31.087
Childhood family:								
Stepfamily I	0.306	0.530	-0.478	-0.090	-0.667	0.016	-0.012	0.187
Mother-only family I	0.374	0.562	0.101	0.969	-0.188	1.216+	-0.229	0.199
Hiatus	0.333	1.257	-0.261	3.571*	-1.378	0.021	0.381	-3.926
Stepfather	-0.057	0.293	-0.104	-0.798	0.052	-0.388	0.165	-0.578
Children in family:								
Child < 4	0.359	-0.491	0.082	-0.227	0.160	-0.034	0.084	-2.815
Child 4-6	-0.257	-0.804*	-0.107	-0.602	-0.160	0.506	0.160	-2.632
Girl 12-18	0.182	1.435**	-0.369	3.126***	-0.693+	0.927	-0.158	-1.193
Boy 12-18	0.319	0.156	-0.032	0.072	-0.165	2.845***	0.076	-0.259
Total number	0.002	0.953**	-0.172	1.046***	0.342*	0.612*	-0.006	-0.825
Black	-0.028	0.997**	-0.447	1.203*	0.005	0.501	0.543*	-0.743
Size	0.060	0.042	0.173*	0.094	-0.095	-0.113	-0.080	0.166

Table 10.5. (continued)

Dependent Variables	Housecleaning		Laundry		Yard, Home Maintenance		Paperwork	
	Husband	Child	Husband	Child	Husband	Child	Husband	Child
South	0.195	-0.237	0.686*	0.025	-0.183	0.968+	-0.235	3.995+
Wife's:								
Schooling	0.076	-0.067	0.068	-0.190	-0.211**	-0.253+	-0.034	1.441*
Employed	-0.474	0.303	-0.571	0.131	-0.122	0.363	-0.043	-3.852
Work hours	0.030*	0.001	0.020	0.008	0.012	0.017	-0.001	0.035
Disabled	0.529	0.359	0.496	2.412*	0.179	1.859	-0.245	-2.414
Income	0.070**	0.090**	0.070*	0.040	0.020	-0.050	0.000	-0.120
Age	-0.081	-0.073	-0.103	-0.270	0.092	0.114	-0.042	1.050
Sex-role attitudes:								
Family roles	0.393*	0.035	0.382+	0.097	0.023	0.769*	0.105	1.309
Job roles	-0.324	-0.533+	-0.103	-0.272	-0.293	-1.612**	-0.257	-3.600
Husband's:								
Schooling	0.072*	0.038	0.045	-0.008	0.121**	0.096	0.089**	0.158
Work hours	0.006	0.012	-0.002	-0.001	0.016+	0.003	-0.006	-0.024
Income	-0.000	0.020	-0.010	0.030	0.010	0.010	0.010	-0.070
Disability	-0.113	0.973*	-0.020	1.249	-1.169**	-1.428+	0.148	-1.900

Two-tailed tests of significance:
** = p ≤ .01
* = .01 < p ≤ .05
+ = .05 < p ≤ .10

Table 10.6. *Effects of Maternal Employment, Hours of Employment, and Earnings on Teenage Girls' and Boys' Shares in Household Tasks*

	Grocery Shopping	Dishes	Cooking	Child Care	Cleaning	Laundry	Yard Work
Girls 12–18							
1. Girl 12–18	.036**	.217**	.089**	.008	.253**	.109	.036**
Mother's employment	-.019	.044	-.006	.016	.010	-.021	-.004
EMP * G1218	-.022	.029	.071**	.031*	-.005	.094**	-.020
2. Girl 12–18	.027**	.217**	.102**	.009	.248**	.129**	.032**
Mother's hours of employment	.001**	.000	.001	-.001*	.001	.000	.000
Hours * G1218	-.000	.001	.002**	.001**	.000	.002**	-.000
3. Girl 12–18	.027**	.230**	.140**	.032**	.252**	.135**	.034**
Mother's annual earnings (*000)	.000	.000	-.000	.000	.004**	.002*	.002*
Earnings * G1218	-.000	.000	.001	-.000	-.000	.005**	-.002
Boys 12–18							
4. Boy 12–18	-.000	-.001	-.005	-.009	-.031	.005	.052**
Mother's employment	-.031**	.059**	.026	.028*	-.006	.013	-.019
EMP * B1218	.007	-.008	-.008	-.001	.034	.008	.017

Table 10.6. (continued)

	Grocery Shopping	Dishes	Cooking	Child Care	Cleaning	Laundry	Yard Work
5. Boy 12–18	–.010	.001	–.008	–.013	–.015	.009	.048**
Mother's hours of employment	–.028**	.001	.001**	.028**	.001	.001	–.000
Hours * B1218	.000	–.000	–.000	.000	.000	.000	.001
6. Boy 12–18	–.012	–.004	–.022	–.013	–.034	–.000	.047**
Mother's annual earnings (*000)	.000	.001	–.001	–.000	.002	.003**	.000
Earnings * B1218	.002*	–.000	.002	.001	.004*	.002	.003*

Note: Each model includes all the variables in table 10.2.
Two-tailed tests of significance:
** = p ≤ .05
* = .05 < p ≤ 0

Notes

1: The New Decline of the Family

1. The new privacy may have allowed some families not only independence from unwanted intrusion, but also from social control, so that levels of incest and family violence have come to match those of the Appalachian farm.

2: Family Trends Since the Baby Boom

1. We put "know" in quotations here because many of the things about social trends that are "generally known" are either misunderstood or are not true. Similarly, we put "used to" in quotations because the sense of the social past is also very shallow. With few exceptions, people feel that a current change is the first change, and that the past—of their childhood, or their mythology—is what has always been (Goode, 1970).

2. The baby boom was unique in several ways. Nevertheless, it was hardly a return to the demographic patterns of the preindustrial past, since the long-term rise in divorce slowed, but did not really reverse, and the long-term decline in *very large* families continued.

We must still begin with the 1950s for several reasons. It is the first decade of "normalcy"; to start earlier is to encounter two more decades of even greater distortion and difficulty—the Great Depression of the 1930s and World War II and its aftermath of the 1940s. There was also a drastic improvement in the quality and flexibility of data on families that started in this period. It is much more difficult to peer into the deeper past, when many fewer data were published, and then rarely in a form to answer questions not yet thought of.

3. This has especially been the case for black women, whose husbands could earn relatively little, primarily as a result of discrimination, and who hence were forced

into domestic service, caring for other homes before they could tend their own (Jones, 1985).

4. There is still a great deal of concern about the care of preschool children.

5. We are indebted for this and other evidence of changing attitudes we present below to an important study by Thornton (1989), although he would probably not interpret his results in exactly the same fashion.

6. Population growth continues in the United States, in part because the long-term consequences of fertility decline take a while to be felt and in part because of high levels of immigration. At current levels of fertility and mortality, there will be more deaths than births by the year 2022, even including births to new immigrants (Espenshade, 1983). The United States could maintain stability or growth at some level by varying the numbers of immigrants allowed in (since those applying continue to exceed by large numbers the spaces legally available) or by weakening enforcement against illegal immigrants.

7. This actually represents a slight decline in the proportion expecting to be childless, from 9 percent for girls and nearly 7 percent for boys, among high school seniors 10 years earlier (Thornton, 1989).

8. The effect of the decline in marriage and the rise in divorce on men's parental roles is a dramatically under-researched area. We know that there has been a decline in the proportion of adult years spent living with a spouse for both men and women (Schoen, Urton, Woodrow, and Baj, 1985), but there has been a much greater decline in the proportion of years spent living with children for men than for women (Eggebeen and Uhlenberg, 1985). Furstenberg (1988) presents an interesting speculative analysis of trends in fatherhood that parallels in some respects the approach we take here. He speaks of a growing trend toward "good fathers" who are very much involved in parenting and "bad fathers" who, when not living with their children, relinquish their support responsibilities, interact rarely with their children, or both.

9. The major important exception is Burch and Mathews (1987), discussed in more detail below.

10. As recently as 1962, only 32 percent of a sample of young married women disagreed with the statement "Most of the important decisions in the life of the family should be made by the man of the house." By 1985, 78 percent of these same women (still married to the same men) disagreed (Thornton, 1989).

11. Can you imagine a column called "Can this Marriage be Saved?" in *Field and Stream*? The only major exception to this generalization is the development in the 1970s of such popular magazines as *Psychology Today*.

3: Studying Family Change:
Approach and Data

1. See particularly Cowan (1983), Zelizer (1985); Demos (1986); Matthews (1987).

2. In fact, only in controlled experiments can we really be sure that the observed difference in outcomes was "caused" by the event or characteristics of interest to us (Lieberson, 1985). In reality, those raised by two natural parents probably differ from those raised by one parent in many ways besides their family structure, not all of which can be controlled statistically, either because the survey does not contain information

on a key point of difference, or because *we do not know* what a key point of difference actually is. This latter problem is called the problem of inference; we think the sun will rise tomorrow because we think we have studied all the factors leading to that outcome, but we can never truly *know*. Controlled experiments can overcome this problem, up to a point, by randomly assigning people to "treatment" and "control" groups, as in the medical testing of new drugs. This process makes two groups similar both on the factors people know can bias their results, as well on those they don't know about. We cannot assign people randomly to the experiences of parental divorce or nonfamily living, or to growing up black or wealthy.

As researchers, we try to minimize the impact of this problem both by holding constant as many of the other factors that might affect the outcome of interest, and by remaining sensitive to omitted factors, events, or characteristics that we think might bias the view of the process, but that we cannot measure. In all the analyses that follow, we control for characteristics of the individual, the family, the environment, and the situation that might affect the attitudes or behaviors we are examining.

3. Prospective studies pose a different set of problems. No such study has been successful at returning to *everyone* that was originally interviewed. This problem, called "attrition," increases with the length of a survey, and can cumulate to an impressive level of loss. At some point, it becomes difficult to trust results of such data, since those who remain to be interviewed may no longer be representative of the population meant to be studied. Such studies lose the poor and less educated, who often have good reason not to leave a forwarding address; they also lose young unmarried men, whose lives are rarely as glamorous as myth would make them. Among prospective surveys, the NLS has extraordinarily low levels of attrition, although they are greater for young men than young or mature women. See Appendix A for details on attrition in these panels.

4. We are oversimplifying this to a certain extent, since another dimension, usually related to resources, is *costs*. Those with the same preferences and resources might not be as able to attend college in the 1980s as easily as in the 1970s because of the increase in tuition costs; rising rents have also altered people's calculations about living arrangements. And costs need not be economic, linking more closely to tastes or preferences than to resources. Young women starting a job as a welder normally encountered very different "social costs" than young men do in that job, even if they earn the same income; the same problem is experienced by male compared with female secretaries. Little boys whose newly arrived brother leads them to want to play for a while with dolls also find it more costly to exercise this preference than do little girls.

5. This is often not possible, however, in current surveys. No one has figured out how to take into account the resources of prospective spouses in the decisions young women (or young men) make about whether and whom to marry.

6. For ideal statistical conditions, one needs a total history, with every change dated, although many studies are forced to make do with repeated measurement over fairly long time periods. Observing people married at each of two time periods can mean that they stayed married to the same person throughout, or it could mean that some of them divorced and remarried rapidly in the interim.

7. The dependent variable in these analyses are dichotomous. We estimated all models with logistic regression, using maximum-likelihood, a technique appropriate for analysis of dichotomous dependent variables (Goodman, 1976). To permit com-

parison of the effects of the independent variables within and across equations, we transformed the logit coefficients by multiplying by $P(1-P)$ to yield measures analogous to unstandardized ordinary least squares (OLS) regression coefficients (Hanushek and Jackson, 1977). The transformed logit coefficients reflect the estimated effect of a unit change in the independent variable on the probability of marriage, childbearing, or divorce during a given year, evaluated at the sample means. Table 5.2 in Appendix C presents these transformed logit coefficients for probability of marriage at various ages. Tables 6.2 and 6.3 in Appendix C present comparable models for first birth and for marital disruption.

8. We sometimes feel, however, that an important part of the burden of performing household chores lies not in loading the washing machine and turning it on, but in being the one who everyone else complains to if they don't have clean underwear.

9. Similarly, the "good provider" role for men means that husbands' work will continue to be more important in family decision making than wives' work as long as married men earn considerably more than married women. While it is important in families to encourage children who are "C" students to do their best and to try not to laugh at one another's incompetencies at changing tires and folding laundry, it is difficult entirely to ignore the bottom line.

4: Planning for New Families

1. For a vivid analysis of women changing career plans—both of those who decided that their family and children were too rewarding to sacrifice to the demands of a full-time career, as well as those whose jobs moved from temporary to permanent, see Gerson (1985).

2. Scanzoni (1975) has done a particularly insightful analysis of these links. Like others, however, he sees sex-role modernity primarily as an emphasis on individualism (although he makes this equation reluctantly) and summarizes his results by concluding that the "greater the individualism [that is, sex-role modernity] the less the familism" (p. 187). Clearly, he was referring only to traditional families. In a paper that presents some of the results of this chapter (Waite et al., 1986), we, too, took this narrow view.

3. Much more information on these subjects was collected from young women than young men, perhaps reflecting the view that women are changing their lives and men are not (although it is likely that men's attitudes are much more salient in the establishment of modern families than are women's).

4. We divided this measure into those who planned to work and those who planned not to or were undecided.

5. The questions on fertility were asked in 1971, 1973, and 1978.

6. Young women answered these questions in 1968, 1972, and 1978, and young men in 1971 and 1976. None of the young men were asked whether they would be willing to share half their family's domestic tasks to qualify as holding a "modern" sex-role attitude. *Women* were asked a question about whether men should share tasks around the house with women at all, but men were not. Few women felt that men should be totally exempt, so this question was not useful in constructing any of the scales we used.

7. Since these scales approximate a normal distribution, we will present the results

for factors influencing them in terms of percentiles, based on standard deviation scores (z-scores). For example, among women otherwise average for this sample, never-married women are on average more modern than 45 percent of the sample (and less modern than 55 percent); married women are more modern than 53 percent of the sample, an 8 percentile difference.

8. Finding two distinct dimensions of sex-role attitudes in this series of questions replicates results from a number of other studies. Mason and Bumpass (1975) and Mason et al. (1976) found, using questions overlapping to some extent with those that we use, that respondents answered relatively consistently all questions on the appropriateness of the traditional division of labor within the family, and those on rights of the sexes in the labor market, but apparently saw little need to connect their views across these two dimensions.

9. Our sample is restricted to those 14 to 17 in the first year of the survey to allow us to observe and measure a complete history of nonfamily living prior to marriage or the last date of the survey. We use data on young women from 1968 through 1978, and on young men from 1966 through 1976; each group was 24 to 27 years old at the last interview analyzed here.

10. We include here families headed by a divorced, separated, or never-married woman, families headed by one of the young person's parents and a stepparent, and families headed by someone other than a parent, for example an aunt or grandparent.

11. McLanahan and Bumpass (1988) find that childhood experience in a female-headed family *increases* the chances that a young woman has a birth while a teen, or marries at this young age. So experiences of this type may push young women toward independence to escape an unpleasant home situation.

12. Each of the figures presented in this chapter shows the effect of the factor being considered, net of all the other factors we include in our models. Table 4.1 in Appendix C presents definitions of all independent variables.

See tables 4.2–4.4 in Appendix C for the detailed regression and logistic regression tables underlying this analysis, which give the complete equations, including statistical significance for individual variables. We will occasionally discuss results from tests of specific subgroups or for interactions between two measures. We present results for these models in the Appendix as they appear in our discussion.

13. More than half of these young women expect to be working at age 35. Among those who grew up in two-parent families, 53 percent expect to work compared with 63 percent among those who did not. Although these results are intrinsically interesting, we found that presenting these percentages in the midst of percentiles was too confusing, both in the text and the figures, even for quite sophisticated readers. However, we will continue to present them in our endnotes.

14. The effect for young men, however, is less consistent, and so does not meet the standards of statistical significance.

15. This measure uses the *proportion* of potential years of nonfamily living actually away from home, rather than the *number* of years, to control for the differences among individuals in the potential number of years. Since all young people we examined were living at home and unmarried when we first observed them, only those who married at age 18 had no opportunity to be observed living away from home prior to marriage in these annual interviews.

One disadvantage of the use of proportion rather than number of years is that the smaller the number of potential years of nonfamily living, the easier it is to have either all or none of it lived away. If we assume that individuals have an underlying propensity to live away from home, then we have fewer observations on this propensity for individuals with a small number of potential years away. This gives us inefficient but unbiased estimates of these underlying propensities for these individuals.

The use of proportion of years away rather than number implies that the first year of nonfamily living has a larger effect than subsequent years, with the effect of each year declining at a rate of (years - 1/ years), a slow to moderate decay function. This function makes sense theoretically, as we expect that the new experiences a young adult undergoes by living away, as well as the new skills acquired, are largest in the first year, with additional skills and experiences added at a declining rate with more years of nonfamily living.

One could also argue that *family* living should include both time living with parents and time living with a spouse. Just as young people may decide to leave the family to live away, so they may decide to form a new family of their own with which to live. This argument implies that we should measure the proportion of potential years of nonfamily living actually away by including all the years from age 17 until the survey date in question, including years after marriage, since the person could have lived away during those years if he or she had not married. We created such a measure and include a discussion of it in our results.

16. The effect of nonfamily living at age 20 is equally as great at age 22, although it becomes smaller at age 24, suggesting that the effects of nonfamily living may be short-lived. However, by age 24, a much greater proportion of *all* young women plan to be working by age 35, increasing from 45 percent at age 17 to 65 percent at age 24.

17. The greater stability of ideals relative to concrete plans is also evident from the lack of effect from all the new experiences we measure in our statistical model (with the exception of school enrollment), and from the somewhat larger effect of the prior measure for this than for birth expectations in analyses that control for a prior measure. (See below.)

18. The effect for young men is also less consistent than for young women, and so does not meet the standards of statistical significance.

19. We tested the argument that we should include years married as years of family living by replacing the proportion of years prior to marriage lived away with a measure that incorporated years married. We found essentially the same pattern with either measure of nonfamily living. We found our conclusions on the impact of nonfamily living to hold in a number of different ways of ferreting out these effects.

20. This particular attitude provides the strongest evidence for our arguments about the impact of nonfamily living on family related attitudes and plans. The other attitudes were reported only occasionally. For them, we used the latest available measure to reflect the consequences of nonfamily or nontraditional family experiences, with the earliest measure held constant to provide an approximate baseline. In these cases, we cannot be absolutely sure that the earliest reported attitudes do not reflect nonfamily experiences already underway.

21. Among those who attended college, 69 percent of young women who experienced nonfamily living from age 17 to 22 planned to work at age 35, compared with 59 percent of young women who lived at home during their college years. For the

group who did not attend college, 49 percent expected to be working at age 35, whatever their living arrangements in young adulthood.

22. These differences can be observed by comparing tables 4.2 and 4.3 in Appendix C with table 6 in Waite et al. (1986).

23. The effect of nonfamily living on the college group is also *not* the result of having attended a "higher quality," that is, residential college, since the same effect characterizes the small group of women who attended college while living at home, but lived independently at some other age (Waite et al., 1986).

24. This suggests that the negative effect on fertility of college attendance found in other studies may be an artifact of the greater likelihood that those who attend college live away from their parental home.

25. By age 24, however, there is no difference by race, wholly because young white women had dramatically increased their plans for working by that age.

26. These results differ from those of Mason et al. (1976), who found southern women to be more traditional on questions about mothers' working, although not on other issues. In their analysis, however, the question focused on how "warm" such mothers' relationships could be with their children, whereas the question we are analyzing assumes perfect conditions for children ("a trusted relative available for care") but variation in *the husband's* approval.

27. The effects are only significant for the oldest age at which work plans was asked, suggesting that a lot of young women working in early adulthood expect not to be working during their family-building years. And the effect of working on fertility plans is only statistically significant when a prior measure of fertility plans is included in the analysis, suggesting that the employment experience is particularly important in causing young women *to change* their fertility plans.

28. So little material was collected on fatherhood for the young men that we must assume either that it had no effect on their lives, or that the survey personnel though that it should not.

5: The Transition to Marriage

1. In a few cultures, one-parent families (always female-headed) are the predominant family form. However, this pattern occurs in a context of strong kin support, in which a woman's male relatives (most commonly her brother) bear major financial responsibility for her children (Blumberg and Garcia, 1977).

2. As people can ignore physical differences in a classroom (where the teacher is often physically weaker than the students) or status differences in a brigade (where the lieutenant's parents might be able to "buy and sell" the captain's).

3. A review either of the major feminist works (a useful starting point is the collection, *Sisterhood is Powerful* [Morgan, ed., 1970] or of such statements as "The Playboy Philosophy" [Heffner, 1963]) should demonstrate the extent of the confusion between family roles, per se, and traditionally defined gender roles.

4. Certainly, the parents of the generation of the 1960s were not enthusiastic about their children cohabiting—or even spending a weekend together—under the parental roof. This "generation gap" may be changing, however, as parents are increasingly

themselves children of the 1960s, taking some pressure of young adults to finance separate housing.

5. For an extensive and thought provoking discussion of this point, see Ehrenreich (1983).

6. Horn, 1977. Given the substance of the article, it is noteworthy that the editors chose to accompany it with this cartoon, which seems rather to be a clear illustration of denial.

7. The results that follow are drawn from three separate analyses: Kobrin and Waite (1984); Goldscheider and Waite (1986; 1987). Most appeared in Goldscheider and Waite (1986), whose table 2 is presented here in modified form as table 5.2 in Appendix C.

8. Each of the figures presented in this chapter shows the effect of the factor being considered, net of all the other factors we include in our models. See table 5.1 in Appendix C for definitions of the variables used in the analysis and table 5.2 for the detailed logistic regression underlying this analysis, which give the complete equations, including statistical significance for individual variables. We will occasionally discuss results from tests of specific subgroups or for interactions between two measures. We do not present detailed results for these models in the Appendix since they are quite voluminous.

9. The increase is shown to be significant at ages 17–18, as shown in Kobrin and Waite (1984).

10. Thus, this life-course patterning in which the experience of nontraditional family forms in childhood differs over the transition to adulthood means that studies of the effects of childhood family structure are strongly affected by the ages that are chosen over which to look for possible effects. Those looking at teenagers have typically found that young women who experienced mother-only households during childhood were *more likely* to marry (McLanahan and Bumpass, 1988). But studies that looked at marriages during early adulthood (ages 21 to 22), found that such experiences had *no effect* (Michael and Tuma, 1985). Our results indicate that the early positive effect of mother-only families on marriage becomes negative in the early twenties.

11. The comparison, however, is not completely fair, since those with remarried parents probably experienced divorce at an earlier age than those whose parents have not remarried. Data that can be used to examine these relationships in more detail are needed to confirm the extent to which these experiences have parallel effects on marriage.

12. This effect is greater than that for most of the other variables in the model (see table 5.2, Appendix C).

13. This measure is more appropriate than the young adults' own education in an annual analysis of marriage, since variation in educational attainment for young adults of a given age at least partially reflects being grade-advanced or grade-retarded, at least during the early years of the marriage transition when many are in or just finishing school.

14. We are unable to use the broader attitudinal questions, such as sex role attitudes and attitudes toward a woman's working, since these questions were asked too rarely to be used in an annual analysis of the probability of marriage. In most cases, the questions were asked after most of the sample had married.

15. It is possible that the somewhat higher rate of attrition of young black males, which is associated with their greater likelihood of serving in the armed services, means that those remaining in the sample are somewhat more likely to be married than those who were lost.

16. These effects have been often documented (Smith, 1980; Becker, 1981; Korenman and Neumark, 1988). However, a similar problem arises when considering the effect of female resources on the likelihood of divorce. Research often finds that women who are working are more likely to divorce. At least some evidence suggests that in many cases, the divorce was not the *result* of their working; rather they went back to work because of concerns about their marriage (Johnson and Skinner, 1986).

17. Although this effect should have been reduced by the inclusion of work plans in our model.

18. The demographic squeeze had already eased by the mid–1980s, and will begin to turn strongly against men in the 1990s, as those born during the rapid declines in fertility of the late 1960s and early 1970s enter the marriage market. In many parts of the country, the job market for young people has also started to improve.

19. This should not create a major problem, however, since we have controlled the effect of actual enrollment.

6: Transitions in the Early Years of Marriage

1. National Center for Health Statistics (1989). We are indebted for many of these ideas to Daniels and Weingarten (1982), who have thoughtfully expanded upon the life course approach of Eriksen (1968) and focused it on marriage and parenthood for both men and women.

2. Being employed appeared to have an exceptional effect on young women, since it both increases modern attitudes and facilitates marriage.

3. See particularly Presser (1978), Kiernan and Diamond (1983), Trussell and Bloom (1983), Michael and Tuma (1985), and Rindfuss, Morgan, and Swicegood (1988). The growth of childbearing outside of marriage has encouraged scholars to want to include these women, and led one author to propose a paper called "Does Marriage Matter?" The answer was a resounding, "Yes" (Rindfuss, 1986).

4. Hence, we would ideally like to include not only married women, but couples in committed relationships, even if they had decided to forgo the formalities of legal marriage. However, a high proportion of couples who are "living together" expressly deny that their relationships are based on such commitment (Bumpass et al., 1989). Since in these data, it is difficult to distinguish couples who are living together from married couples, and since most, in any event, are not in committed relationships, we chose to focus on legally married couples.

5. We saw in chapter 5 that young women pregnant at the start of an interval were substantially more likely to marry in the near future than those who were not pregnant.

6. Thus with the exception of the first and last interval, we are estimating yearly probabilities of having a first birth. The final period is 18 months because the chance of a first birth begins to fall with years childless since marriage, so a longer period

becomes necessary to observe a reasonable number of births. We separate the first 6 months of marriage to isolate those births certainly conceived before the wedding.

7. We begin with just over 1,000 young women who had just married, approximately 1 in 10 of whom was pregnant. About 1 young woman in 4 has a baby in each of the next years, leaving a smaller and smaller group who have not become parents. By the end of the 4th year of marriage we are left with only about 400 young women who still remain childless. Our methods of estimation are discussed in chapter 3.

8. See chapter 3 for a full discussion of how we measure variation in family structure in childhood and young adulthood.

9. Because the effects of both living in an intact family during childhood and of independent living during young adulthood were very similar in all periods after the first 6 months of marriage, we pooled observations on these 3 intervals. Each of the figures presented in this chapter shows the effect of the factor being considered, net of all other factors we include in our models. Table 6.1 in Appendix C presents definitions of all independent variables. See tables 6.2 and 6.3 in Appendix C for the detailed regression and logistic regression tables underlying this analysis, which give the complete equations, including statistical significance for individual variables.

10. Waite and Stolzenberg, 1976. We realize that some of the results we have examined suggest that nontraditional family experiences both in childhood and young adulthood affect young women's sex-role attitudes and plans for later work, so that including these factors in our analysis of fertility risks *underestimating* the total effect of having these experiences. However, these attitudes and plans are also influenced by other factors that we cannot measure, so that omitting them risks *overestimating* the effects of measures correlated with them. We estimated these models with and without controls for sex-role attitudes and work plans, and none of the other effects was significantly affected by their omission.

11. Pebley's (1981) comparison of changes in ideal age at first birth for women respondents to the 1970 and 1975 National Fertility Surveys strongly suggests this interpretation.

12. See Oppenheimer (1988) for a detailed discussion of the relationship between young men's career demands and marriage.

13. F. Goldscheider and C. Goldscheider, 1989. This was particularly the case among those with doctorates or professional degrees, who actually married rather young, but had children very slowly.

14. We will not be able to consider these issues directly, since the lack of information on religion in these data led us not to focus on this dimension of attitudinal differences (chapter 3).

15. Martin and Bumpass, 1989. However, differences between black and non-Hispanic white couples appear to have diverged rather than converged.

16. As we did with the transition to parenthood (and with the transition to marriage in chapter 5), we examine the factors that influence separation or divorce over separate periods after marriage—in this case, each of the first 5 years—to see whether factors that increase very early divorce differ from those that lead to separation later in marriage. Since we found no consistent differences, we pooled the intervals, and refer only to these results in the text.

17. For a discussion of this problem, see chapter 3.

18. For example, some surveys include information on dating frequency, to indicate how actively a young adult has searched for a mate (Marini, 1978) and others include measures of physical attractiveness (Glenn, 1976), which might indicate potential success in the remarriage market. But no large-scale survey has measured interpersonal communication skills, to our knowledge.

19. Since men and women tend to choose a spouse of a similar age (although the husband is normally a few years older than the wife), these two measures are too closely related for us to include both. There have been few, if any, studies on the effects of *male age* on marital dissolution.

7: Family Structure and Husbands' Share in Household Tasks

1. There is no generally accepted term for women who have not added paid employment to their domestic responsibilities. This term may be least problematic. It is sexist, but reflects a sexist reality; househusbands face many, quite different problems.

2. The traditional division of labor can also lead to the opposite imbalance, at least in families that feel strongly that the wife should not work outside the home. During hard times, many men must moonlight, working two and even more jobs to support their families. Housebound wives have relatively little more that they can effectively contribute to the family economy, since in modern urban households there are many fewer options for taking in boarders, for sewing, or for gardening to supplement the family diet than there were in the not-very-distant past. So in most cases, wives in this situation take a job.

3. We discuss the precise measurement of sharing in specific household tasks, as well as how we measure overall sharing, in Appendix B.

4. Thus, all families include both a husband and a wife. In some families, other adults were included. We cannot examine the effect of such family extension on sharing tasks with husbands, since the number of such households was too small; only 5 percent of all husband-wife households include another adult who is not a child of the couple.

5. Fuller details on these measures and on our composite measure of overall sharing can be found in Appendix B.

6. Only one study considers the impact of the allocation of household tasks among an individual's parents on their own division of labor within marriage. A study of couples in New Zealand (Koopman-Boyden and Abbott, 1985) compares their expectations for household division of labor prior to marriage and actual division of labor one year after marriage. This study finds that the way that parents allocated household tasks between themselves had no effect on young people's expectations for division of labor, and had no effect on household tasks for males. For young women, traditionality of parents' division of housework increased *nontraditionality* of their own marital allocation of chores, suggesting some backlash across generations. However, no other study has corroborated this finding and in our view it remains highly speculative.

7. Each of the figures presented in this chapter, with the exception of figure 7.1, shows the effect of the factor being considered, net of all other factors we include in

our models. So in this case, the possibility that those growing up in female-headed families have less education, or are more likely to be black, is taken into account through statistical controls. The values presented show the predicted amount husbands share in the family if they all had the *same level* on all the other variables in the multivariate regression equation (taken at the mean of the sample, for each variable), and only differed on, in this example, childhood family structure. Table 7.1 in Appendix C presents definitions of independent variables. See tables 7.2 and 7.3, Appendix C, for the detailed regression tables underlying this analysis, which give the complete equations, including statistical significance for individual variables. We will occasionally discuss results from tests of specific subgroups or for interactions between two measures. We present results for these models in the Appendix as they appear in our discussion.

8. We say "nearly" because there is evidence that couples with boys are less likely to divorce than couples with girls. Morgan, Lye, and Condran (1988) have demonstrated this phenomenon, and argue that it is the result of the very great likelihood that mothers will get custody of minor children and the greater closeness of fathers to their sons than to their daughters. Hence, fathers with sons are more willing to keep their marriage together at given levels of marital discord than fathers with daughters.

9. There is some evidence that such marriages work as well as first marriages (White and Booth, 1985).

10. Stepfather families are defined as the families of women in second or later marriages in which at least one of the children in the household was born before the current marriage began and hence is unlikely to be the child of both parents. These families may also include children of the remarried couple.

8: Change in Husbands' Share in Household Tasks?

1. See Stafford, Beckman, and Dibona (1977), Huber and Spitze (1983), Ross (1987), and Kamo (1988). Ross (1987) reports that only the husband's attitudes affect his participation in housework; the wife's attitudes have no impact. And one study (Coverman, 1985) finds that men's domestic labor time is actually *lower* among those husbands with liberal sex-role attitudes.

2. Our measures are only available for women, and not their husbands. This presents a problem, since, as we noted above, most studies of couples have shown that *his* attitudes are much more important than hers, when they differ. Weighed against her feelings are not only his feelings, but also tradition, the attitudes of the general community, and those of his family and friends, all of which are likely to be traditional, if his are. However, those studies also show that husbands and wives tend to share similar attitudes on a wide variety of issues (Williams and Thomson, 1985). Thus, for our analysis, the measure of the wife's attitudes can be thought of as probably reflecting those of her husband, as well.

3. Each of the figures presented in this chapter shows the effect of the factor being considered, net of all other factors we include in our models. So in this case, the pos-

sibility that those with more traditional attitudes have less education or work fewer hours is taken into account through statistical controls. The values presented show the predicted amount husbands share in the family if they all had the *same level* on all the other variables in the multivariate regression equation (taken at the mean of the sample, for each variable), and only differed on their scores on the FAMILY ROLES index. See table 7.2 and table 7.3 in Appendix C for the detailed regression tables underlying this analysis, which give the complete equations, including statistical significance for individual variables.

4. As we will see in chapters 9 and 10, this may reflect the characteristics of the authors, who are thus least likely to involve their own children in housework or apparently even to think of involving them.

5. To some extent, this result is an artifact of the way questions were asked. Since women could not respond that *both* their children and spouse shared a given task, naming a child as principal sharer precludes recording the husband's smaller contribution (and vice versa). However, on the total share index, this is not such a problem, since the likely pattern of task specialization means that husbands could continue to be responsible for many tasks, and could increase their responsibility for those tasks, even while children were being included as principal sharers in other tasks.

6. We cannot, unfortunately, compare the same couples at the 2 stages of the family cycle, since the survey has not lasted the 20 to 25 years needed for substantial numbers of young couples to marry, have children, and see those children mature and leave home.

7. There is also some evidence that women who think that they are particularly attractive to men wield greater power over their husbands through their sense of having alternatives (Udry, 1981).

8. This point was brought to our attention by Spitze (1986).

9. Previous studies have measured the wife's earnings, the husband's earnings, and the ratio between them. Most studies find little impact on relative earnings of spouses on the division of household labor; absolute levels of earnings and education have more effect. See in particular, Farkas (1976), Hannan, Tuma, and Groneveld (1977), Berk and Berk (1979), Maret and Finlay (1984), Coverman (1985), Kamo (1988). However, Ross (1987) finds that the smaller the gap between the husband's earnings and those of his wife, the greater his relative contribution to housework.

10. At some point, however, if the tasks the wife is more prepared to do overwhelm her, because of a sick child or her own disability, then the husband will step into the breach to get the job done. Similarly, where the husband's efforts are not enough, such as in a small business, the wife (and children) will cover the counter for periods when the proprietor stocks, or orders, or goes out to arrange financing, or eats his dinner. Hence, when there are extraordinarily many tasks, and the excess is particularly on the tasks of one partner, the other feels called in to "help out." In many ways, modern two-job couples are increasingly finding themselves in this situation. The double pressure is on the wife, who is now doing two jobs, one at home and one in the workplace.

11. Those with "very traditional" attitudes are represented by scale scores of −1.5 on JOB ROLES and FAMILY ROLES; those with "very modern" attitudes scored + 1.5 on each scale.

9: Children's Share in Household Tasks

1. We thank Viviana Zelizer (1985) for this vivid term.

2. But see Berk (1985), a small study that reinforces many of our findings and interpretations.

3. White and Brinkerhoff (1981b) explored this issue in a study of families in Nebraska; they also reviewed the ambivalence the scientific community has shown on the subject of children's work in the home. Among the small set of studies on children's household work, this is perhaps the most valuable.

4. Many children are likely to feel that this is a rationalization for the parents' getting out of doing "their work," since aren't they learning responsibility at school?

5. There is some evidence that parents are attempting to establish more more egalitarian roles in the home for their children. Duncan and Duncan (1978) found that mothers in 1971 were less likely to endorse sex differentiation in children's chores than mothers in 1955, although what they did in practice is unknown.

6. Unfortunately, we must focus only on women in this chapter because neither of the samples of males included in the NLS asked fathers about sharing chores with children. Since men's experience of living in a nonintact family affected their participation in household tasks more than their wife's experience (chapter 7), it is important to see if this is also the case for sharing with children. Clearly, better data are needed to settle this issue.

As in our analysis of sharing with husbands, we include both samples of women (those aged 14–24 in 1968 and those aged 30–44 in 1967). For the analyses looking at the effect of living outside a family prior to marriage, we look only at the subset of women aged 14–17 in 1968, in order to track the histories of their living arrangements.

7. We confirmed this inference directly in families with only one child, since the patterns we show below by age and gender of child are essentially the same for these families as for all families.

8. Each of the figures presented in this chapter, with the exception of figure 9.1, shows the effect of the factor being considered, net of all other factors we include in our models. See tables 9.2 and 9.3, Appendix C, for the detailed regression tables underlying this analysis, which give the complete equations, including statistical significance for individual variables. We will occasionally discuss results from tests of specific subgroups or for interactions between two measures. We do not present detailed results for these models in the Appendix since they are quite voluminous.

9. This concept is powerfully developed in Berk (1985).

10. Kiecolt and Acock (1988) find suggestive effects of childhood family structure on adults' views of political power for women. Those who grew up up in a household headed by a divorced mother favor greater political power for women.

11. Unfortunately, we cannot test this proposition for fathers with nontraditional family experiences, since the male samples were not asked about sharing with children.

12. We will examine patterns of substitution directly among men, women, and children in chapter 10.

13. For "very traditional women" we took the value of –2.0 on the FAMILY

ROLES scale; for "highly egalitarian women" we took the value of $+1.5$ on the FAMILY ROLES scale.

14. Living in the South was a strong and significant predictor of hiring help with household cleaning.

15. We also tried to compare our methods with those of other studies to see why our results differ from theirs. However, there were so many differences in methods— in samples, definitions of children's work, and variables included as controls in the analysis—that it was impossible to pinpoint likely reasons to account for the differences in results.

16. As we will see in chapter 10, however, on issues other than availability, children generally substitute for their mothers, not their fathers.

10: The Domestic Economy: Husbands, Wives, and Children

1. See notes in chapters 7 and 8 for references to important studies of the division of labor between husbands and wives, and in chapter 9, for studies of children's roles. However, an important exception to this generalization is the path-breaking work of Sarah Fenstermaker Berk (1985), which, in an analysis that aptly portrays the home as a "gender factory," looks at the apportionment of work in American households. The study considers the roles of husbands, wives, and teenage children in housework, as well as the effects of the volume and apportionment of these tasks on the employment of wives and mothers.

Unlike our study, which analyzes a relatively small amount of information on a representative sample of 10,000 Americans, Berk studied 335 California couples, collecting a rich array of data from both husbands and wives, including attitudes toward housework and the perceptions of both husbands and wives of the fairness of their own division of labor. Many of our interpretations are buttressed by reference to her findings. However, most of the results we report below, including the central finding that men's labor substitutes for that of their children far more than children's labor does for their fathers', did not appear in that study because of the small size of her sample.

2. A higher proportion of *middle-class* families had servants for work in the household in the past, but a much smaller proportion of families were middle class (Dudden, 1983).

3. White and Brinkerhoff, 1981b.

4. Here, as in chapter 9, we must focus only on women respondents because neither of the samples of males included in the NLS asked fathers about sharing chores with children. Studies that included both husbands and wives (such as Berk, 1985) report that husbands and wives systematically underestimate each other's efforts, so this biases our understanding of husband-wife sharing. No scientific study has examined whether maternal reports underestimate children's involvement in household tasks, or how this would affect our understanding of *father-child* trade-offs.

As in our analysis of sharing with husbands, we include two samples of women (those aged 14–24 in 1968, called "The Young Women" and those aged 30–44 in 1967, called "Mature Women"). For the analyses looking at the effect of living outside a family prior to marriage, we examine only the subset of women aged 14–17 in 1968, in order to track their living arrangements' histories.

5. It differs from the group used for the analysis of husbands' sharing in chapters 7 and 8, since that included childless couples in order to see whether children— their arrival or departure—influence how much husbands share with their wives. It also differs from that in chapter 9, since there we included mother-only families, learning that boys share female-type tasks more in such families than girls do in two-parent biological families.

6. Because all of these families include both husbands and children, the families are larger and more complex than those in our previous analyses. This will bias our results in favor of the wife somewhat more than in those analyses, since in cases where both the husband and one or more children share in the task, only the proportion of the most important sharer is recorded, and the residue necessarily credited to the wife. However, this bias should not affect the balance between husbands and children.

7. These results differ slightly from those reported in earlier chapters because of the differences in the samples analyzed.

8. These results resemble those found in more detailed analyses of the *time* family members spend on these household tasks: Of these 10 hours per day, husbands contribute about 1.7 hours per day, children 1.2 hours, and wives 6.8 hours (Sanik, 1981).

9. We did an expanded analysis of sharing household cleaning, including as possibilities sharing with husbands, children, and hired help (whom we call a cleaning woman, reflecting the extent of gender segregation in this occupation, although we do not know how many of our sample households actually hire men for this task). We summarize these results here. We will refer to them later in the analysis to underline their limited role in the results we are reporting.

The significant predictors of using a cleaning woman are husbands' and wives' income (but not their employment hours); the disability of both spouses; having a toddler in the household (age <4); and the education of the wife. The wife's income has much more effect on hiring a cleaning woman than the husband's—our results predict that most or all household cleaning would be contracted out in this fashion when the wife's income reaches $30,000; men do not provide such help to their nonworking wives until their incomes reach $70,000.

The disability results (which are about twice as strong for her disability as for his) and the effect of toddlers suggests that role overload is an important problem in housecleaning; it is not simply a question of wealth. The positive effect of wife's education is the most intriguing. It suggest strongly the importance of modern attitudes in lowering the prestige of housework. It is likely that more educated women received the least education for doing work in the home, and we know that they are helping their daughters avoid learning about it, as well, while also providing little training for their sons.

Including the option of hiring help with household cleaning changes the results presented in Appendix C, table 10.2 very little, increasing the positive effect of wives' education on husbands' share of this task above the threshold of statistical significance while reducing the negative effect of her education on children's share, so that it is no longer statistically significant *for this chore*.

10. We approach the problem of division of household labor between wives, hus-

bands, and children somewhat differently than we have approached any of the outcomes considered to this point. The analysis of the scale of sharing with husbands and children is done with two-stage least squares, a system of simultaneous equations (Hanushek and Jackson, 1977). The analysis of each chore uses an approximation to polytomous logistic regression developed by Haggstrom (1983).

Our model of the extent of overall sharing with husbands and children includes three types of influences: the husbands' share is expected to affect the children's share and vice versa; some factors influence both sharing with husbands and children; and other factors are expected to influence the husbands' share only as a result of their effect on the children's share (since by sharing the task with children there is less work to do) or to influence sharing with children only as a result of its effect on sharing with husbands.

We reason that the number of the husband's hours of paid work should directly affect his ability to take responsibility for household tasks, but should not directly influence the children's level of participation, affecting their share only indirectly through the greater amount of work remaining to be done. Our position with regard to sharing with children was somewhat more complex: we reason that parents in families with teenage daughters feel a responsibility to train them in domestic tasks, a training function that few husbands would be able to provide. Hence, the presence of such children will increase a woman's reported sharing with children, but affect sharing with her husband only through the effect that sharing with children has on sharing with husbands.

So we assume in our examination of overall sharing that husbands' hours at work do not directly affect sharing with children and that the presence of teenage daughters does not directly influence sharing with husbands. We do expect teenage girls to affect the amount of housework children do, and that this, in turn, will affect the amount that husbands pitch in. In the same way, the number of hours the husband works will affect the amount children do *because* it affects the amount that husbands do around the house. We expect this chain of effects and our model takes them into account.

For each individual chore, we examined whether the wife shares with the husband, the children, or neither, sharing either with no one or with other relatives or nonrelatives. Since the level of sharing with other relatives and nonrelatives is too small to examine separately (rarely more than 1 percent) and since the supervision of such others usually is the wife's responsibility, we felt that the wife's sharing with other relatives or hired help was likely to be most similar to the wife having sole responsibility for the chore. Each coefficient shows how a change in the variable affects the log odds ratio of sharing with either husband or children relative to the wife having complete responsibility. The interested reader can see the complete results in tables 10.1–10.4 in Appendix C.

11. An alternative interpretation is that husbands are much more efficient than children, so that their sharing a task reduces the amount of work to be done far more than is the case with children. This could happen if, to earn the response that they "share responsibility" for these tasks, children are only cleaning their rooms, or doing their own laundry. No data are currently available anywhere to resolve this puzzle, since what is needed is not only information on housework hours but on *the efficiency* of housework by various family members.

12. Some portion of the differences between this chapter and the previous three, of course, reflects the different populations under study. Factors affecting children's share disproportionately in mother-only households would be less likely to appear in this analysis, as would be the case for those affecting husbands' sharing patterns in empty-nest families.

13. As in previous chapters, the results we present are normally based on the appropriate regression results found in our appendix tables, in which we predict the extent to which our results indicate that husbands would share if they were stepfathers or not stepfathers, but otherwise had average values on other variables in the models. In this case, we solved jointly for values of both husbands' and children's shares using iteration.

14. Because of the strong negative effect of nonfamily living on fertility (chapter 6), very few women aged 14–17 in 1968 who were eligible for this analysis because they had married and had children aged 6–19 by 1983 had had this experience. The average proportion of nonfamily living for unmarried women through 1980 was .19 (which is still low, given our difficulty measuring this issue); however, the mean for this sample of married women with post-toddler children was only .05. Most women who experienced nonfamily living in young adulthood had selected themselves *out* of our sample by marrying and/or having children much later than women who had not had this experience. If so, then the effect of nonfamily living on *reducing* sharing grocery shopping with children may simply reflect the much younger age of their children.

15. The overall level of sharing in this group is lower than in others, because these are families with much younger children; we have standardized for this factor in constructing this figure.

16. We define modern wives as those with FAMILY ROLES scale values of + 1.5; traditional wives as those with scale values of –2.0. See chapter 3.

17. That result is evidently the outcome of slight increases for husbands' share, which decreases in children's share. This effect, coupled with a small direct negative effect on children, cumulated to the effect we found earlier.

18. We compare families with both parents with some postcollege education (18 years) with those who did not complete any years of high school (8 years).

19. The questions of who will provide other support services, including caring for elderly relatives, staying home with sick children, arranging family parties, and maintaining kinship and social ties when the women who took over this task are employed full time are also of great importance.

20. Coverman, 1985; Spitze, 1986.

21. However, *employed* mothers less often share grocery shopping with either children or husbands. Working women apparently can shop by simply stopping on their way home from work.

22. This issue is discussed at length in chapters 8 and 9.

23. Presser and Cain, 1983.

24. See footnote 10.

25. We should note, here, that we are not studying *housework hours*; rather our focus is on *sharing responsibility* for housework. If families purchase substitutes— dinner at Wendy's, take-out Chinese, ordering pizza—for the wife's labor, then family

members could be increasing their *share* of household chores simply because the wife has reduced her contribution. So the husband and children take responsibility for a large proportion of the chores, but the chores themselves have shrunk. And families may simply be shifting responsibility for arranging for a given chore—rather than for doing it—to children or husband. For example, the husband could call in an order or stop and pick up dinner on the way home.

26. U.S. Bureau of the Census, 1989b.

27. In part because their earnings are contributing to hiring outside help.

11: The Future of the Home in the Twentieth-First Century

1. In his most recent analysis of the American family, Victor Fuchs (1988) hopes that we can achieve population replacement primarily through the efforts of Mormons, Hispanic Catholics, fundamentalist Protestants, and Orthodox Jews.

2. A recent example is a fine study by Hochschild (1989).

3. The alternative of going back to large family sizes in the modern context presents even greater problems which can only be ignored by a powerful religious faith that population explosion is not a problem.

4. For a useful discussion of some of these issues see Bart (1970) and Hartmann (1982).

5. Most women use accumulated vacation time or sick leave to finance their maternity leaves, which are most often 6 weeks.

6. Isaac Asimov (1983) has explored what society might look like if each adult lived in a separate dwelling and most social interaction was done over high-tech view phones.

7. In one, we are told that "arguments about housework are the leading cause of domestic violence in the United States" (Fuchs, 1988, p. 74). The second reference is paired with two versions of what the author evidently sees as related, far-out scenarios; one in which sex-change operations are painless, inexpensive, and easily reversible; the other a distant fictional society in which individuals are sometimes female and sometimes male (Fuchs, 1988, p. 144).

8. Other evidence, however, suggests that most of the pay gap must come from other sources, such as discrimination. Studies that have tried to measure the impact of domestic responsibilities on *how hard* women work on the job have not been able to find a strong effect. Women do not seem to allocate less effort to paid work than men; in fact, they appear to work harder in the workplace than men, with substantial differences when those in similar family situations are compared (Bielby and Bielby, 1985).

9. Huber and Spitze, 1983. This relationship should also be tested to see whether divorce actually occurs. We were not able to include this dimension in our analysis of divorce, since measurement of *who* shares household tasks was not included in the survey until the last year of observation. Other data (or later years of this survey) are needed to test the effect of a more egalitarian division of labor on the actual likelihood of divorce.

10. Thornton, 1989.

11. Gershuny and Robinson, 1988; Robinson, 1988.

12. Increasing proportions of men have recently been adding "likes to cook" in their ads in the personals columns that have become such an important feature of dating in the 1980s and 1990s.

Appendix A: The National Longitudinal Surveys

1. A newer cohort of youth (NLSY) was begun in 1979.

2. Additional detail on the NLS cohorts is available in the NLS Handbook, available from the Center for Human Resource Research, 921 Chatham Lane, Suite 200, Columbus, OH 43221–2418.

3. The young women were interviewed annually from 1968 through 1973 and seven more times: 1975, 1977, 1978, 1980, 1982, 1983, and 1984. The young men were interviewed annually from 1966 through 1971, and then 6 more times: 1973, 1975, 1976, 1978, 1980, and 1981. The mature women were interviewed annually from 1967 through 1969, and then 10 more times: in 1971, 1972, 1974, 1976, 1977, 1979, 1981, 1982, 1984, and 1986.

Appendix B: The Creation of Key Measures

1. Walker and Woods, 1976; see also Spitze, 1986.

2. The same series of questions was asked in other years as well, but the analyses reported here use data from the interviews listed above.

3. This answer applies in many cases: if she has no children; or if she has, but has sole responsibility, shares with someone other than children, or has no responsibility and the children also have none.

4. Analysis of the scale characteristics of the household tasks was performed with ANLITH (analysis of item-trait homogeneity). The relationship between each item and the scale was corrected for overlap between the item and the scale, since the scale is the sum of all household tasks. An item-scale correlation corrected for overlap is the correlation between the item score and the sum of the items in the scale other than the item in question. All items needed a corrected correlation of 0.30 or higher to be included in the final scale and were generally much higher (Donald and Ware, 1982).

5. Goldscheider, 1985.

6. Speare, 1970.

7. Virtually none of the respondents of either sex were living away at these ages (for example, 4 of the young women 14 to 17 were not living with their parental family); we eliminated from the sample those very few who were not living at home at these ages.

References

Abrahamse, Allan, Peter Morrison, and Linda J. Waite, "Teens Who Would Be Single Mothers," *Family Planning Perspectives*, 20, no. 1 (January/February 1988): 13–18.

Alwin, Duane, "From Obedience to Autonomy: Changes in Traits Desired in Children, 1924–1978," *Public Opinion Quarterly*, 52 (Spring 1988): 33–52.

Asimov, Isaac, *The Naked Sun*, New York: Ballantine, 1983.

Baldwin, Wendy, and Virginia S. Cain, "The Children of Teenage Parents," *Family Planning Perspectives*, 12, no. 1 (January/February 1980): 34–43.

Bart, Pauline, "Portnoy's Mother's Complaint," *Transaction* (November 1970).

Becker, Gary S., *A Treatise on the Family*, Cambridge: Harvard University Press, 1981.

Beller, Andrea H., and John W. Graham, "Child Support Awards: Differentials and Trends by Race and Marital Status," *Demography*, 23, no. 2 (May 1986): 231–245.

Berk, Richard A., and Sarah Fenstermaker Berk, *Labor and Leisure at Home: Content and Organization of the Household Day*, Beverly Hills: Sage, 1979.

Berk, Sarah Fenstermaker, *The Gender Factory*, New York: Plenum, 1985.

Berkman, Lisa F., and Leonard M. Syme, "Social Networks, Host Resistance, and Mortality: A Nine-Year Follow-Up Study of Alameda County Residents," *American Journal of Epidemiology*, 190, no. 2 (February 1979): 186–204.

Bernard, Jessie, *The Future of Marriage*, New York: World Publishing, 1972.

Bernard, Jessie, "The Good-Provider Role: Its Rise and Fall," *American Psychologist*, 36, no. 1 (January 1981): 1–12.

Berryman, Sue E., and Linda J. Waite, "Young Women's Choice of Nontraditional Occupations," in Christine Bose and Glenna Spitze, eds., *Ingredients for Women's Employment Policy*, Albany: State University of New York Press, 1987, 115–136.

Bielby, Denise D., and William T. Bielby, "She Works Hard for the Money: Household Responsibilities and the Allocation of Effort," paper presented at the annual meetings of the American Sociological Association, Washington, 1985.

Blake, Judith, "Coercive Pronatalism and American Population Policy," in R. Parke, Jr. and C. Westoff, eds., *Aspects of Population Growth Policy*, The Commission on Population Growth and the American Future Research Reports, 6, Washington: U.S. Government Printing Office, 1972.

Blake, Judith, *Family Size and Achievement*, Berkeley: University of California Press, 1989.

Bloom, David E., "What's Happening to Age at First Birth in the United States? A Study of Recent Cohorts," *Demography*, 19, no. 3 (August 1982): 351–370.

Blumberg, Rae Lesser, and Maria-Pilar Garcia, "The Political Economy of the Other-Child Household," in Robert Winch, ed., *Familial Organization: A Quest for Determinants*, New York: Free Press, 1977, 144–175.

Bongaarts, John, and Robert Potter, *Fertility, Biology, and Behavior: An Analysis of the Proximate Determinants*, New York: Academic Press, 1983.

Bowlby, John, "Mother-Child Separation," in K. Soddy, ed., *Mental Health and Infant Development*, 1, New York: Basic Books, 1956.

Brody, Charles J., and Lala Carr Steelman, "Sibling Structure and Parental Sex-Typing of Children's Household Tasks," *Journal of Marriage and the Family*, 47, no. 2 (May 1985): 265–273.

Bumpass, Larry, "Changing Family Patterns in the United States," paper presented at the Census Analysis Workshop: Families and Households, Data and Trends, Madison, October 1987.

Bumpass, Larry, James Sweet, and Andrew Cherlin, "The Role of Cohabitation in Declining Rate of Marriage," paper presented at the annual meeting of the Population Association of America, Baltimore, 1989.

Burch, Thomas, and Beverly Mathews, "Household Formation in Developed Countries," *Population and Development Review*, 13, no. 3 (September 1987): 495–511.

Bureau of Labor Statistics, "Labor Force Participation Unchanged Among Mothers with Young Children," USDL 88–431, Washington: U.S. Government Printing Office, 1988.

Burgess, Ernest, and Henry Locke, *The Family: From Institution to Companionship*, New York: American Book, 1945.

Caldwell, John, *Theories of Fertility Change*, New York: Academic Press, 1982.

Cogle, Frances L., and Grace E. Tasker, "Children and Housework," *Family Relations: Journal of Applied Family and Child Studies*, 31, no. 3 (July 1982): 395–399.

Coverman, Shelley, "Gender, Domestic Labor Time, and Wage Inequality," *American Sociological Review*, 48 (October 1983): 623–637.

Coverman, Shelley, "Explaining Husbands' Participation in Domestic Labor," *The Sociological Quarterly*, 26, no. 1 (1985): 81–97.

Coverman, Shelley, and Joseph F. Sheley, "Change in Men's Housework and Child-Care Time, 1965–1975," *Journal of Marriage and the Family*, 48 (May 1986): 413–422.

Cowan, Ruth S., *More Work for Mother: The Ironies of Household Technology from the Open Hearth to the Microwave*, New York: Basic Books, 1983.

Cromartie, John, and Carol Stack, "Reinterpretation of Black Return and Nonreturn

Migration to the South, 1975–80," *Geographical Review*, 79, no. 3 (July 1989): 297–310.

D'Amico, Ronald, R. Jean Haurin, and Frank L. Mott, "The Effects of Mothers' Employment on Adolescent and Early Adult Outcomes of Young Men and Women," in Cheryl D. Hayes and Sheila B. Kamerman, eds., *Children of Working Parents: Experiences and Outcomes*, Washington: National Academy Press, 1983, 130–219.

Dambrot, Faye H., Mary E. Papp, and Cheryl Whitmore, "The Sex-Role Attitudes of Three Generations of Women," *Personality and Social Psychology Bulletin*, 10, no. 3 (September 1983): 469–473.

Daniels, Pamela, and Kathy Weingarten, *Sooner or Later: The Timing of Parenthood in Adult Lives*. New York: W. W. Norton, 1982.

Davis, Kingsley, "The American Family in Relation to Demographic Change," in C. Westoff and R. Parke, Jr., eds., *Demographic and Social Aspects of Population Growth*, Washington: U.S. Government Printing Office, 1972, 235–265.

Demos, John, *Past, Present and Personal: The Family and the Life Course in American History*, New York: Oxford University Press, 1986.

Di Leonardo, Micaela, "The Female World of Cards and Holidays: Women, Families, and the Work of Kinship," *Signs*, 12, no. 3 (1987): 440–453.

Dudden, Fay, *Serving Women: Household Service in Nineteenth Century America*, Middletown, CT: Wesleyan University Press, 1983.

Duncan, Beverly, and Otis Dudley Duncan, *Sex Typing and Social Roles: A Research Report*, New York: Academic Press, 1978.

Dyer, Everett D., "Parenthood as Crisis: A Re-study," *Marriage and Family Living*, 25 (1963): 196–201.

Easterlin, Richard A., "What Will 1984 Be Like? Socioeconomic Implications of Recent Twists in Age Structure," *Demography*, 15, no. 4 (November 1978): 397–432.

Eggebeen, David, and Peter Uhlenberg, "Changes in the Organization of Men's Lives: 1960–1980," *Family Relations*, 34, no. 2 (April 1985): 251–257.

Ehrenreich, Barbara, *Hearts of Men: American Dreams and Flight from Commitment*, Garden City, NY: Doubleday, 1983.

Ellwood, David T., and Mary Jo Bane, "The Impact of AFDC on Family Structure and Living Arrangements," Report to DHHS Grant No. 92-A–82, Cambridge: Harvard University, 1984.

Ericksen, Julia A., William L. Yancey, and Eugene P. Ericksen, "The Division of Family Roles," *Journal of Marriage and the Family*, 41, no.2 (May 1979): 301–313.

Erikson, Erik, *Identity, Youth and Crises*, New York: Norton, 1968.

Espenshade, Thomas J., "Paths to Zero Population Growth," *Family Planning Perspectives*, 15, no. 3 (May/June 1983): 148–149.

Espenshade, Thomas J., "Marriage Trends in America: Estimates, Implications, and Underlying Causes," *Population and Development Review*, 11, no. 2 (June 1985): 193–245.

Farkas, George, "Education, Wage Rates, and the Division of Labor Between Husband and Wife," *Journal of Marriage and the Family*, 38, no. 3 (August 1976): 473–483.

Farley, Reynolds, "Trends in Racial Inequalities: Have the Gains of the 1960s Disappeared in the 1970s?" *American Sociological Review*, 42, no. 2 (April 1977): 189–208.

Freedman, Deborah, "The Relation of Economic Status to Fertility," *American Economic Review*, 53, no. 3 (June 1963): 414–426.

Freedman, Deborah, Arland Thornton, Donald Camburn, Duane Alwin, and Linda Young-DeMarco, "The Life History Calendar: A Technique for Collecting Retrospective Data," in Clifford C. Clogg, ed., *Sociological Methodology*, Washington: American Sociological Association, 1988.

Frey, W., and Frances Kobrin, "Changing Families and Changing Mobility: Their Impact on the Central City," *Demography*, 19, no. 3 (August 1982): 261–277.

Fuchs, Victor R., *Women's Quest for Economic Equality*, Cambridge: Harvard University Press, 1988.

Furstenberg, Frank, "Good Dads—Bad Dads: Two Faces of Fatherhood," in Andrew Cherlin, ed., *The Changing American Family and Public Policy*, Washington: The Urban Institute Press, 1988.

Gershuny, Jonathan, and John P. Robinson, "Historical Changes in the Household Division of Labor," *Demography*, 25, no. 4 (November 1988): 537–554.

Gerson, Kathleen, *Hard Choices: How Women Decide about Work, Career and Motherhood*, Berkeley: University of California Press, 1985.

Glenn, Norval, "The Utility of Education and Attractiveness for Females' Status Attainment through Marriage," *American Sociological Review*, 41, no. 3 (June 1976): pp. 484–498.

Glenn, Norval, and Michael Supancic, "The Social and Demographic Correlates of Divorce and Separation in the United States: An Update and Reconsideration," *Journal of Marriage and the Family*, 46, no. 3 (August 1984): 563–576.

Glenn, Norval, and Charles N. Weaver, "A Note on Family Situation and Global Happiness," *Social Forces*, 57, no. 3 (March 1979): 960–967.

Glick, Paul C., and Arthur J. Norton, "Marrying, Divorcing, and Living Together in the U.S. Today," *Population Bulletin*, 32, no. 5 (October 1977).

Goldscheider, Frances K. *Crossvalidating Data from National Longitudinal Surveys Measuring the Transition to Adulthood*, N-2293-NICHD, Santa Monica: The RAND Corporation, 1985.

Goldscheider, Calvin, and Frances K. Goldscheider, "Moving Out and Marriage: What Do Young Adults Expect?" *American Sociological Review*, 52, no. 2 (April 1987): 278–285.

Goldscheider, Calvin, and Frances K. Goldscheider, "The Intergenerational Flow of Income: Family Structure and the Status of Black Americans," paper presented at the annual meetings of the Population Association of America, New Orleans, 1988.

Goldscheider, Calvin, and Frances K. Goldscheider, "Leaving Home and Marriage," unpublished manuscript, 1990.

Goldscheider, Frances Kobrin, and Celine LeBourdais, "Growing Up and Leaving Home: Variation and Change in Nestleaving Patterns, 1920–1979," *Population Studies and Training Center*, Brown University (1986).

Goldscheider, Frances Kobrin, and Linda J. Waite, "Sex Differences in the Entry into Marriage," *American Journal of Sociology*, 92, no. 1 (July 1986): 91–109.

Goldscheider, Frances Kobrin, and Linda J. Waite, "Effects of Nestleaving Patterns on the Transition to Marriage," *Journal of Marriage and the Family*, 49, no. 3 (August 1987): 507–516.

Goode, William, *World Revolution in Family Patterns*, New York: The Free Press, 1970.

Goode, William, "Why Men Resist," in Barrie Thorne and Marilyn Yalom, eds., *Rethinking the Family: Some Feminist Questions*, New York: Longman, 1981.

Goodman, Leo A., "The Relationships Between Modified and Usual Multiple-Regression Approaches to the Analysis of Dichotomous Variables," in D. Heise, ed., *Sociological Methodology* (1976): 83–110.

Gove, Walter R., "Sex Roles, Marital Roles and Mental Illness," *Social Forces*, 51, no. 1 (September 1972): 34–44.

Gove, Walter R., "Sex, Marital-Status, and Mortality," *American Journal of Sociology*, 79, no. 1 (July 1973): 45–67.

Greif, Geoffrey L., "Children and Housework in the Single Father Family," *Family Relations*, 34, no. 3 (July 1985): 353–357.

Haaga, John, "The Revival of Breastfeeding in the United States, 1963–81," unpublished paper, Santa Monica, The RAND Corporation, December 1988.

Haggstrom, Gus W., "Logistic Regression and Discriminant Analysis by Ordinary Least Squares," *Journal of Business and Economic Statistics*, 1, no. 3 (July 1983): 229–238.

Hannan, Michael T., Nancy Brandon Tuma, and Lyle P. Groeneveld, "Income and Marital Events: Evidence from an Income-Maintenance Experiment," *American Journal of Sociology*, 82, no. 6 (May 1977): 1186–1211.

Hanushek, Erik A., and John E. Jackson, *Statistical Methods for Social Scientists*, New York: Academic Press, 1977.

Hartmann, Susan M., *American Women in the 1940s: The Home Front and Beyond*, Boston: Twayne Publishers, 1982.

Heer, David M., and Amyra Grossbard-Shechtman, "The Impact of the Female Marriage Squeeze and the Contraceptive Revolution on Sex Roles and the Women's Liberation Movement in the United States, 1960 to 1975," *Journal of Marriage and the Family*, 43, no. 1 (February 1981): 49–65.

Heffner, Hugh, "The Playboy Philosophy," *Playboy*, January 1963: 41.

Henshaw, Stanley K., and Greg Martire, "Abortion and the Public Opinion Polls: 1. Morality and Legality," *Family Planning Perspectives*, 14, no. 2 (March/April 1982): 53–55, 59–60.

Hill, Martha S., "Marital Stability and Spouses' Shared Time: A Multidisciplinary Hypothesis," *Journal of Family Issues*, 9, no. 4 (December 1988): 427–451.

Hochschild, Arlie, *The Second Shift: Working Parents and the Revolution at Home*, New York: Viking, 1989.

Hofferth, Sandra L., "Updating Children's Life Course," *Journal of Marriage and the Family*, 47, no. 1 (January 1985): 93–115.

Hoffman, Lois W., "Increasing Fathering: Effects on the Mother," in Michael E. Lamb and Abraham Sagi, eds., *Fatherhood and Family Policy*, Hillsdale, New Jersey: Lawrence Erlbaum Associates, 1988.

Horn, Jack, "The Life-Giving Properties of Marriage," *Psychology Today* (January 1977): 20–21.

Huber, Joan, and Glenna Spitze, *Sex Stratification: Children, Housework, and Jobs*, New York: Academic Press, 1983.

Johnson, William R., and Jonathan Skinner, "Labor Supply and Marital Separation," *American Economic Review*, 76, no. 3 (June 1986): 455–469.

Jones, Jacqueline, *Labor of Love, Labor of Sorrow: Black Women, Work and the Family from Slavery to the Present*, New York: Random House, 1985.

Kamo, Yoshinori, "Determinants of Household Division of Labor: Resources, Power, and Ideology," *Journal of Family Issues*, 9, no. 2 (June 1988): 177–200.

Katz, Michael, *The People of Hamilton, Canada North*, Cambridge: Harvard University Press, 1975.

Kett, Joseph F., *Rites of Passage: Adolescence in America, 1790 to the Present*, New York: Basic Books, 1977.

Kiecolt, K. Jill, and Alan C. Acock, "The Long-Term Effects of Family Structure on Gender-Role Attitudes," *Journal of Marriage and the Family*, 50, no. 3 (August 1988): 709–717.

Kiernan, Kathleen E., and I. Diamond, "The Age at Which Childbearing Starts—a Longitudinal Study," *Population Studies*, 37, no. 3 (November 1983): 363–380.

Kobrin, Frances, "The Primary Individual and the Family: Changes in Living Arrangements Since 1940," *Journal of Marriage and the Family*, 38, no. 2 (1976): 233–239.

Kobrin, Frances E., and Gerry Hendershot, "Do Family Ties Affect Mortality? Evidence from the United States, 1966–68," *Journal of Marriage and the Family*, 39, no. 4 (May 1976): 233–239.

Kobrin, Frances E., and Linda J. Waite, "Effects of Family Stability on the Transition to Marriage," *Journal of Marriage and the Family*, 46 (1984): 807–816.

Komarovsky, Mirra, *Dilemmas of Masculinity: A Study of College Youth*, New York: W. W. Norton and Company, 1976.

Koopman-Boyden, Peggy G., and Max Abbott, "Expectations for Household Task Allocation and Actual Task Allocation: A New Zealand Study," *Journal of Marriage and the Family*, 47, no. 1 (February 1985): 211–219.

Korenman, Sanders D., and David B. Neumark, "Does Marriage Really Make Men More Productive?" Finance and Economics Discussion Series, Division of Research and Statistics, Washington: Federal Reserve Board, 1988.

Kuznets, Simon, "Size and Age Structure of Family Households: Exploratory Comparisons," *Population and Development Review*, 4, no. 2 (June 1978): 187–233.

Laslett, Barbara, "The Family as a Public and Private Institution: An Historical Perspective," *Journal of Marriage and the Family*, 35, no. 3 (August 1973): 480–494.

Lawrence, Frances Cogle, Grace E. Tasker, and Deborah K. Babcock, "Time Spent in Housework by Urban Adolescents," *Home Economics Research Journal*, 12, no. 2 (December 1983): 199–205.

Lawton, Leora, "The Quality of Parent and Adult-Child Relationships and Family Structure," paper presented at the annual meetings of the Population Association of America, Toronto, 1990.

Lieberson, Stanley, *Making It Count: The Improvement of Social Research and Theory*, Berkeley: University of California Press, 1985.

Light, Harriett K., Doris Hertsgaard, and Ruth E. Martin, "Farm Children's Work in the Family," *Adolescence*, 20, no. 78 (Summer 1985): 425–432.

Lopata, Helena Z., *Widowhood in an American City*, Cambridge: Schenkman, 1973.

McLanahan, Sara, and Larry Bumpass, "Intergenerational Consequences of Family Disruption," *American Journal of Sociology*, 94, no. 1 (July 1988): 130–152.

Maret, Elizabeth, and Barbara Finlay, "The Distribution of Household Labor Among Women in Dual-Earner Families," *Journal of Marriage and the Family*, 46, no. 2 (May 1984): 357–364.

Marini, Margaret M., "The Transition to Adulthood: Sex Differences in Educational Attainment and Age at Marriage," *American Sociological Review*, 43, no. 4 (August 1978): 483–507.

Marini, Margaret M., "Age and Sequencing Norms in the Transition to Adulthood," *Social Forces*, 63, no. 1 (September 1984): 229–244.

Martin, Theresa Castro, and Larry L. Bumpass, "Recent Trends in Marital Disruption," *Demography*, 26, no. 1 (February 1989): 37–51.

Mason, Karen O., *Women's Labor Force Participation and Fertility*, Research Triangle Park: Research Triangle Institute, 1974.

Mason, Karen O., and Larry L. Bumpass, "U.S. Women's Sex-Role Ideology," *American Journal of Sociology*, 80, no. 5 (March 1975): 1212–1219.

Mason, Karen O., John L. Czajka, and Sara Arber, "Change in U.S. Women's Sex-Role Attitudes, 1964–1974," *American Sociological Review*, 41, no. 4 (August 1976): 573–596.

Matthews, Glenna, *"Just a Housewife": The Rise and Fall of Domesticity in America*, New York: Oxford University Press, 1987.

Mead, George H., *Mind, Self, and Society*, Chicago: University of Chicago Press, 1934.

Michael, Robert T., and Nancy Brandon Tuma, "Entry Into Marriage and Parenthood by Young Men and Women: The Influence of Family Background," *Demography*, 22, no. 4 (November 1985): 515–544.

Michael, Robert T., Victor R. Fuchs, and Sharon R. Scott, "Changes in the Propensity to Live Alone: 1950–1976," *Demography*, 17, no. 1 (February 1980): 39–56.

Miller, Joanne, and Howard H. Garrison, "Sex Roles: The Division of Labor at Home and in the Workplace," *Annual Reviews of Sociology*, 8 (1982): 237–262.

Moore, J., and A. Mata, *Women and Heroin in Chicano Communities*, Los Angeles: Chicano Pinto Research Project, 1982.

Moore, Kristin A., and Linda J. Waite, "Marital Dissolution, Early Motherhood and Early Marriage," *Social Forces*, 60, no. 1 (September 1981): 20–40.

Morgan, Carolyn Stout, and Alexis J. Walker, "Predicting Sex Role Attitudes," *Social Psychology Quarterly*, 46, no. 2 (June 1983): 148–151.

Morgan, Robin, ed., *Sisterhood is Powerful: An Anthology of Writings from the Women's Liberation Movement*, New York: Random House, 1970.

Morgan, S. Philip, and Linda J. Waite, "Parenthood and the Attitudes of Young Adults," *American Sociological Review*, 52, no. 4 (August 1987): 541–547.

Morgan, S. Philip, Diane N. Lye, and Gretchen A. Condran, "Sons, Daughters, and the Risk of Marital Disruption," *American Journal of Sociology*, 94, no. 1 (July 1988): 110–129.

Mortimer, Jeylan T., Jon P. Lorence, and Donald S. Kumka, "Work and Family Linkages in the Transition to Adulthood: A Panel Study of Highly Educated Men," paper presented at the American Sociological Association Meetings, San Francisco, 1982.

National Center for Health Statistics, "Advance Report of Final Natality Statistics, 1986," *Monthly Vital Statistics Report*, 37, no. 3 Supplement, Washington: U.S. Government Printing Office, July 12, 1988.

National Center for Health Statistics, "Advance Report of Final Divorce Statistics, 1986," *Monthly Vital Statistics Report*, 38, no. 2, Supplement, Washington: U.S. Government Printing Office, June 6, 1989.

National Research Council, *Who Cares for America's Children? Child Care Policies for the 1990s*, Washington: National Academy Press, 1990.

Neal, Arthur G., H. Theodore Groat, and Jerry W. Wicks, "Attitudes About Having Children: A Study of 600 Couples in the Early Years of Marriage," *Journal of Marriage and the Family*, 51, no. 2 (May 1989): 313–328.

Oakley, Ann, *The Sociology of Housework*, New York: Pantheon Books, 1974.

Oppenheimer, Valerie K., *The Female Labor Force in the United States: Demographic and Economic Factors Governing Its Growth and Changing Composition*, Berkeley: University of California Institute for International Studies, 1970.

Oppenheimer, Valerie K., *Work and the Family: A Study in Social Demography*, New York: Academic Press, 1982.

Oppenheimer, Valerie K., "A Theory of Marriage Timing," *American Journal of Sociology*, 94, no. 3 (November 1988): 563–591.

Pebley, Anne R., "Changing Attitudes Toward the Timing of First Births," *Family Planning Perspectives*, 13, no. 4 (July/August 1981): 171–175.

Peters, Jeanne M., and Virginia A. Haldeman, "Time Used for Household Work," *Journal of Family Issues*, 8, no. 2 (June 1987): 212–225.

Pfeffer, Jeffrey, and Jerry Ross, "The Effects of Marriage and a Working Wife on Occupational and Wage Attainment," *Administrative Science Quarterly*, 27, no. 1 (March 1982): 66–80.

Pleck, Joseph H., *Working Wives/Working Husbands*, Beverly Hills: Sage, 1985.

Pope, Hallowell, and Charles W. Mueller, "The Intergenerational Transmission of Marital Instability: Comparisons by Race and Sex," in George Levinger and Oliver C. Moles, eds., *Divorce and Separation*, New York: Basic Books, 1979.

Popenoe, David, *Disturbing the Nest: Family Change and Decline in Modern Societies*, New York: Aldine De Greyter, 1988.

Population Reference Bureau, "Speaking Graphically," *Population Today*, 17, no. 12 (December 1989): 2.

Presser, Harriet B., "The Timing of the First Birth, Female Roles and Black Fertility," *Milbank Memorial Fund Quarterly*, 49, no. 3, part 1 (July 1971): 329–359.

Presser, Harriet B., "Social Factors Affecting the Timing of the First Child," in W. Miller and L. F. Newman, eds., *The First Child and Family Formation*, Chapel Hill: Carolina Population Center, 1978.

Presser, Harriet B., and Virginia S. Cain, "Shift Work Among Dual-Earner Couples with Children," *Science*, 219 (1983): 876–879.

Propper, Alice Marcella, "The Relationship of Maternal Employment to Adolescent

Roles, Activities, and Parental Relationships," *Journal of Marriage and the Family*, 34, no. 3 (August 1972): 417–421.

Pruett, Kyle D., *The Nurturing Father: Journey Toward the Complete Man*, New York: Warner Books, 1987.

Rank, Mark R., "Fertility Among Women on Welfare: Incidence and Determinants," *American Sociological Review*, 54, no. 2 (April 1989): 296–304.

Rexroat, Cynthia, and Constance Shehan, "The Family Life Cycle and Spouses' Time in Housework," *Journal of Marriage and the Family*, 49, no. 4 (November 1987): 737–750.

Rindfuss, Ronald R., "How Much Does Marriage Matter, Anyhow?" paper presented at the annual meetings of the Population Association of America, San Francisco, 1986.

Rindfuss, Ronald R., S. Philip Morgan, and Gray Swicegood, *First Births in America; Changes in the Timing of Parenthood*, Berkeley: University of California Press, 1988.

Robinson, John P., "Who's Doing the Housework?" *American Demographics* (December 1988): 24–28, 63.

Rodgers, Willard, and Arland Thornton, "Changing Patterns of First Marriage in the United States," *Demography*, 22, no. 2 (1985): 265–279.

Ross, Catherine E., "The Division of Labor at Home," *Social Forces*, 65, no. 3 (March 1987): 816–833.

Ross, Catherine E., John Mirowsky, and Joan Huber, "Dividing Work, Sharing Work, and In-Between: Marriage Patterns and Depression," *American Sociological Review*, 48, no. 6 (December 1983): 809–823.

Ross, Catherine E., John Mirowsky, and Patricia Ulbrich, "Distress and the Traditional Female Role: A Comparison of Mexicans and Anglos," *American Journal of Sociology*, 89, no. 3 (November 1983): 670–682.

Rossi, Alice S., "Transition to Parenthood," *Journal of Marriage and the Family*, 30, no. 1 (February 1968): 26–39.

Rossi, Alice S., "A Life-Course Approach to Gender, Aging, and Intergenerational Relations," in *Social Structure and Aging: Psychological Processes*, Hillsdale, NY: Lawrence Erlbaum, 1989, 207–236.

Roth, Phillip, *Portnoy's Complaint*, New York: Random House, 1969.

Rotundo, E. Anthony, "American Fatherhood: A Historical Perspective," *American Behavioral Scientist*, 29, no. 1 (September-October 1985): 7–25.

Roy, Prodipto, "Maternal Employment and Adolescent Roles: Rural-Urban Differentials," *Marriage and Family Living*, 23, no. 4 (November 1961): 340–349.

Rubin, Lillian Breslow, *Worlds of Pain: Life in the Working-Class Family*, New York: Basic, 1976.

Ruggles, Steven, *Prolonged Connections: The Rise of the Extended Family in Nineteenth Century England and America*, Madison: University of Wisconsin Press, 1987.

Russell, Graeme, "Primary Caretaking and Role Sharing Fathers," in Michael Lamb, ed., *The Father's Role: Applied Perspectives*, New York: John Wiley and Sons, 1986.

Sanik, Margaret Mietus, "Division of Household Work: A Decade Comparison—

1967–1977," *Home Economics Research Journal*, 10, no. 2 (December 1981): 175–180.

Sanik, Margaret Mietus, and Teresa Mauldin, "Single Versus Two Parent Families: A Comparison of Mothers' Time," *Family Relations*, 35, no. 1 (January 1986): 53–56.

Scanzoni, John H., *Sex Roles, Life Styles and Childbearing*, New York: Free Press, 1975.

Schoen, Robert, William Urton, Karen Woodrow, and John Baj, "Marriage and Divorce in Twentieth Century American Cohorts," *Demography*, 22, no. 1 (February 1985): 101–114.

Schultz, T. W., "The Value of the Ability to Deal with Disequilibria," *Journal of Economic Literature*, 13, no. 3 (September 1975): 827–846.

Schwartz, Felice, "Management Women and the New Facts of Life," *Harvard Business Review*, 67, no. 1 (1989): 65–76.

Smith, James P., *Female Labor Supply: Theory and Estimation*, Princeton: Princeton University Press, 1980.

Smith, James P., and Michael Ward, *Women's Wages and Work in the Twentieth Century*, Santa Monica: The RAND Corporation, 1984.

Spitz, Rene, "Anaclitic Depression," in *Psychoanalytic Study of the Child*, 2 (1946): 313–342.

Spitze, Glenna D., "Role Experiences of Young Women: A Longitudinal Test of the Role Hiatus Hypothesis," *Journal of Marriage and the Family*, 40, no. 3 (August 1978): 471–480.

Spitze, Glenna D., "The Division of Task Responsibility in U.S. Households: Longitudinal Adjustments to Change," *Social Forces*, 64, no. 3 (March 1986): 689–701.

Stafford, Frank P., "Women's Use of Time Converging with Men's," *Monthly Labor Review* (December 1980): 57–59.

Stafford, Rebecca, Elaine Beckman, and Pamela Dibona, "The Division of Labor Among Cohabiting and Married Couples," *Journal of Marriage and the Family*, 39, no. 1 (February 1977): 43–56.

Straus, Murray A., "Work Roles and Financial Responsibility in the Socialization of Farm, Fringe, and Town Boys," *Rural Sociology*, 27, no. 3 (September 1962): 257–274.

Strecker, Edward, "Their Mother's Sons: A Psychiatrist Examines an American Problem," Philadelphia: Lippincott, 1946.

Terhune, Kenneth W., *A Review of the Actual and Expected Consequences of Family Size*, Washington: U.S. Government Printing Office, 1974.

Thornton, Arland, "Changing Attitudes Towards Family Issues in the United States," *Journal of Marriage and the Family*, 51, no. 4 (November 1989): 873–893.

Thornton, Arland, "Influence of the Marital History of Parents on the Union Formation Experience of Children," paper presented at the annual meetings of the Population Association of America, Toronto, May 1990.

Thornton, Arland, and Deborah Freedman, "Changes in the Sex Role Attitudes of Women, 1962–1977: Evidence from a Panel Study," *American Sociological Review*, 44, no. 5 (October 1979): 831–842.

Thornton, Arland, and Deborah Freedman, "Changing Attitudes Toward Marriage and Single Life," *Family Planning Perspectives*, 14, no. 6 (November/December 1982): 297–303.

Thrall, Charles A., "Who Does What: Role Stereotype, Children's Work, and Continuity Between Generations in the Household Division of Labor," *Human Relations*, 31, no. 3 (March 1978): 249–265.

Tilly, Louise, and Joan Scott, *Women, Work, and Society*, New York: Holt, Rinehart & Winston, 1978.

Timmer, Susan Goff, Jacquelynne Eccles, and Kerth O'Brien, "How Children Use Time," in F. Thomas Juster and Frank P. Stafford, eds., *Time, Goods, and Wellbeing*, Ann Arbor: University of Michigan, 1985, 353–382.

Townsend, Bickley, and Kathleen O'Neil, "American Women Get Mad," *American Demographics*, 12, no. 8 (August 1990): 26–32.

Treiman, Donald J., and Patricia A. Roos, "Sex and Earnings in Industrial Society: A Nine-Nation Comparison," *American Journal of Sociology*, 89, no. 3 (November 1983): 612–650.

Trussell, James, and David E. Bloom, "Estimating the Co-variates of Age at Marriage and First Birth," *Population Studies*, 37, no. 1 (1983): 403–416.

Udry, J. Richard, "Marital Alternatives and Marital Disruption," *Journal of Marriage and the Family*, 43, no. 4 (November 1981): 889–897.

Udry, J. Richard, "Biological Predispositions and Social Controls in Adolescent Sexual Behavior," *American Sociological Review*, 53, no. 5 (October 1988): 709–722.

Umberson, Debra, "Family Status and Health Behaviors: Social Control as a Dimension of Social Integration," *Journal of Health and Social Behavior*, 28, no. 3 (September 1987): 306–319.

U.S. Bureau of the Census, "Household and Family Characteristics: March 1980," *Current Population Reports*, Series P–20, no. 366, Washington: U.S. Government Printing Office, 1980.

U.S. Bureau of the Census, "Marital Status and Living Arrangements: March 1983," *Current Population Reports*, Series P–20, no. 389, Washington: U.S. Government Printing Office, 1983.

U.S. Bureau of the Census, "Fertility of American Women: June 1988," *Current Population Reports*, Series P–20, no. 436, Washington: U.S. Government Printing Office, 1989a.

U.S. Bureau of the Census, "Money Income of Households, Families, and Persons in the United States: 1987," *Current Population Reports*, Series P–60, no. 162, Washington: U.S. Government Printing Office, 1989b.

U.S. Department of Labor, Bureau of Labor Statistics, unpublished data from the May 1988 *Current Population Survey*, 1990.

U.S. Riot Commission, *Report of the National Advisory Commission on Civil Disorders*, New York: Bantam Books, 1968.

Waite, Linda J., Frances Kobrin Goldscheider, and Christina Witsberger, "Nonfamily Living and the Erosion of Traditional Family Orientations Among Young Adults," *American Sociological Review*, 51, no. 4 (August 1986): 541–554.

Waite, Linda J., and Glenna D. Spitze, "Young Women's Transition to Marriage," *Demography*, 18, no. 4 (November 1981): 681–694.

Waite, Linda J., and Ross M. Stolzenberg, "Intended Childbearing and Labor Force Participation of Young Women: Insights from Nonrecursive Models," *American Sociological Review*, 41, no. 2 (April 1976): 235–252.

Walker, Kathryn, and Margaret E. Woods, *Time Use: A Measure of Household Production of Goods and Services*, Washington: American Home Economics Association, 1976.

Wallerstein, Judith S., and Sandra Blakeslee, *Second Chances: Men, Women and Children After Divorce*, New York: Ticknor & Fields, 1989.

Weiss, Robert S., "Growing Up A Little Faster: The Experience of Growing Up in a Single-Parent Household," *Journal of Social Issues*, 35, no. 4 (1979): 97–111.

Weitzman, Lenore J., *The Divorce Revolution*, New York: The Free Press, 1985.

Westoff, Charles F., "Perspective on Nuptiality and Fertility," *Population and Development Review*, Supplement to 12 (1986): 155–170.

White, Lynn K., and Alan Booth, "The Quality and Stability of Remarriages: The Role of Stepchildren," *American Sociological Review*, 50, no. 5 (October 1985): 689–698.

White, Lynn K., and David B. Brinkerhoff, "The Sexual Division of Labor: Evidence from Childhood," *Social Forces*, 60, no. 1 (September 1981a): 170–181.

White, Lynn K., and David B. Brinkerhoff, "Children's Work in the Family," *Journal of Marriage and the Family*, 43, no. 4 (November 1981b): 789–798.

Williams, Richard, and Elizabeth Thomson, "Can Spouses Be Trusted? A Look at Husband/Wife Proxy Reports," *Demography*, 22, no. 1 (February 1985): 115–123.

Wylie, Phillip, *A Generation of Vipers*, New York: Rinehart and Company, 1942.

Young, Christabel, *Young People Leaving Home in Australia: The Trend Toward Independence*, Canberra: Australian National University Printing Press, 1987.

Zelizer, Viviana, *Pricing the Priceless Child: The Changing Social Value of Children*, New York: Basic Books, 1985.

Index

Abbott, Max, 275 n. 6
Abortion, 32
Abrahamse, Allan, 88
Acock, Alan C., 278 n. 10
Age: childbearing and, 87; children's share in household tasks and children's, 147–149; children's share in household tasks and mother's, 168–169, 170f; marital disruption and women's, 98, 101
Alcoholism, 4, 98
Alwin, Duane, 16
ANLITH, 284 n. 4
Arber, Sara, 32, 41, 218
Asimov, Isaac, 283 n. 6
Attitudes: blacks and, 32, 33; children's influence on, 57–58, 58f; community size and, 55; divorce and, 32; effect of marriage on, 57, 72–74; family values and, 198; measurement of men's, 42–45; measurement of women's, 31–33, 34–35, 42–45, 218; mother's working and formation of, 29; nonfamily living's effect on, 46–50, 49f; nontraditional family's effect on, 45–46
Attrition, 267 n. 3

Babcock, Deborah K., 144
Baj, John, 266 n. 8
Baldwin, Wendy, 21
Bane, Mary Jo, 62
Bart, Pauline, 283 n. 4
Becker, Gary S., 273 n. 16
Beller, Andrea H., 62

Berk, Richard A., 130, 277 n. 9
Berk, Sarah Fenstermaker, 9, 111, 130, 137, 146, 277 n. 9, 278 n. 2, 9, 279 n. 1, 279 n. 4
Berkman, Lisa F., 202
Bernard, Jessie, 60, 62
Berryman, Sue E., 45, 64
Bielby, Denise D., 283 n. 8
Bielby, William T., 283 n. 8
Births. *See* Childbearing
Blacks: attitudes of, 32, 33; childbearing among, 95; children's share in household tasks, 161–162, 163; and division of household labor, 182–183, 183f, 184; family disruption among, 67, 102; husband's share of household tasks, 127–128, 128f; marriage among, 73
Blake, Judith, 13, 43, 46
Blakeslee, Sandra, 15, 24
Bloom, David E., 87, 273 n. 3
Blumberg, Rae Lesser, 271 n. 1
Bongaarts, John, 89
Booth, Alan, 276 n. 9
Bowlby, John, 10
Brinkerhoff, David B., 110, 142, 145, 159, 278 n. 3, 279 n. 3
Brody, Charles J., 146
Bumpass, Larry, 1, 3, 14, 15, 41, 90, 98, 103, 218, 269 n. 8, 269 n. 11, 272 n. 10, 273 n. 4, 274 n. 15
Burch, Thomas, 18, 266 n. 9
Bureau of Labor Statistics, 9
Burgess, Ernest, 4

297

Designer: U.C. Press Staff
Compositor: Prestige Typography
Text: 10/12 Times Roman
Display: Helvetica
Printer: Edwards Bros., Inc.
Binder: Edwards Bros., Inc.